The Combat PTS(D) Resilience and Reintegration Workbook Copy.
The Combat PTS(D) Training Program is a registered trademark of Project Healing Heroes ⓒ
CombatPTSD.org®, a veteran-owned, 501(c)(3) nonprofit corporation.

Legal Disclaimer: The opinions and interpretations expressed in this book are those of the authors and do not reflect those of anyone else. The views and opinions expressed in this book do not represent those of the United States Air Force, the Department of Veterans Affairs, Texas A & M University, Project Healing Heroes, Project Sanctuary, Baylor Scott & White Hospital or any other organization.

This book is not intended to replace therapy in any way. There is no client-therapist relationship intended or unintended by the use of the materials in this book. We strongly encourage you to reach out to a mental health provider and share with them your intent to get healthy and regain your life. If you or someone you know is experiencing thoughts of suicide, please contact 911 immediately or the suicide hotline at 1-800-273-8255. If you or someone you know is experiencing post-traumatic stress disorder and are a veteran, contact the Department of Veterans Affairs at 1-800-827-1000. All other symptoms that require immediate attention, please contact 911.

The story, all names, characters, and incidents portrayed in this book are fictitious except for those whom we honor that have died in war. No identification with actual persons, places, or buildings is intended or should be inferred.

All pictures in this book are in the public domain unless otherwise noted. If there is erroneous credit, please contact the authors, and we will make appropriate changes in future editions.

Lt Col David F. Tharp, PsyD, M. Div.
Capt Katherine A. Tharp, MD
Visit the Project Healing Heroes website at www.ProjectHealingHeroes.org

Printed in the United States of America
First Printing: Aug 2017
ISBN-9781092158145

TABLE OF CONTENTS

ABOUT THE AUTHORS

Lt Col (Dr.) David F. Tharp, Psy.D., M.Div., M.A., M.A.S.W., is a Lieutenant Colonel in the United States Air Force Reserve. He was triple-hatted as a NATO commander in Kandahar, Afghanistan, where he deployed in support of Operation Enduring Freedom. He is a two-time national award winner: The 2014 Air Force Association (AFA) Department of Veteran's Affairs employee of the year and the 2014 Disabled American Veteran (DAV) Department of Veterans Affairs National Commander's Award. He also received the Texas District 17 Congressional Award by Congressman Bill Flores.

Katherine Tharp, M.D., is a Captain in the U.S. Air Force Reserves (USAFR). She is in her fourth year of residency at Baylor Scott & White Hospital in Temple, TX. There, she earned the top Psychiatry Residence in Training Exam (PRITE) score and was in the 99th percentile nationwide. She has also received the Medical Student Teaching Award and was inducted into the John L. Montgomery, MD Resident and Fellow Chapter of the Gold Humanism Society.

By Lt Col (Dr.) David F. Tharp:

While in Kandahar, I served as the medical advisor (MEDAD) and was responsible for 28 countries' medical assets. Like most commanders, I had multiple responsibilities and served as the preventative medicine (PREVMED) liaison and environmental engineer (ENVENG). During my tour of duty, I suffered a spinal cord illness that caused me to lose most of the functioning below T3. I continued for another month in that condition while being treated by a Navy neurologist until after my tour was complete. I refused to leave, and I was going to finish my tour at all costs. In theater, I saw and identified well over 100 people who died. It was my job to notify the country or the service of the real casualties of war. It was then and there that I was changed forever. Thankfully, I went on to recover from most of my physical challenges and continue to serve at the Air Force Academy in Colorado Springs, CO.

I entered the military as a psychologist after the attacks of 9/11. I was so furious by what I saw, I was not about to stand by and do nothing. After being on the cover of the *Air Force Magazine* for innovative treatment of PTS(D), I then volunteered to deploy to Kandahar for many reasons, one of which is that too many so-called PTS(D) "experts" have no comprehension of what it's like to go to war. I refuse to be one of them, and I joined to serve and make a difference. While in a war zone, I saw and experienced firsthand the devastating effects of war. I have the deepest respect for our men and women who fight this battle on a continual basis. With fewer resources, the men and women of the United States Armed Services are now deploying throughout multiple tours of duty and in multiple locations throughout the world. This takes a toll not only on them, but I believe at times, even more so on their families who have to go on with life without them. We, the American people, owe you a debt beyond anything we could ever repay. You are willing to sacrifice your life for this country, and you deserve anything and everything a true servant and warrior should have. This willingness to risk one's life for freedom is on the shoulders of less than one percent of our population. You are the less than one percenters.

This book goes beyond the insights gained from our direct experience in a war zone and in working with warriors. This program is personal in many ways. We have watched as the military and the VA continue to try to force warriors into a certain mold we call trauma therapy. After experiencing war firsthand, I realized many researchers just don't get it because they haven't been there. This, in my opinion, needs to change.

"We use military training, language and concepts to face military trauma."

We believe it only makes sense to work from the framework already etched in the minds of the warrior. We are also spiritually grounded, open and inclusive, something many psychologists and psychiatrists seem to shy away from. We will "not leave behind" any resource to help warriors, including the hope that God can bring. No other known resource addresses PTS(D) from the vantage point of military training, language and concepts, combined with the belief that God has a purpose for our life. It is in that context that the authors want to encourage each struggling warrior, because we see people get better every day, and there is hope. There is nothing more rewarding and exciting than watching warriors claim victory, lead rewarding and fulfilling lives, and then sharing what they have learned with others. Please join us in this fight together.

* * *

Drs. David and Katherine Tharp have two children: Joshua and Peyton. They are happily married and live in Waco, TX.

INTRODUCTION

Welcome to your new mission. It may have taken you years to get here, experiences you never expected, or symptoms sometimes beyond what you can bear, but we believe we have exactly what you need: surgically precise weapons that will give you a future and hope. It is our promise that if you truly give your all to this process, you will undoubtedly get better—a lot better.

You know the truth: *you will never forget.* Trauma is biologically wired and permanently engrained in your brain, even to the point of shrinking the hippocampus, but you will be successful, educated, seasoned, and ready for what lies ahead. We will contradict conventional logic that says there is something wrong with you, that you are broken beyond repair, and that what you are experiencing cannot be changed. *It can be changed.*

Unlike the most widely used, evidence-based trauma treatments that stem at their core from female sexual assault[1][2][3][4][5], our program focuses on needs specific to combat veterans who desperately need a resource coded in their own unique warrior language. Through feedback, we have also heard from police, firefighters, trauma personnel, and first responders who have found this material helpful as well. Our intent is to create a resource specifically for them. Veterans and first responders are warriors who naturally run *toward* danger, not away from it. They have leadership abilities and capabilities that are groomed through formal training. They are experts in their craft.

---

[1] Resick, P. A., Jordan, C. G., Girelli, S. A., Hutter, C. H., & Marhoefer-Dvorak, S. (1988). A comparative outcome study of behavioral group therapy for sexual assault victims. Behavior Therapy, 19, 385–401.

[2] Resick, P. A., Nishith, P., Weaver, T. L., Astin, M. C., & Feuer, C. A. (2002). A comparison of cognitive-processing therapy with prolonged exposure and waiting condition for the treatment of chronic posttraumatic stress disorder in female rape victims. Journal of Consulting and Clinical Psychology, 70, 867–879.

[3] Foa, E. B., Dancu, C. V., Hembree, E. A., Jaycox, L. H., Meadows, E. A., & Street, G. P. (1999). A comparison of exposure therapy, stress inoculation training, and their combination for reducing posttraumatic stress disorder in female assault victims. Journal of Consulting and Clinical Psychology, 67, 194–200.

[4] Resick, P. A., & Schnicke, M. K. (1993). Cognitive processing therapy for rape victims: A treatment manual. Newbury Park, CA: Sage.

[5] Chard, K. M. (2005). An evaluation of cognitive processing therapy for the treatment of posttraumatic stress disorder related to childhood sexual abuse. Journal of Consulting and Clinical Psychology, 73, 5, 965–971.

The Combat PTS(D) Resiliency and Reintegration Workbook is a culmination of research and practical observations based on the training and experience of being in a war zone. As we begin, let us set the stage...

Human beings are naturally resilient. A trauma survivor is not sick or broken beyond repair.
Resiliency Formation Training (RFT) seeks to awaken and strengthen this resilience.

Post-Traumatic Stress (PTS) and, specifically, Post-Traumatic Stress Disorder (PTSD) treatment programs have better results when they are flexible and invidualized. Enough of manualized, "cookie cutter" treatment programs that force people into the same box as if we have all been affected the same way. Resiliency Formation Training (RFT) is designed to educate trauma survivors and provide them with a precision-targeted, individualized training plan, much like the coordinates required by our most sophisticated weaponry in order for their payloads to reach their intended targets.

While we insist that PTS(D) is not primarily a medical problem, that does not mean we abandon the hard-earned, scientific approach that ultimately led us to create this educational program. No, the scientific method is still extremely valid, helpful, and informative. For example, when we use the following training modules in our respective psychiatric and psychological treatment programs, we borrow an age-old training approach from our colleagues in medical education. It is known as the *medical teaching model* in which you "see one, do one, teach one." If a medical student is learning how to draw a blood sample, they would watch it once first, do it themselves second, and teach it to someone else the third time.

Thus, we encourage you to strategically and dynamically work on your own issues and then, after you begin to gain hopefulness and confidence in your own recovery, reach out to others. Veterans trust other veterans. Who better to help than those who have been through the fire?

We need to be crystal clear: *The Combat PTS(D) Training Series* does not replace medical, psychiatric, and psychotherapeutic care that occurs in-person at your local clinic or hospital. Modern medicine is simply too complicated to allow us to safely design an educational program such as this, while taking into consideration all possible issues of each warrior. As such, we encourage you, even implore you, to get your own therapist, at the very least. This may seem daunting now, but our intention is to provide you with a vehicle to overcome some of the common stigmas that hinder people from getting the help they desperately need. We also hope we convey that this is a real biological disorder that can be tackled, and the more tools you engage to defeat it, the better your chances of success.

There are places in this workbook with fill-in-the-blank sections. Please fill these out as you progress through the training program and take the completed worksheets to a trusted therapist in your area for actual treatment. This will give them the detailed data they need to pinpoint how to make the best use of your therapy time. Years down the road, you will also be able to see how far you've come. You should also seek a prescribing psychiatrist or primary care physician because medications require a prescription. Keep in mind that a good psychiatrist who is well versed in PTS(D) is thoroughly trained not only in medications but drug-drug interactions. Given the potency of medications, their potential side effects and their efficacy, it is important to have an expert in drug-drug interactions to ensure safety and compliance. There are many influeincing factors that play a role in medications. Having confidence in your physician and their expertise is invaluable.

We also caution you to be careful about whom you entrust your trauma work with.[6] Not all therapists are trained the same or even as effective, just as the quality of cars differs. I would never put a Yugo up against a Lamborghini, no matter how much the makers of the first car argue they are equivalent "transportation." The adage of "you get what you pay for" was created for a reason.

RFT can be completed either by an individual or within a group. For many combat veterans, distance from a competent and knowledgeable therapist creates a challenge. Or they may often find themselves wanting to isolate, thus not desiring to go outside of their comfort zone, which is directly related to safety and security issues. Our hope is that by using these materials, it may build a bridge from isolation to integration.

The families and friends of combat veterans, and even sometimes the veterans themselves, find that they have made noticeable changes in their behavior. This may include installing cameras and purchasing weapons for increased security, only going out at certain times of the day/night, being more isolated, trusting people less, and feeling that the world is more unsafe than they did previously. They may encounter dramatic changes in their sleep patterns, rethinking and reexperiencing what they have been through, health challenges, anxiety, weight gain, depression, and an increase in over-the-counter or prescribed medications. If this has been your experience, then this book is for you.

Others may wish to use this in a group setting with veterans who have "been there" and experienced firsthand what they have gone through. It takes time to build trust with people in a group,

---

[6] Some states now allow providers who never went to medical school and have only four months of training specific to psychotropic medication to have prescriptive authority. Somehow they are viewed as equivalent to someone who completed medical school and a four-year residency and is board eligible or board certified. Likewise, we now have providers who have a degree from a two-year masters program providing therapy when psychologists are required to have four years of doctoral training, a year of internship and often times a post-doctoral fellowship. This is not to say that there are some providers with far less training who are not effective. However, statistically, it has been shown that some providers can't even pass the most basic requirements. One specific example is Nurse Practitioners (NP) and their fight for independent practice. All psychiatrists not only have to get into medical school, complete it and then do a four-year residency, but they also have to pass three tests (Step 1, Step 2 and Step 3) prior to taking their National Board Exam. When NPs were given Step 2 as an argument for independent practice as compared to psychiatrists, 40 percent failed. Every single psychiatrist must pass Step 1 and 2; otherwise, they do not progress to Step 3. We simply let the statistics speak for themselves. But given how healthcare is deteriorating, it should come as no surprise that lesser-trained providers are arguing for independent practice and reimbursement. What is even more astounding is that naturopathic medicine providers are prescribing substances that are not even FDA regulated. This is a debate which we will not enter as it is beyond the scope of this book. However, if you aren't getting what you need from your provider, you might want to get a more qualified and trained person that helps you accomplish your goals. Your life is on the line, and this is not a place to leave to the lesser trained.

even with other veterans. But once that trust is built, there is strength and comfort in knowing that you are not alone and that what you are experiencing is normal, at least for combat veterans. If you are interested in becoming a part of a small group of veterans that can encourage and help each other in this process, please contact us for information about the REACH VET peer-to-peer program. This program encourages veterans to create their own support network within the community, similar to the buddy system in the military. It sets the stage for support, encouragement, accountability, trust, and an "I've got your back" mentality. We all have blind spots and need encouragement. And who better to help in the healing process than those who have been there? Finally, we encourage you to think about this as your new mission. As we teach the various modules, our hope is that you will have a better understanding of what is happening and experience the "weight off your shoulders" relief.

In the REACH VET meetings, we believe in an "iron sharpens iron" mentality. Simply put, other veterans can help you see and confront unhealthy mantras, which are defined as a series of beliefs that, over time, you have told yourself repeatedly and now accept as fact. Unfortunately, many of these mantras are actually the source of the problem. These unhealthy mantras actually prevent you from being resilient and may be the source of relational, financial, occupational, legal, and/or other problems.

Combat veterans take into account what other veterans have to say to a higher degree than nonveterans. It is not unusual to hear someone say, "Well, you just don't understand; you haven't been there." These resources are focused on the people who have been through the trenches. Those trenches do not have to be overseas. In order to prepare for war experiences, many first responders and trauma personnel work in our inner cities and are in the CONUS[7] trenches and see some of the same types of injuries and other environmental stressors that may be more specific to the war theater.

Warrior defined: In order to best serve the reader, it is imperative that we define our audience. We would like to respect the service and sacrifice made by all of the combat veterans, first responders, firefighters, police, EMTs, and other emergency personnel. For easier reading throughout the book, we attempt to use one word to describe our audience: warrior. We define a warrior as someone who has been in the trenches fighting for, at a minimum, safety and security. This could be at the local level or halfway around the world. Either way, we are all warriors because we answered the call and stepped forward. We leaned into this fight to make the world a better place, no matter the cost.

RFT focuses in on the one resource that we all have to help us overcome traumatic events: resilience. The term *resiliency* is often used to describe a person's innate ability to be flexible and adaptive regarding life's stresses. It is the ability to bounce back in life. Similar to a bobber in the water, no matter how much we are tossed and thrown about in the ocean, or how much water engulfs and crashes over and around us, we consistently rise to the surface. For some of us, it's to gain another breath and battle on.

---

[7] CONUS is the acronym for Continental US.

Resilience can be stressor specific. Certain stressors or traumas can overwhelm a person's ability to cope with life, creating a need to develop resiliency to match that situation. We believe that a person can develop the skills, characteristics, and behaviors that equip them to deal with what may often feel overwhelming. Sometimes, people even respond by saying things like, "God won't give you more than you can handle." In this fight, we believe it is best to address one specific stressor at a time. And as you tackle them and subdue them, it builds confidence and success to tackle the next one until all have been driven into submission.

Each stressor may require different types of responses and *brain flexibility*. RFT is a military-focused training program that uses military language and concepts to draw out the warrior's ability to bounce back from the stressors in life and re-engage with their goals, priorities, and lifestyle.

In Post-Traumatic Stress (PTS), warriors often feel overwhelmed and can become despondent as their symptoms, such as sleep deprivation and depression, begin to manifest in their lives. This results in emotional withdrawal and social avoidance, which can, in turn, compound the problem. We call this **Resilience Deficiency**. In order to deal with these resiliency challenges, we created Resiliency Formation Training.

RFT has three distinct phases:

In **Phase 1: Assessment and Preparation,** warriors learn to prepare themselves for an intense program that takes a sincere commitment to complete. Distractions in life seem to abound at the same time someone seeks to recover from PTS. From legal problems and relationship stress to committing to stop any drugs and alcohol for the duration of your participation in this educational program, warriors are asked to pause in Phase 1 to reflect on just how ready and prepared they really are. Just like going into battle, you don't do so lightly, without an "O" plan[8], or without weapons at the ready. Warriors will process their trauma using the Resiliency Formation Nodal Events Timeline. This looks at each warrior's entire life to discover other traumatic events that may have occurred. Unlike other approaches that focus on one single trauma, we focus on the totality of issues and address them from a holistic perspective. For example, a therapist might ask, "What was the date of your trauma?" when filling out his or her worksheet, not realizing that, while deployed, multiple people were killed throughout your tour of duty. Trying to focus on one single situation or date minimizes a deployment full of experiences and stressors.

In **Phase 2: Resiliency Formation Training Modules,** warriors learn how to utilize preexisting military training, including concepts, strategy, and expertise, to mitigate PTS(D) symptoms. This phase introduces perspective, balance, and appropriate risk assessment in their thinking. Warriors are often surprised to learn that complicated psychological education leads them to some simple changes in their perspective with profound effects. Relief in the overall hypervigilance and insomnia is usually felt after this phase of treatment. We also encourage our warriors to create their "End State" vision and a New

---

[8] Operational plan

Mission about which they are passionate. This involves plugging in and giving back so that they can help enrich others' lives in some way. For those who have experienced loss, we have found that this helps by honoring the memory of the fallen. We then introduce the REACH VET worksheet of changing negative mantras and beliefs. The modules can be completed in any order based on your interest, but we encourage you to complete all of them to gain a holistic perspective and increase resiliency.

In **Phase 3: Reintegration and Reinvestment,** we focus on trying to get you all the way home and plugged in, not just physically, but emotionally. You will be prepared to address any setbacks that may occur and create a crisis plan if one is needed. We even provide a process by which you can answer difficult questions that people may ask. We also believe in positive affirmation and encourage those who use a group format to take time to share their words of encouragement with each other. Extra REACH VET worksheets are available at the end of this workbook for you to process any remaining unhealthy beliefs/mantras,

As we increase resiliency, a healthier response to trauma can occur. Again, fill out the "fill in the blank" questions, even though you may be tempted to skip them. We want your brain to be fully involved in the process. Similar to writing things down in preparation for taking a test, versus trying to remember information, you will heal better by engaging more neuronal pathways. Reading and then writing your responses helps you to process the information. Don't shortchange your healing.

 Key Takeaway: By writing things down, it actually involves more aspects of your brain than simply reading the material.

Our Resiliency Formation Training is broader in scope and more specific to warriors than the two leading treatments in the field today, namely Cognitive Processing Therapy (CPT) and Prolonged Exposure Therapy (PE). While we greatly appreciate and applaud these treatment efforts to help warriors recover from trauma, superimposing rape victim trauma onto combat veterans is not the answer. We believe these treatments have significant weaknesses that require a very different approach—a military-focused approach. Both of these trauma treatments were created to treat female rape victims, who are often a very different population than that of most warriors who have been in a war zone. The standard course of CPT does not include survivor guilt, moral injury, or grief work as part of therapy for veterans, yet these are three of the most common issues facing warriors today. Up until now, there has not been a program specifically created to address combat veterans using military training, language and concepts. This, along with an intense passion to reduce veteran suicide, is the reason we felt compelled to create such a resource.

Resiliency for Emotional and Cognitive Health, Veterans Education and Training (REACH VET) Worksheets

When our patients use the REACH VET Worksheets explained in Module XVII, they discover that negative lessons learned earlier in life have been compounded in the wake of their trauma. Compound trauma can help explain incredibly intense reactions to military trauma that otherwise may not have warranted as strong a response. By using the worksheets, trauma themes will surface, oftentimes including some you never even knew existed. A concerted effort is made to uncover the overarching unhealthy trauma themes and mantras throughout a person's lifetime so that the healing can begin. As an example, if you have bone cancer and the skin's surface begins to deteriorate, you don't simply put a bandaid on it and call it good. You go after the source of the problem.

In psychology, there is a term called **factor analysis**. It's when you take multiple related things and narrow them down to one or two descriptive words. After working on various life issues, and hopefully uncovering different concepts, we hope that a clearly defined, common theme will surface. When you factor various problems into one particular theme, we can then focus on that theme and make specific improvements in your life (i.e., target the problem). Unfortunately, many of our brothers and sisters in arms don't even know what their themes are, or they may have developed blind spots to them as a subconscious coping mechanism. That is why we created the various modules in Phase II. By addressing these various themes in the modules, we believe that you will be able to not only relate to them because you are living them, but also discover a way out from under them. Moreover, when resolution of themes occurs, this is when people feel the "weight" lift from their shoulders.

You have carried enough burdens from your experiences and the weight of the world on your shoulders. This price of freedom you continue to pay was not designed to be carried or handled alone. Remember, you are not alone, and we will not leave you behind! *It is time to unload.*

In conclusion, what RFT provides that differs from other trauma approaches is the purposeful use of military training, concepts and strategy to help warriors increase resilience. This is accomplished through an intense, educational program with REACH VET Worksheets to identify the trauma themes that have been the most impactful in your life. The resulting trauma themes, nodal events, and mantras are mapped to the specific beliefs, emotions, and behaviors that warriors find problematic. Therefore, this approach is essentially warrior-style training for leaving the combat zone and returning to civilian life. *These are the missing briefings that you never received, because they didn't exist—until now.*

PHASE 1: ASSESSMENT AND PREPARATION

WHAT IS COMPOUND TRAUMA, AND HOW IS IT DIFFERENT FROM SINGLE-EPISODE TRAUMA?

One of the most challenging issues that combat veterans experience when they return from the battlefield and are assessed for psychological issues is the notion of single-episode trauma. Therapists and assessment personnel at the Veterans Health Administration (VHA), and the Veterans Benefit Administration (VBA) continue to ask veterans about <u>one</u> specific trauma event, often called an index trauma, along with follow-up questions that include who, what, when, where, why, and how about this single experience? It's simple. When I approached the leading expert in the United States Air Force about this issue, the response was quite clear. He asked if I had anything better to treat PTS(D) and I indicated I did not. His response, "Well then, until you do, we have to do something". It was at that point, out of necessity, that the military chose to use a trauma treatment approach based on female sexual assault. The assumption was that trauma is trauma, and if nothing else, it's better than nothing. Unfortunately, these treatment approaches that are specific to female sexual assault victims have been superimposed onto combat veterans. More than 15 years post 9/11, the DVA and the military are still using this same boxed approached to combat trauma. Given the rape victim approach to trauma, it should come as no surprise that roughly 30-40 percent of people are considered "non-responders". That means, they did not respond to the treatment of choice.

However, something is truly better than nothing and 60-70 percent to report a positive outcome. We are thankful for the trauma treatment that was supplied to our men and women in combat. However, we believe that a solution for the "non-responders" is warranted. Remember, we leave no one behind!

We also believe that translational research should be done specifically for combat veterans as their unique needs are not necessarily the same as those of female sexual assault victims, except possibly in the area of military sexual trauma (MST).

As for a specific example, it is not surprising that current trauma treatment, such as Cognitive Processing Therapy (CPT), talks about "intimacy" as one of their top five issues. So, what's the problem? Addressing intimacy issues makes perfect sense if you are a rape victim but doesn't make sense for combat veterans. Again, we believe that combat trauma is <u>very</u> different than female sexual assault. We are of the opinion that there should be combat-specific trauma treatment options available to assist those who are labeled as non-responders.

There has been a new term coined "complex trauma."[9] This is trauma that is not a one-time event but instead accounts for multiple occurrence trauma, including the trauma of military members who are deployed on a continual basis, as well as the trauma of those who are experiencing ongoing child abuse. We believe a more precise term is "compound trauma." In essence, trauma that is experienced later on in life may well be compounded by earlier, childhood or adult trauma experiences. This is often the case in combat trauma. Although children and young adults are resilient, the memories of the traumatic experiences may have been suppressed throughout their lifetime. However, a person joins the military and is exposed to traumatic circumstances, and because that person has previously experienced trauma, this compounds the problem. Not only does the person have to deal with what he or she has seen in the military but may also have issues from unresolved trauma as a child, thus complicating treatment.

Combat compound trauma is more than a one-time experience; it's the result of a deployment full of experiences. Although there can be one specific trauma that was the most difficult, combat trauma happens over an extended period and is often a culmination of multiple stressors and life-threatening experiences, often on foreign soil. This is the reason why asking about a single-event trauma makes it difficult for combat veterans to answer the question. How can we begin to even address issues of combat trauma if we, as providers, aren't even asking the right questions? And when we do finally ask the right questions, we are using treatment approaches that aren't specific to warriors.

Now that we have defined compound trauma, let's begin the process of specifically addressing combat trauma. Combat trauma is defined as having witnessed or experienced war-related death and destruction in which the resiliency of psychological, moral, ethical, spiritual, and emotional responses is inadequate to address the trauma. It often manifests itself in embedded, vivid, reexperienced memories, which forever change the person.

Subsequent difficulties may include insomnia; moral injury; survivor guilt; relationship problems; job difficulties and loss; questioning of leadership decisions, political motives, the purpose of war; war crimes; distress when in public; reactions and responses to multiple triggers; disclosure challenges; feelings of isolation, shame, guilt, and remorse, just to name a few.

Because combat trauma is very different from sexual assault, we have found that the constructs, although sometimes helpful, are not necessarily specific to the challenges that warriors experience. And, thus, there was a necessity to create a combat trauma-focused resource that specifically addresses combat-related issues and triggers.

It is our intent to create the most comprehensive resources for combat veterans, but we need your input. If you find examples or content that may need to be added, revised or removed, please contact us.

---

[9] https://www.psychologytoday.com/blog/compassion-matters/201207/recognizing-complex-trauma

We will address them in subsequent revisions. We are in this fight together, and we will not leave you behind.

Phase 1: Assessment and Preparation

If you go to a private therapist, the Department of Veterans Affairs, or other psychological professionals to get treatment for PTS(D), you will most likely be asked a series of standardized questions. This is done so that clinicians and researchers can determine if a specific diagnosis is warranted and which of the few treatment approaches may work best for you. The scope of this book does not attempt to diagnose PTS(D), and you do not have to have PTS(D) to benefit from this book. However, understanding some of the symptoms you struggle with and specifically addressing those throughout this book may be helpful. That being said, we highly recommend that a full psychiatric and developmental history be completed with a qualified, licensed provider who specifically understands and is empathetic to these issues. This book is not intended to replace therapy, nor should it be interpreted or construed that there is a patient-client or therapist-client relationship within it.

You know yourself better than anyone. Please, take a few minutes to do your own assessment. This self-assessment will prepare you to launch fully into Phase 2, which is primarily educational in nature. A strategic approach for the warrior may be to work on the modules you feel are most pertinent first. The modules do not have to be completed sequentially.

Identifying specific content areas in which you may need additional support can be helpful at the outset. You can use the following checklist to assess specific issues that will need attention. Please check off any issues that you are currently experiencing, and try your best to quantify the issue, or put N/A for not applicable.

	Select All That Apply	**Quantify your answers where appropriate (i.e., 3–4 hours of sleep per night)**
☐	Sleeping problems	
☐	Nightmares	
☐	Avoidance issues	
☐	Hypervigilance, "extreme situational awareness"	
☐	Death of a child	
☐	Death of a warrior	
☐	Guilt from actions in war	
☐	Anger	
☐	Relationship problems	

☐	Self-esteem	
☐	Lack of community resources	
☐	Loss of motivation	
☐	Memory problems	
☐	Spiritual issues	
☐	Self-hate	
☐	Financial challenges	
☐	Suicidal/homicidal issues	
☐	*Other issues:*	
☐		
☐		
☐		

AM I READY FOR THIS?

Working on your trauma is probably not on the short list of your favorite things to do in life. You've probably gone to great lengths to avoid actually having to deal with this and may even view asking for help as a sign of vulnerability. Vulnerability is often viewed as weakness, and the opposite of what we are taught in the military. Our mission is to utilize power and take control. We dictate how things go, and the definition of vulnerability is quite the opposite. Throughout this book, remember that everything needs to be put in context. If you were competing in the Olympics, you would want to wear something that has the least amount of resistance for a swimsuit, such as a Speedo. However, showing up in that on your prom night may result in lasting memories you may not wish to have throughout your lifetime.

I argue that only the truly strong are capable of being vulnerable. It takes courage to know that we are not always in control and that we can't always dictate what happens in life. In reality, sometimes it's an illusion. We are taught and believe we are in control, oftentimes because being vulnerable means we cannot direct the outcome of things to come. We see this played out in war, all the time. We do everything possible to dictate the outcomes of war, but in the end, we know we are not the ones who are in control. As a matter of fact, wars can be fought, and even lost, based on weather conditions.[10] And when someone close to us dies, we are especially vulnerable. But in all honesty, the more we embrace this reality, the healthier and more resilient we become.

Think about your experiences in war as you read this paragraph. Courage is defined as the ability to do something that frightens one. It can also be interpreted as strength in the face of pain or grief. God knows that both of these definitions can apply to veterans. In my sometimes mathematical mind:

Vulnerability = Courage = Warriors

---

[10] In the Battle of Gettysburg, which has aptly been named the Bloodiest Battle of the American Civil War, 46,286 Union and Confederate soldiers died in a three-day period from 1-3 July 1863. It was on 4 July 1863 when the weather played a significant role. Rev. Dr. Michael Jacobs recorded 1.39 inches of rain that day. Many of the wounded had not yet been removed from the low-lying areas by the Plum Run Creek which had overflowed its banks. It is recorded that near the flood waters is where all the injured Confederates drowned. It not only affected those injured but also the Confederates who were attempting to retreat. During the 17-mile long trek with wounded soldiers as they headed back to Virginia, the Potomac river overflowed and severely impacted the ability of the wagons to move freely. The Confederate Army remained trapped there until 13 July.

The journey you are starting on now will undoubtedly bring back memories and cause you to replay some of the trauma scenes in your mind but with a different focus. We chose to do this on purpose—because it helps get you to a more healthy state.

You have probably found that "stuffing" the emotions and memories down deep into the subconscious isn't working very well for you, or you wouldn't be reading this right now. Something has to change; you may not know what or even how to do it. The good news is that as you continue to better understand and learn how trauma affects the psyche, or even how Post-Traumatic Stress and Post-Traumatic Stress (Disorder) comes about in the first place, your emotions will most likely begin to calm down. Some people who often experience anxiety and panic attacks find that they do a better job of dealing with their emotions after the use of our program. Even more so, our thought processes that affect outcomes dramatically improve. And this improvement means increased resiliency.

We have found that trauma work takes an enormous amount of energy. There is clearly enough internal distress that we encourage you to do everything you can to *minimize external stress*. We know it's hard to limit external stress, but the better job you do with this, the more energy you can use to work on what you are experiencing internally.

That said, some people have too many life distractions which make it unwise to start this program because it would be too much to handle at the moment. You may need to wait until your life situation becomes more stable. You are the best person to make that decision. To help you make an informed decision, we have included some basic assessment questions you may want to ask yourself prior to committing to the process:

• If I am partaking in alcohol or drugs, can I commit to sobriety during the course of PTSD treatment? Sobriety is a requirement for treatment. If this is not an issue for you, check it off the list. If this cannot be done, we recommend this training program be postponed until you are ready to handle the emotional challenges while sober.

• Do I have a stable support situation? Are there people I can count on who will be there for me? Are there unstable people that will distract or discourage me?

• Can I afford this psychologically? Am I at a place where I can look at my issues with objectivity and be willing to make the changes necessary to get better?

• Am I willing to invest the time and energy necessary to see this through? Can I commit myself to this program for weeks to months before seeing results? Remember, it isn't time that heals; it's what you do with the time that heals. If time healed, every WWII and Vietnam veteran would have resolved all of their issues. Unfortunately, this is simply not the case.

THREAT OF LOVE AND THE LAW

What is your motivation for change? What is it that has brought you to this place in your life? Did you ever think you would be here? Did you ever think that, at your age, you would be dealing with the consequences of war to this degree? Most people do not.

That being said, there are often multiple reasons why people seek help. We will address at least two of these, but there are many more: threat of love and the law.

For some of us, the threat of love is just that. It's the threat from loved ones that, if you do not get help, they will leave. They have had enough, but they still care. As a matter of fact, people who don't care don't threaten; they just leave. Many of you have already experienced that pain. If loved ones are still around, be thankful.

If someone has threatened to leave, the good news is that they are still holding out hope for you. We believe this book you are holding in your hands may provide answers to the questions you may have. It may also provide some answers to questions you aren't even asking. We will support and encourage you and help you to understand *why* you react and respond the way you do. This knowledge alone can be your pathway to freedom.

We have consistently seen that warriors struggle with PTS and PTS(D). Most veterans wish others could understand why they do what they do. The reality is this: we cannot change other people. We can only change ourselves. You cannot change the civilian population, your loved ones, your boss, etc. In reality, *they* are not working through this program—*you* are. When I ask most veterans if civilians can understand what they have been through, they inevitably say "no." At that point, I ask what it would take for them to understand, and the response is "to walk in my boots and see the things I have seen." At that point, they no longer are civilians but veterans of war. There is no possibility that all of the people in your life, if even a handful, will ever experience war. Since that is the case, expecting them to "get it" becomes difficult, if not impossible. Therefore, we need to focus on what we can change and not put that expectation on others.

Remember, if you do have loved ones who have threatened to leave you, count it a blessing. At least they threatened, and now you can do something about it. And even if your motivation is to change so that they won't leave, at least it's motivation.

Another reality for many veterans is the threat of the law. Judges, Veteran Service Organizations, Veteran Justice Outreach, probation officers, etc., often try to find solutions for veterans because they know that the experiences of war can take their toll. Unresolved issues can influence really bad decisions—sometimes even to the point of legal trouble. Chances are you have made some bad decisions because of these experiences, and they may or may not have landed you in legal trouble. Either way, whether forced to deal with it or not, this program will help to address these issues, increase your resiliency and give you your life back.

EXTINCTION BURST

Hopefully, you have said *yes* to the question, "Am I ready?" And let's be honest, you aren't crazy, but you have had some very difficult life experiences. As a matter of fact, our responses to some of these experiences may lead us to question ourselves, but we will talk more about this specifically in "Module VII: It's Not Rocket Science; It's Classical Conditioning."

 Key Takeaway: Just like any mission you go on, there are risks. The risk of addressing some of your thoughts, feelings, and emotions about what you have experienced can be daunting. As a matter of fact, what I tell every one of my clients is this: it *will* get worse before it gets better. But we have good news for you.

Now, isn't that just exactly what you want to hear? That things get worse before they get better? No, it is not! I get that, but we have to be honest about this process and mitigate the risk. Remember, mitigating risk is what we do in the military.

Chances are you have been using avoidance, numbing, alcohol and/or drugs, or anything you can to make this all go away. Now, here you are, in some ways forced into dealing with your struggles differently than you have before. Clearly, what you have been doing isn't working, at least in some areas of your life, so you have found yourself in this place. We are excited you are here, to be honest. Because it's where you can get the help you need. **And it *will* get better.** I can assure you that if you do not quit, it is true, you will get better.

That being the case, let me give you this analogy. If you've ever been on a roller coaster, it can be incredibly exhilarating *and* scary at the same time. It's that moment when you feel as if you are no longer in control that something bad could happen, and yet you trust the equipment and the equipment operator to bring you back safely. While you stand there, in preparation for the thrill, you often get excited—some people so much so that they get too excited. Their sympathetic nervous system kicks in. Their heart starts pounding; they start feeling weak in the knees, maybe even nauseous. But finally, the time arrives; you get on.

Click, click, click, click goes the back-and-forth jerky motion at a 60-degree angle up into the sky. And then it hits you: I WANT OFF!

You see, the roller coaster ride isn't designed for you to get off. As a matter of fact, there is nothing at the very top to let you off: no platform, no elevator, no stairs, nothing. Once you start, you are on, and getting off is not an option. And—think about it—if you thought you were scared for the few moments while going up, think about what it would be like if you were to attempt to get off and actually try to get down at the peak. I would bet most people would just freeze. They wouldn't even let go of the bar to get off, completely stuck and gripped with fear.

Thus, you are not given the option at the peak of a roller coaster. The intent is not for you to experience heart throbbing fear, but instead it is designed to increase fun. Most people experience parasympathetic symptoms of heart racing, exhilaration, impending excitement, some sweating of the hands as it makes a person feel alive. However, too much of the parasympathetic system and you end up in a panic with your heart beating out of your chest, profuse sweating, gripping fear and an attempt to escape the situation at all costs. If people only experienced the latter response, not very many people would go to amusement parks.

Doing this program can be much the same way. You've been using all types of avoidance mechanisms not to have to deal with these issues. But getting started and then stopping when things start to get difficult, when you are actually doing the work and confronting difficult things, would be akin to wanting to get off at the peak of the roller coaster. That's a really bad idea.

We have to make difficult life choices, but we care enough about you to be honest. This program is difficult, but it can impact your life, your marriage, your finances, and your health. And before each mission, we count the costs and mitigate as many risks as possible. Now that we are post-deployment, we have the luxury of asking ourselves the question, "Is doing this program and confronting my issues worth it?" Only you can answer that question. I no longer question whether I can help people work through their issues as I have experienced traumatic breakthroughs throughout my career. What we have to offer can definitely help. The only question is, are you willing to do the work? Are you willing to give it everything you have? For some of you, it may be a matter of life and death. We don't want to be dramatic, but we do face the realities of war. DVA research indicates that 20 veterans kill themselves every day. We believe even one is too many. It's time to give people the tools to bring about a hope and a future.

RESILIENCY FORMATION TRAINING (RFT)

The following visual will hopefully illustrate the resiliency-deficit challenge that most people experience. Remember, resiliency can be thought of as the warrior's ability to bounce back in life after stressful or traumatic events.

When we start out in life, our resiliency capabilities are normally rather large, because we haven't had to experience significant life stressors that tax our systems. As we begin to experience stressors in life, depending upon how we deal with them, our capability to tolerate things diminishes. As a matter of fact, on a scale from 1–10, if 10 is our threshold and inability to no longer tolerate things, the closer our stress baseline starts out (for example, it may be a 7 that day), our ability to tolerate stress is decreased. You may know people like this. I relate resiliency deficits to a fuse. Some people have so much stress in life that their stress baseline is highly elevated, and their ability to tolerate stress is quite low. So, when a stressor comes along, they have a micro-second fuse which explodes in the form of anger.

It's equivalent to holding a large firecracker during a 4th of July celebration. With such a short fuse, the risk of it going off in your hand is significant. We are tired of getting burned. We cannot afford any more explosions in our lives. The answer may *not* be simply counting to ten, because, for some warriors, that's just a countdown to an explosion. Instead of counting 1–10, these folks start at 10 and go to 1. Our answer is in reducing the stress baseline when the person is not under duress. If all we do is focus on the trigger, it is oftentimes too late. And this, in our opinion, is one of the significant problems with many of today's therapeutic interventions. They intervene at the point of the triggering event. Our Resiliency Formation Training (RFT) approach addresses the problem at the stress baseline *before* the triggering event.

It's akin to a bank account. Let's say you have $5,000 in your bank account. If you owe a friend $2,000, your resiliency threshold is not exceeded with the stress of owing them that amount of money. Thus, you have a resilience factor that can handle it. On the other hand, if you owe your friend $7,500, your threshold is exceeded, and your bank account would be overdrawn, creating a resilience deficit. You will then have no choice but to worry about how you will resolve this problem. In this illustration, if you wait until payday to solve it, you've waited too long. You either have to decrease the stress (the amount you owe) or increase the threshold (the amount you have) in your bank account. From a psychological standpoint, we cannot afford to wait until the triggers occur. There is an urgency to prepare now. And resolving problems is at the heart of RFT.

Following is an example of Brian, a warrior, and the significant events that have happened in his life. Notice the stress levels early in life compared to when he was deployed, and then finally, when he was able to address his stressors. The baseline of stress changes, and so does his ability to tolerate it.

Resiliency Formation

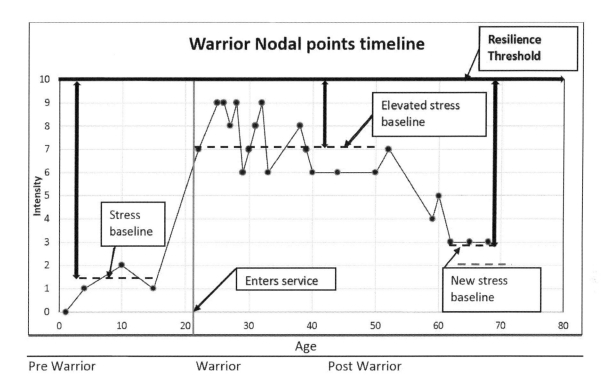

Nodal Points in Brian's Life

Age

4   Had an asthma attack
10 Saw his dad get injured in a motorcycle accident. Childhood stress baseline average (mean) is 1.5
22 Left for war and experienced his first death
24 Experienced an Intermittent Explosive Device (IED) that killed his friend Kyle
24 Saw the massacre of three children
25 Saw an Afghan woman kill herself in an IED mishap
26 Returned home from war
28 Experienced a second deployment
29 Experienced a divorce
30 Received a second article 15 for alcohol use and loses rank
31 Experienced a TBI from MRAP explosion
32 Got remarried, spouse had their first child after he was away on another deployment. (Stress baseline is now elevated compared to pre-military trauma. The average (mean) is now a 7.0.)

38   Experienced a promotion but feels stress due to responsibility

40   Retired from military service

44   Had difficulty interpreting life events as non-threatening. Adrenaline continued to be elevated, including insomnia, sleep apnea, and depression.

50   Experienced a loss of job

52   Experienced a second divorce

59   Sought out therapy

60   Experienced extinction burst challenges due to confronting trauma experiences

61–65   Was in therapy, confronting issues, and baseline reduced his average to a mean of 3.0, still higher than before joining the military but lower than after deployment and not being able to resolve issues

Stress Threshold: The issue is that if you use a scale from 0–10, with 10 being threshold, then the real issue isn't just the new experiences one has that can push a person "over the edge." It's the reality that the baseline is now changed. Resiliency is the amount of "tolerance" one has between one's baseline and threshold. If the tolerance number exceeds the tolerance capabilities, threshold is exceeded, and bad things happen. Warriors often focus on the triggers or events that happen to them. And this is what they try to control. Instead, once the trigger has happened, time is not on their side, and people who have a short fuse often find themselves irritable and angry and have outbursts that can be costly.

Answer: The real answer lies not solely in dealing with the triggering event but in one's stress baseline. If you have a lower stress baseline, your ability to tolerate things will be increased. The stress baseline number becomes key. As you resolve issues, you most likely will not get back to pre-service baseline; however, you will see improvement compared to your elevated stress baseline when triggers/issues came up and were unresolved. Let's take this to a personal level.

NODAL EVENTS TIMELINE

Your first assignment is to create your own personal nodal events timeline. This exercise is very helpful in listing out the various nodal points (significant points) in your life that have brought you to this point. It is recommended that you list out all of the nodal points you can think of and and then go back and write in the age it occurred. That way, you can then put it in chronological order.

Significant Nodal Points

Age   Nodal Points

____ – _____

____ – _____

____ – _____

____ – _____

____ – _____

____ – _____

____ – _____

____ – _____

____ – _____

____ – _____

____ – _____

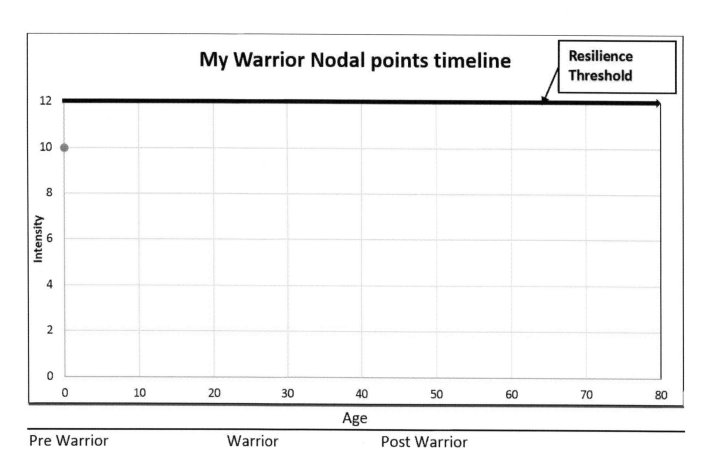

Now that you have listed out your nodal points and charted them, do one last thing. Put a plus or minus next to each one on your list, right next to where it says Age. Plus for positive, minus for negative. Then, count them up.

How many positive nodal events have you had in your life? _____

How many negative nodal events have you had in your life? _____

What trends do you notice in your life? _____

_____

_____

_____

_____

_____

Most warriors list out more negative nodal points than positive ones. This shouldn't surprise us because nodal events are often tied to emotional experiences that contain a lot of emotional turmoil. This is exactly why we need to write the next few chapters in our life in a positive manner.

PERCEPTION MATTERS

Any police officer who has to interview witnesses to the same accident will get as many different responses as there are people to the question "What happened?" Why? Because people see things and interpret things from a different perspective. This perspective includes our vantage point, the language the interviewer uses and the "lenses" we are using at the time. There are things we cannot control, but we do have influence, especially over how we perceive things: either through a positive or negative lens.

You may know people who are very negative. No matter what good things happen in life, they are the ones who always play the role of Eyore in the Winnie the Pooh movies. They always see the glass half empty and will give you every possible negative scenario that can happen. They are the ones who also call themselves realists, not pessimists. And oftentimes, they end up being right because they are the first to tell you when something goes wrong. Very seldom do they say they were wrong when everything goes right. Instead, they will say, "give it time."

We will encourage you to put on lenses that look at the world in the light of genuine, healthy solutions. There are enough negative things in the world, and we don't need to add to it.

PHASE 2: RESILIENCY FORMATION TRAINING MODULES

When people become overwhelmed with PTS(D) and depression, most of them focus on material issues, because they are the most immediate and pressing.

Some of the more common material issues include:

- Finances
- Jobs
- Volatile Relationships
- Living situation
- Activities of daily living
- Transportation
- Access to health care
- Changes in identity/life station (i.e., from military to civilian life, student, disability, etc.)

By the end of PTS(D) recovery, much of the emphasis shifts to strengthening healthy relationships and putting energy into things greater than oneself. Some of the more common themes include:

- Faith
- Family
- Meaning
- Purpose
- Selfless service

So how do we get there? Our modules are designed to increase resilience by using strategic concepts and thought-provoking questions to challenge mantras (core beliefs) we have accepted as truth. The hard work of this so-called "soft science" is to challenge previous beliefs, better understand emotions, and even expose you to new (and better) core beliefs and mantras.

We actually have a lot of schemas and mantras that we have been taught growing up and in the military. These may include, "Big boys don't cry," "Pain is weakness leaving the body," "Never leave your wingman," etc. Although these messages are meant for a specific time and place, they can carry weight and sting in situations where things don't go as planned.

Remember, do not begin the process of working through psychological issues without having the resources to lean on during difficult times. If you find you do not have the resources you need, it is important to establish them prior to this journey. Otherwise, it's like going on a family vacation to Disneyland only to find out halfway through your trip that you left the tickets at home. You may even want to take the time to write down the answers to some very important questions as you consider moving on to Phase 2.

When times get tough, I can count on (e.g., certain people, working hard, my family, prayer, etc.)
_____.

When I am going through an emotional time, my healthy options include (e.g., exercise, helping others, staying busy, etc.) _____
_____.

If I cannot solve a problem, I could turn to _____ to tell me the truth.

Spirituality is/is not (circle one) a resource for me.

The biggest threat to my success is _____, and I will mitigate   this   by
_____
_____.

When I start thinking negative thoughts, I will intentionally _____
_____.

The   one   healthy   thing   I   really   enjoy   doing   when   feeling   stressed   is –
_____
_____.

Because I cannot change other people and can only change myself, I commit myself to this process fully. My start date for healing is: _____

_____
(signature)

MODULE I: AM I NORMAL?

Intent: To help warriors understand what it means to be normal and answer the questions, "Am I crazy?" or "Is there something wrong with me?"—especially after coming out of a war zone.

Context: Anyone who has ever been deployed will understand why these questions are important. We often wonder how we've changed, and if we don't wonder, it doesn't take very long after we get out of theater to quickly discover that the world has continued on. As a matter of fact, you may even begin to wonder, "Was it all worth it?" After all, you've been to war, seen all kinds of things, and been involved in situations that you never thought possible, and then, come to find out, the world has not skipped a beat. People are going about their business as if we aren't even at war. And yet, it feels as if you want the world to stop, or at least for you to stop the world and say, "Hey, do you people not know that we are at war?!"

I'm not sure what it was like for you, but here's the question: how long after you came out of the Area of Responsibility (AOR) did it take you to realize that the world had just kept going on as if nothing was happening or that we were even at war? Was it when you flew home? Was it when you saw color for the first time and heard sounds that you hadn't heard since you left, such as a baby crying? Was it when you got home and things were very different than when you left, or possibly when you went back to work stateside? Was there a distinct time when it happened for you?

Take a moment, and as you contemplate these questions, think back. And then finish this sentence: "I realized that the world continued on without me and that people seemed oblivious that we were in war when _____

_____

_____

_____

_____

_____."

For me, it was on the commercial flight home. It was the first time since being deployed that I had not worn my military uniform and was in civilian clothes. I had a commercial flight from Germany to Baltimore, MD, after my spinal cord illness. As I sat in the airport and then actually got on the plane, I looked around, and everyone was going about their business—using cell phones, reading magazines, and getting out their computers to either work or watch a movie. I didn't say much; I was still thinking about what I'd been through. There wasn't any time to process in theater, and now I was left to myself with my thoughts. People began to order drinks on the plane, and I just shook my head. It was as if I was living in two different worlds—two totally different worlds. And then it happened.

One guy, who clearly was not in a happy mood, began complaining about the temperature of his coffee about 30 minutes into our flight. I'm not sure what you experienced, but I quickly realized that I compared everything that was going on around me to what I had experienced in war. As the medical advisor in Kandahar, I saw everyone who had serious injuries as they went to the Role 3 trauma hospital for care. If anyone died, it was my responsibility to ensure that the appropriate service or country knew the identity of the person. And when people came to the Role 3, they usually had suffered some pretty serious and gruesome injuries. My body and my mind had begun to acclimate to this as reality. It's what you do in theater. You begin to get used to seeing trauma. It's normal.

Trauma surgeons,[11] nurses, and techs all experience this as they have to find a way to cope with this new normal, day in and day out. That's why they are often there only four months. It's very, very difficult work. And we are affected not only by what happens to others who get injured or die, but often also when we think about how it is that we survived. And, since you are reading this book, you, too, are likely a <u>survivor</u>.

Unfortunately, these experiences take their emotional toll, as if you were literally at a tollbooth with cars lined up behind you, and you find that there is a price to be paid, but you left your wallet at home. You're stuck, can't move, and confused as to how this happened, and all the while people are waiting for you to hurry up and move on (i.e., get on with your life). You feel rushed to make decisions, and you feel as if people are honking their horn saying, "Come on, hurry up." But "getting back your old self" doesn't seem possible, given what you've been through.

These thoughts run through my head, and I wonder if they go through yours as well? I flash back to reality, and there remains this guy complaining about his coffee on the flight. He is impatient, irritable, and downright rude. You may find that your patience runs out much quicker than it normally would have before you deployed. You may think to yourself, "I mean, seriously, in light of people dying in a war zone, while you sit in your nice comfy suit on a multimillion dollar plane, going somewhere safe, all you can think about is the temperature of your coffee when there are people dying for your <u>freedom?" Your frustration buil</u>ds to anger, and all you want to do is shut him up. Your eyes scan back

---

[11] If you are interested in reading more about what medical personnel go through, you might want to consider reading *No Place to Hide* by W. Lee Warren, M.D. He was a neurosurgeon in Iraq and details incredible stories of what he, as a doctor, went through.

and forth as you look around, and everyone is just sitting there. Alone in your thoughts, it's a pull between contemplating horrific acts of harm like throat punching this guy and realizing you shouldn't even be having these thoughts.

In your mind, you didn't fight for freedom in this country to have some jerk be mean to a flight attendant because of the temperature of his coffee! And then you realize it's happening. You find yourself getting angry, very quickly, over people who are rude, selfish, etc., or with people who just like drama. Why? Because we compare it to our ideal of what we went to war for: to create a safe, secure, and peaceful world. People who jeopardize that, well, we don't have much tolerance for them.

Chances are you get it when I say, "A new normal." Take just a few moments to think about that concept. Do you have a new normal? Did you change? Or are the world and the people in it just selfish and full of drama, only caring about their personal well-being and what they get out of life? Or both? How would you define your new normal? What do you notice about yourself that has changed?

When it comes to my new normal, I realize:

_____

_____

_____

_____

_____.

Whatever you do, don't leave that blank. Think about how things, or you, have changed. And if so, how did this happen?

FRAME OF REFERENCE

Let me give you the top ten reasons why I believe that we change.

First, things are different because of experiential learning. Whenever you go through an experience of war, it changes you. You see things differently because in war things oftentimes come down to life and death. When your safety has been jeopardized, you quickly realize that you may be the one who dies. You have to deal with mortality issues, issues related to friends dying, or what life would be like for your family if you don't make it home. You learn to judge things in regard to how bad they are based on life and death. That just makes sense, given the context. So, when someone complains about their coffee, you may think, "Are you kidding me? Do you not know that we are at war? And *you* certainly aren't going to go! You sit in your comfortable world and demand that others cater to you, all while people are sacrificing and dying for your 'rights'!" Does this sound familiar?

 Key Takeaway: One's frame of reference changes when everything around one in a theater of war could mean the difference between life and death.

Second, less than one percent of the American population serves in the military. We hear that number thrown around, but what it often means to us is that we are willing to go and serve and possibly die for our country, and others will not. Others would rather enjoy all the benefits of freedom and not have to pay one minute of their lives to earn it. On top of that, people have died so that they could enjoy that freedom. For those who are selfish, the one word that came to my mind was ungrateful. What words would you use?

_____

_____

Third, we are expendable. The intense, gut realization hits that it could have been you who died in the war zone. You probably saw the effects of war that are quite costly. You may even wear a bracelet or run in a 5K race to honor those who have died. They have names, and those names mean something. When you go to Veterans Day events and see or hear the names of the fallen, you know it very well could have been you. Some people even experience survivor guilt.

In my case, it became very up close and personal. All of the nine Air Force officers were killed in the JDOC in Bagram when I was in Kandahar. None survived—not one. They were killed by an Afghan pilot who was supposed to be on our side. And the JDOC is supposed to be in the inner sanctuary of the green zone. The holiest of holies, if you will. This is where command and control is, but there was no controlling death, even in the safest place in a war zone. Had my orders been to Kabul instead of Kandahar, the only other NATO command location in Afghanistan, *I would be dead—period*. And that carries a weight all by itself. Oh, sure, I tell myself, "I would have been prepared; I could have killed him instead," and it somehow would have turned out differently. I wonder if any of our brothers or sisters in the Air Force on that day thought the same thing. The reality is that it was nine against one, and they still died.

How about you: what was your experience like? What was the loss of life that you experienced? What were the names of the dead? How did they die? You can honor them by writing down the names of the people (if you know them) who died and how it happened. If you don't know their names, just put a symbol there and describe what happened.

_____

_____

_____

_____

_____

_____

_____

Without making this experience too personal, I do wish to honor those who gave the ultimate sacrifice that day in Kabul. These are the men and women who died that day and changed my perspective on mortality forever. They deserve honor, respect and our remembrance of them and their sacrifice.

Lt. Col. Frank D. Bryant Jr., 37, of Knoxville, TN, who was assigned to the 56th Operations Group at Luke AFB, Arizona;

Maj. Philip D. Ambard, 44, of Edmonds, WA, an assistant professor of foreign languages at the US Air Force Academy in Colorado Springs, CO;

Maj. Jeffrey O. Ausborn, 41, of Gadsden, AL, a C-27 instructor pilot assigned to the 99th Flying Training Squadron at Randolph AFB, TX;

Maj. David L. Brodeur, 34, of Auburn, MA, an 11th Air Force executive officer at JB Elmendorf-Richardson, AK;

Maj. Raymond G. Estelle II, 40, of New Haven, CT, who was assigned to Air Combat Command headquarters at JB Langley-Eustis, VA;

Maj. Charles A. Ransom, 31, of Midlothian, VA, a member of the 83rd Network Operations Squadron at Langley-Eustis (posthumously promoted to the rank of major on May 3);

Capt. Nathan J. Nylander, 35, of Hockley, TX, who was assigned to the 25th Operational Weather Squadron at Davis-Monthan AFB, AZ; and

MSgt. Tara R. Brown, 33, of Deltona, FL, who was assigned to the Air Force Office of Special Investigations at JB Andrews, MD.

Fourth, people say stupid things, and we have a reaction to that. When I came home, one of my civilian peers asked me, "David, would you let your kids join the military after all you experienced?" I said, "Well, it's their choice, but of course, if that is what they would want to do, it would be honorable, especially since I know firsthand the sacrifice." And then the person stated, "Well, I would never let my kid join. I would never let them go in harm's way."

Right then my anger started building up inside to a point I never thought possible. My response (thank God, inside my head) went like this: "Oh, so it's OK for my kid to serve and go to war and possibly die, but it's not OK for your kid. So you want to enjoy all of the benefits of freedom without any sacrifice. You want to stay here in your cushy job, have people like me sacrifice so that you can get your Starbucks, do nothing but 'research' those of us that come back, and then you have the audacity to say that! I love my kid just as much as you love yours! Get out of my face!" I was beyond angry, and I have never forgotten this experience.

Do you find that people say some really stupid things, and you have a reaction, too? Do you find yourself getting frustrated, irritable, and impatient? What is it that, when you think about it, triggers a strong emotional reaction?

_____

_____

Fifth: triggers, triggers, triggers. When you come out of a war zone, you have been forced to do things in a very specific way in order to stay safe and to stay alive. To not do so can literally cost you or others their lives. Anyone in that position would then take things seriously. We will talk about classical conditioning in Module V and how we are constantly trained in situational awareness, risk assessment, threat mitigation, you name it. On top of that, you probably experienced risk to your own life on multiple occasions and that feeling of despair that others didn't make it home. You are not crazy; it's classical conditioning. It's not complicated either—you've been conditioned to have certain responses. So, there is no wonder that you continued this behavior when you came home.

You stay home, and when you do go out, you watch people and size up situations. You check exits, your six,[12] and you don't do well in crowds. You think about threats and how to mitigate them. And all of this is because of self-preservation. All of us want to come home and bring everyone else back alive, but that doesn't always happen. One thing is for sure: there are triggers that often go back to safety and security, because that is what was threatened, and not coming home alive was not an option. Think about some of the triggers that you have experienced. What triggers you, and what is your response? Think of at least three incidents that have happened to you.

---

[12] When using an analog clock, the six is behind you, so it means, "watch your back."

Trigger	Response

Sixth, I am a pawn in the analogy of a chess piece. When I ask people, "If war was a chess match, what chess piece would you be?" almost inevitably, they say, "a pawn." Some people do pick other pieces, but very few. The piece you pick is probably highly correlated to how much power and control you felt you had in theater. And although we have a lot of weapons on us and around us, there are times we felt as if we were a pawn, with very little significance, power, or influence, especially when it came to decisions and what we were allowed to do. That is often left for others to decide.

We are usually told what to do in the military. And no matter what position you hold, someone is directly above you. So, we learn to take orders and do so efficiently and effectively. To not do so is a UCMJ violation, an article 15, or, at minimum, a letter of reprimand (LOR).

When people are in the military, they are not allowed to speak poorly about their superiors, especially the commander in chief. But when you leave the military, this seems to change quickly. Have you found yourself saying things and having strong feelings about what goes on in the world, maybe even involving politics? What are your reactions when you see things happening around you?

_____

_____

_____

_____

_____

Seventh, we tend to perceive things through "all or nothing" glasses. Did you notice what you did in response to the media, television, or, specifically, the news? Some people stay completely away from the news because they get easily triggered. Others want to watch it so that they know exactly what's going on. It's like a light switch; you are either on or off, all or nothing. Which way do you lean when it comes to the news media? Where else have you noticed "all or nothing thinking" in your life?

_____

_____

_____

Eighth, we experience difficulty in knowing what to share, if anything at all. "Do I share, or do I not share what happened in theater?" That is the question. On one hand, you want to share or talk about what you've been through. On the other, you may find it difficult to do so for various reasons, possibly because you don't want to bring it back home with you. By talking about it, you then do what I call "adulterate" the happy, content, safe home life that you fought to protect. You may also wonder what others might think of you if they truly knew what you did. They may judge you, even if they don't say anything. So, you don't risk it. But then it stays bottled up inside, and if we've learned nothing, time doesn't heal. Just ask any of our WWII or Vietnam veterans. If time healed, none of them would have PTS(D). It's not time that heals; it's what you do with the time that heals. Have you felt free to share? Do you go into detail about what happened? Is some of it classified, so you can't? One thing is for sure: when you don't share, people often think the worst. And this is why we created "Module V: You Can't Handle the Truth."

If you do share, great. But if you don't, what stops you from doing so? And even more so, have you noticed that, by not being able to talk about certain things, you have no choice but to internalize them and keep them stuffed down inside? If you respond in this manner, it's a form of self-protection. When you think about the people who you can truly trust with what goes on in your mind, who do you think of? This is your workbook, so keep it safe, but list out those people.

_____

_____

If you do not have anyone, you may feel that you are left with no choice but to go it alone. And humans are not designed to "go it alone." We don't go to war alone, and we can't come home alone. Instead, find a great friend or trained professional who understands the concepts we are talking about in this workbook to help you. Or you can always contact us at www.ProjectHealingHeroes.org. We have a ton of resources available to you, and we want to help. And if what you went through is classified, find someone who has the security clearance and confidentiality who can help without fear of your saying something that will get you into trouble.

Ninth, symptoms can define us if we let them. You may hear veterans talk about how they can't get better because they have PTS(D). Or they may have co-morbid symptoms which include PTS(D) and insomnia. Let's just take sleep as an example. Research shows that over 90% of people who come out of theater have insomnia of some form or another. Why? Because we can die at any moment; we have no idea where or when the enemy will strike; we are vulnerable; we have a high ops tempo; we often live on adrenaline; our schedules are not 8:00 a.m. to 5:00 p.m.; downtime is minimal; we have stressors at home. There are a lot of reasons why we have trouble sleeping. And we haven't even talked about how our brains are trying to make sense of things at night when we no longer have our defense mechanisms active like we do in the daytime. It can literally be a nightmare. Do you have sleeping problems, nightmares, or thoughts that run through your head that you don't want others to know? Congratulations, you're in the 90-percent-or-higher group. If you conclude that you have PTS(D) and cannot get better, continue with this workbook.

Tenth, war is not normal. It has been said that what you are experiencing is "a normal reaction to an abnormal situation." The abnormal situation is war. There is nothing normal about people killing people. There is also nothing normal about living your life as if you may die at any moment. So, let me ask you the same questions that I ask other veterans. And in your head, just say *check* or *yes* if you experience these:

1. Do you have problems sleeping?
2. Do you find yourself irritable and easily angered?
3. Do you get triggered by watching the news?
4. Do you have difficulty talking about certain events that happened?
5. Do you take prescribed or over-the-counter medicine to deal with symptoms since you came home?
6. Do you find yourself watching others, looking for exits, being situationally aware of your surroundings, and possibly thinking about what you would do in certain situations?
7. Do you find yourself going back in time and reliving experiences of war?
8. Do other people say that you've changed or are afraid to say it?
9. Do you have difficulty with relationships both at home and/or at work?
10. Do you have strong political views and not say them out of fear of what others may think or do?
11. Bonus: Do you have homicidal or suicidal thoughts that you keep to yourself?

So, how many times did you answer *check* or *yes*? Are you normal?

The best answer I've heard to date is, "It's normal for those of us that have been to war," and to that I say, "Exactly." There is a *reason* why most of us are the way we are after coming out of a war zone. Our experiences have changed us. We are no longer the same. This doesn't mean we've changed for the worse, but it does mean that we are different. Have you heard others say that you are different or that they want the "old you" back?

The purpose of this module is simple: to realize that what you are experiencing, given the context of war, is normal—normal for warriors, at least. But when you compare it to the so-called "normal" population in the civilian world, it's probably not normal. And our challenge is living in the civilian world. Life may have at times even been simpler in the military or in a war zone, but we didn't join the military to live our lives in a war zone. We did it so that we could ensure a safe world for our loved ones and ourselves. You may want to read the blog on our website called, "Do you want to fight a home or an away game?" It talks about fighting terrorism on *their* soil, not on ours.

Unfortunately, in our minds, we often bring home our "E-bag"—not our A, B, or C bag, but our Emotional bag. And sometimes it's heavier than all three of our other bags. This article is under our blog section also at www.ProjectHealingHeroes.org for you to read if interested.

What I am hoping you will understand is that what you are experiencing is normal *for a war zone.* It kept you alive! But now, even if you are home, *it's time to come all the way home.* If these thoughts, symptoms, issues, and emotions continue to bother you or cause you consequences, it's time to seek out someone or something that can help get you where you want to be. This is where RFT can be helpful.

In conclusion, if many veterans feel and think the same way as you and I do, and the common theme is our experience in a war zone, then it only makes sense that you are not crazy but normal. Remember, "It's a normal reaction to an abnormal situation." That being said, we still live in the civilian world and thankfully so. It's time to address each of these issues, one at a time, and resolve them through various mechanisms. The one we found most helpful in reviewing all of the literature and working through PTS(D) symptoms is using military training to deal with military issues. This is why we created this workbook, because increasing one's resilience to address traumatic experiences and new triggers will give you the resources to handle life's most difficult challenges. It has been said that character isn't built; it's *revealed.* We believe it's actually both. Stress is one of the best ways to unveil a person's character and resiliency. So, now that you know you are more normal than you thought, let's get to work on building resilience.

MODULE II: INSOMNIA

Intent: To help warriors better understand the importance of sleep, why it is elusive, and how it impacts almost everything in your life.

Context: Statistically, over 90% of warriors have struggled with one form of sleep problem or another. In fact, the most commonly diagnosed sleep disorder in the Veterans Health Administration is obstructive sleep apnea. Whether it's a medical condition or insomnia from trauma-related nightmares, sleep deprivation has dire consequences. Sleep problems are typically the biggest complaint in individuals with PTSD, followed closely by anger. Often, when the sleep issue gets resolved, many of the other symptoms improve as well. This cannot be stressed enough!

Let me restate this. Everything improves with quality sleep because it allows the brain to heal. In this module, you'll learn about more than a dozen things that affect sleep so that you can become a student of your own sleep patterns and begin to retrain yourself to sleep more soundly.

Before getting into the specifics of insomnia and its treatment, let's first consider some contributing factors to sleep dysregulation. Make a check next to any of the following that might be affecting your sleep.

- ☐ Nightmares: They either wake us up, or we avoid sleeping so we don't have to experience them.
- ☐ Depression: If you sleep most of the day because you are clinically depressed, you will not need as much sleep at night. Even if you are not sleeping during the day, depression in and of itself disrupts the sleep architecture of the brain.
- ☐ Anxiety: Worrying and thinking a lot at bedtime, trying to solve life's problems while lying in bed at night
- ☐ Chemicals: Caffeine, sugar, and even natural adrenaline can keep us from sleeping. Most people don't think about these issues, but they highly influence insomnia.
- ☐ Drug and or alcohol use or withdrawl: Some people believe that alcohol relaxes them and helps them to get to sleep. In reality, alcohol causes people to wake up more frequently throughout the night, including during stage 4 (REM) sleep.
- ☐ Being overweight: When we're asleep, the muscles of the throat relax and may obstruct the airway, stopping breathing (obstructive sleep apnea).
- ☐ Heart condition: Congestive heart failure can lead to shortness of breath when lying flat.
- ☐ Neurological conditions: Central sleep apnea can occur when the brain doesn't trigger the diaphragm muscle to cause you to breathe.

As you can see from this abbreviated list, there are often a lot of things that could be interfering with sleep. Fortunately, most sleep conditions respond, at least partly, to establishing good sleep habits and educating yourself about what works (and what does not work) for you.

Assuming that medical reasons for insomnia (obstructive sleep apnea, central sleep apnea, congestive heart failure, etc.) are adequately treated, one of the most promising techniques to address insomnia comes from Cognitive Behavior Therapy – Insomnia (CBT–I). Ultimately, the goal of CBT–I is adequate sleep with no need for medications. Think about that for a minute! There are four key components: stimulus control, sleep hygiene, sleep restriction and relaxation training.

STIMULUS CONTROL – The aim is to associate the bed with sleep. People are encouraged to:

- Use the bed for sleep and sex only. Don't read, check your phone, play games, or watch TV in bed. Think of this as training the primitive part of your brain to believe that the bed is only for sleep. Avoid exciting activities such as exercise, sex (unless that helps you sleep), playing games, or watching TV 1–2 hours before bedtime.
- Get into bed only when tired. If you are not tired, it's possible that your body does not need much rest.
- Maintain a consistent pattern. Go to bed and wake up at the same time every day, including weekends. If you can't get to sleep for whatever reason until 2:00 a.m., get up at your normal wake up time. This will help reset your sleeping pattern.
- If you cannot get to sleep within 20 minutes, get out of bed and move to another room. Do something calming and unexciting, such as reading a book. When you get sleepy, return to bed.

SLEEP HYGIENE

The intent here is to control your environment and your behavior before your appointed sleep cycle. Just like brushing your teeth and changing clothes, routines are important in preparing your mind for sleep. The following is a list of things that commonly affect sleep, many that we don't often think about. These tips are for your own behavior modification. Your body will learn to sleep better.

You don't have to do all of these tips, but you should at least try them. Start with one or two that seem relatively easy. Then progress by adding a new one every few nights to build up better sleep habits. The goal will be for you to become a student of your own sleep cycle and the patterns and hours of sleep that you require to feel rested.

RECOMMENDATIONS FOR TRAINING YOUR BRAIN TO SLEEP

Make a check next to the top 2–3 behaviors you want to change first.

☐ Create a soothing, relaxing environment. At least 30 minutes prior to bed, create a low-light environment (switch from incandescent bulbs to candles or 5400 – yellow tint – bulbs), take a warm bath, use aromatherapy, begin to remove or significantly reduce anything stimulating.

☐ Avoid caffeine after noon. Caffeinated drinks have a six-hour half-life. This means if you drank a 32 oz tea at 6:00 p.m. (equivalent to 100mg of caffeine), you would still have 50 mg of caffeine in your system at midnight. Although sensitivity to caffeine varies for each person, having 500 mg a day greatly impacts sleep hygiene. Some people are sensitive to even one cup of coffee (100 mg of caffeine) a day. Caffeine, a natural stimulant, creates problems with insomnia, the number of times one wakes up in the night and interferes with deep sleep. We've included a caffeine chart to give you an idea of the amount of caffeine found in various drinks. (See Attachment A.)

☐ If you cannot sleep after 10-15 minutes of lying in bed, get up. Remember, the bed is only for sleep and sex. If you can't sleep, don't train your body and brain that the bed is also for lying awake, frustrated that you can't sleep. Instead, get up and go to another room that has limited or no stimulus.

☐ Read some relatively dry material for about 15–20 minutes in a low-light environment before bed. For example, keep one of those books you've been meaning to read next to your couch lamp and lie there reading—not in the bed. Also, don't turn on electronics after you've decided to sleep.

☐ Go to sleep and wake up at the same time every day, including weekends. If you can't do this perfectly, try not to vary the time difference by more than one hour.

☐ Invest in a security system so that you don't feel compelled to lie awake, listening for sounds throughout the night.

☐ Exercise during the day, preferably first thing in the morning. Weightlifting to prevent muscle failure is associated with increasing Brain-Derived Neurotrophic Factor (see Module III) and growth hormone release at night.

SLEEP RESTRICTION

Restriction of sleep may seem paradoxical (opposite) to a person with insomnia. In reality, you are trying to find the actual amount of sleep you require in order to function in a normal, healthy manner. Since most people with insomnia are trying to get to sleep, this approach gets to the answer through sleep deprivation. You literally get so little sleep that you are tired and have no problem falling asleep. Then you restrict the amount you are to get, and then gradually add time, until you find the right amount for you.

The mechanism for CBT-I focuses on time in bed (TIB). TIB is based on sleep efficiency (SE). Sleep efficiency is calculated based on the total sleep time (TST), the actual amount of time a person is normally able to sleep, compared to their TIB. That may sound a bit confusing so let's look at it in a bit more detail:

Sleep efficiency = (Total sleep time / Time in bed)
- First, time in bed (TIB) is restricted to the total sleep time (TST).
- Increase or decrease TIB weekly by only 20-30 minutes.
- Increase TIB if SE >90%.
- Decrease TIB if SE <80%.

Here's a specific example:

Let's say you get a total of four hours total sleep time (TST), but the amount of time in bed (TIB) is six hours. TIB (six hours) minus TST (four hours) means you are in bed two hours not sleeping. When you put it into the formula, it looks like this:

Sleep efficiency = (Total sleep time / Time in bed)
4 hours/6 hours = .66 or 66%
So, the sleep efficiency (SE) = 66%

Based on the principles of CBT-I below:
- Increase TIB if SE >90%.
- Decrease TIB if SE <80%.

SE at 66% is less than 80%, so one would decrease TIB. Remember, decrease or increase by 20–30 minutes. So in this case, one would decrease time in bed by 20–30 minutes and then continue to track.

This hopefully makes logical sense to decrease TIB. Laying in bed for an extra two hours and not getting sleep becomes a nightly frustration. And because you have insomnia, you can't make yourself go to sleep (TST). Therefore, the logical solution is to not waste the two hours (TIB) frustrated and trying to get to sleep. Get up, and do something with those two hours.

Things you could do with an extra two hours instead of lying in bed frustrated you can't sleep:

1. Write a book.
2. Read a book.
3. If you have kids or someone special in your life, write them a letter, and mail it. Then tell them they can't open it until a designated date. I do this with my kids so that on their 18th birthdays, they will have at least ten letters to open.
4. Make a video. Sometimes making a video doing something you enjoy, or others would enjoy, can make a lasting impression.

5. Pray for part of the time for people you care about.
6. Start a hobby of something you enjoy. Maybe photography, but don't forget batteries!
7. Try cooking and sharing with a neighbor. What you serve them may depend on how much you like them.
8. Get a dog. Actually, forget that, you will never get any sleep if you get a puppy.
9. Restore a car, a boat, a camper. I renovated a whole house.
10. Think about volunteer opportunities to give back.

Author's note: I have learned that I only require about five hours of sleep a night. I was trying to get the eight hours people indicate, but my body simply didn't need it. I was trying to get my body to do what is recommended, but it had other ideas. So, I decided to quit lying in bed frustrated, get up, and do something productive. This is partly how Project Healing Heroes and CombatPTSD.org came into being and why we have produced multiple books to serve combat veterans.

A final step you can take with CBT-I is relaxation.

RELAXATION TECHNIQUES

The aim is to find find techniques that help you increase your ability to relax. These include using sound machines that imitate nature, sleep pillows, weighted blankets, warm baths, cold rooms, etc.

MEDICATIONS FOR INSOMNIA

The second step for restoring your sleep is to take a hard look at medications that may help—and those that could be making it worse. These are the medications used to treat insomnia related to PTS(D). They are listed from least to greatest side effects and severity.

Stage	Medication	Mechanism	Dose	Cautions
1	Melatonin[13]	Natural hormone that stimulates sleep at night, not during the daytime	3–10 mg	Can cause rapid sleepiness the first few times it is used, then need to be doubled
2	Diphenhydramine (Benadryl)[14]	Antihistamine	50–100 mg	Dry mouth; long-lasting
3	Prazosin (Minipress)	Anti-adrenaline	Starting at 1 mg, usually up to 10–12 mg	Use for nightmares only; lowers blood pressure
4	Trazodone	Antidepressant, anticholinergic	25–200 mg	May cause daytime drowsiness

[13] Over-the-counter
[14] Over-the-counter

5	Cyproheptadine (Periactin)	Anticholinergic	4–8 mg	Dry mouth; lowers blood pressure
	Doxepin	Antidepressant, anticholinergic	3-6 mg	Dry mouth; lowers blood pressure
6	Quetiapine (Seroquel)	Antipsychotic, anticholinergic, anti-adrenaline, antihistamine	50–200 mg	Weight gain, increased cholesterol, diabetes, movement disorders
7	Zolpidem (Ambien)	Acts on the benzodiazepine receptor just like alcohol	5–10 mg	*Temporary last resort*; risk of dementia; lowers intelligence; **worsens sleep**; addictive; deadly when taken with alcohol

Too often, warriors are on high doses of antipsychotics for "anger," Ambien for sleep, and Xanax, Ativan, or Klonopin for anxiety, all while drinking far too much alcohol. Besides the health and safety concerns that abound in these situations, the core issues of post-traumatic stress are not being addressed. Prescribers don't often think about Cyproheptadine and Doxepin, and very seldom take the time to explain the side effects. In fact, it's usually easy to tell by looking at a warrior's medication list just how "trauma-informed" their physician is.

The next step is to get you sleeping. Prazosin is often used for nightmares and another medication for sleep. Within 1–2 weeks, it's possible to begin reversing sleep patterns that have been present for years. We want to emphasize that sleep improvement is best accomplished simultaneously with therapy for post-traumatic stress. If you don't resolve the underlying belief system, hypervigilance, moral injury and survivor guilt, you will be hard-pressed to ever really experience a restful season of life. You'll stay "on guard," with adrenaline pumping through your veins as you try to sleep. And that's simply no way to really live.

INSOMNIA FROM A MOOD DISORDER

The normal biological functions of the body suffer in severely depressed people. Changes in appetite, energy, concentration, motivation, and speed of body movements can all accompany feelings of sadness, depression, and guilt. In fact, five out of eight of these bodily functions must be present in order to diagnose Major Depressive Disorder in the *Diagnostic and Statistical Manual of Psychiatry*.

Fortunately, the treatment of PTS(D) and depression typically go together, so if you treat one, you often treat the other. Next in "Module III—The Biology of PTSD," you will learn that Brain-Derived Neurotrophic Factor is an important protein in the recovery of the hippocampus and other parts of the brain affected bydepression and PTS(D). Prolonged insomnia and its associated high levels of cortisol in the bloodstream cause the hippocampus to shrink—the exact opposite of what is needed for symptom improvement. Therefore, **the warrior must come to terms with restful sleep**, even if that means having to talk about what they have experienced, including the emotional toll it has taken.

The following is a printable weekly chart for you to study your mood and its relationship to sleep:

	Sunday	Monday	Tuesday	Wednesday	Thursday	Friday	Saturday
Predominant mood?							
Number of hours of sleep							
What triggered your mood or sleep problem?							
How long did the mood or sleep problem last?							
Did anything make it better?							
Did anything make it worse?							

MODULE III: THE NEUROBIOLOGY OF THE BRAIN

Intent: To help warriors understand the importance of the biological mechanisms that underlie Post-Traumatic Stress.

Context: The purpose of this module is to increase an understanding of the brain structures as well as the electrical and chemical interactions that contribute to stress reactions.

NEUROBIOLOGY COMPLEXITY

This module could be as complex as trying to explain to a civilian how to do land navigation without any verbal instructions. For example, can you imagine trying to explain to someone how to obtain a car key that is inside a watermelon after guiding them through a five-mile mountainous region while providing only hand signals for directions? Good luck! Now that you have that visual in your head, and some of you are actually thinking to yourself that you could do that, let's just say it's possible, but quite challenging. The same goes for explaining the neurobiology of the brain.

We will attempt to simplify this incredibly complex, integrated and ever evolving knowledge and understanding of how the brain works. The complexity in explaining this organ is that you have to understand both electrical and chemical interactions. In our attempt to simplify things, there are those who may read this and feel we left out important details or concepts. For those of you who are intrigued by the brain processes and wish for a more in-depth analysis, we refer you to resources such as *The Body Keeps the Score* by Bessel Van Der Kolk.

First, we will talk about stress responses, and then second, we will divide the chapter into three brain structures in order to better understand the underpinnings of the brain and its influence on stress:

1. Brainstem
2. Limbic system
3. Prefrontal cortex

STRESS RESPONSES

Let's start with what most warriors know, understand and can relate to because of what they have experienced personally: stress from war. In 1929, Walter Cannon came up with three factors in which stress can manifest itself: fight, flight or freeze. Another word for stress could be trauma or even terror. According to his conceptual framework, during stressful times in a person's life, a person will react and respond in one of these three ways. We, however, believe that there are a few other ways that people respond, beyond his original ideas.

The authors would have added at least two more factors to stressful reactions. The two additional responses to include in this list of stressful responses: Faint and Fail.

The fourth factor is **Faint.** In certain cultures, fainting is a response to incredibly stressful events. As an example, during the wake for a mother whose son had died, the mom began to weep uncontrollably and then subsequently fainted when seeing him lying in the casket. It was heart breaking to see this mother have to go through the stress of losing her son, let alone her physiological response.

The fifth factor is **Fail**. We have seen a person, under incredible stress, experience the failure of the brain to function properly. A perfect example is a person who experiences blindness,[15] limb weakness, or a convulsive episode[16] that may be interpreted as a grand mal seizure after a significant stressor. Medical work ups including in-depth ophthalmology examinations and testing, EEG monitoring, or other neurological assessments/tests will often show no evidence of pathology. However, the individuals are experiencing very real symptoms. Unfortunately, with our current knowledge base, there is no definitive answer as to why our most complex organ responds in such a manner. Hopefully, going forward, that riddle will be solved. I believe that, in time, it will, we are just not there yet.

Remember, the brain is extremely complex.

In the end, the authors propose the following five factors of stress that we will term the 5F stress responses. In summation, the 5F stress responses are:

1. Fight
2. Flight
3. Freeze
4. Faint
5. Fail

Self-assessment: Now that we have listed out our 5F stress responses, consider your life history and your responses to intense stress. Have you had a situation that you can remember where you reacted in one or more of these five ways? Which one, or ones did you experience, and what happened? Place a check next to the stress response you have experienced, and write some key words surrounding the context and what happened. These could be stressors in war, or it could even be things that

[15] Psychogenic blindness
[16] Non-epileptic convulsive spell

happened in childhood. Stress and trauma have no respect for age. Put an X by those you have not experienced or that do not immediately come to mind.

1. _____ Fight – _____

2. _____ Flight – _____

3. _____ Freeze – _____

4. _____ Faint – _____

5. _____ Fail – _____

BRAIN SYSTEM AND THE STRUCTURES

There are three important areas of the brain that we need to explore in order to better understand what is happening to a person before, during and after a stressful experience. We will review these three areas from the most basic (primitive) to complex (sophisticated):

1. Brainstem
2. Limbic system
3. Prefrontal cortex

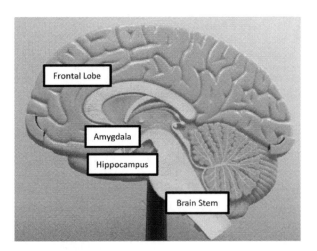

1. Brainstem

Let's look at the brain from a bottom-up approach, beginning with the brainstem. The brainstem is the most primitive (oldest) part of the brain, often called the reptilian brain. The brain stem is the underside of the brain, located just above the spinal cord. It controls our body's autonomic functions. This simply means it controls areas that we don't have to think about like breathing, temperature regulation, hunger, food digestion, blood pressure, sleep/wake cycles, alertness, and startle response.

The reason why this is important to combat veterans, besides the fact that absence of a brainstem means the absence of life, is because the brainstem response is highly correlated to the 5F stress response. Think about how many combat veterans have insomnia, hyperarousal, gastrointestinal problems, appetite issues, intense startle response, etc. The brainstem is very relevant, but it is just one component of the brain as a whole. This brings me to the next important area of the brain for discussion.

2. Limbic System

The limbic system sits right above the brainstem. It includes a few structures, including the amygdala (emotions, fear), hippocampus (memory), thalamus (receives outside information via sight, touch, smell, and hearing) and hypothalamus (regulates body functions). The hypothalamus works closely with the brainstem. If the brainstem is referred to as the reptilian brain, the limbic system can be thought of as the mammalian brain. The mammalian brain, in part, determines what is important for survival. It can be thought of as the first line of defense to alert the body to danger or a threat. Limbic system development depends on a person's genetic makeup in combination with the individual's experiences. We have learned through genetic research that identical twins (with the same exact DNA) can express (utilize/manifest) DNA differently based on their environmental influences. In other words, your trauma history can result in real and measurable physiological changes. This validates people's beliefs that they are different after going to war.

 Key Takeaway: Your trauma history can result in real and measurable physiological changes.

These changes affect things like how your limbic system responds to a perceived threat, for example. Ultimately, the goal of this system is to look out for your welfare and keep you alive. The limbic system interprets information in a non-specific way. For example, a child that has been bitten by a dog may generalize this experience and automatically experience terror any time he or she sees a dog, even a small, lovable, fluffy shih-tzu. The limbic system makes no distinction and automatically initiates one of the 5F stress responses through physiological reactions (increased heart rate and breathing, blood pressure changes, pupil dilation, etc.) and hormone secretion (cortisol, epinephrine, etc.) without any thought on our part. This reaction could mean the difference between life or death under certain threats. But if we have these reactions in non-threatening circumstances, our quality of life suffers. And for some of us, that suffering is not only significant, it permeates our life.

So, what allows some individuals to successfully dial down the 5F stress response after the limbic system has set off an alarm, especially to a "false alarm"? Let's continue talking about the brain in order to make sense of it all. That brings us to the top of the brain, or the cerebral cortex, and more specifically the prefrontal part of the cerebral cortex.

3. Prefrontal Cortex

All mammals have a cerebral cortex; however, the human cerebral cortex is much larger than that found in other mammals. When most people visualize what the brain looks like, they are visualizing the cerebral cortex, which kind of looks like a huge pinkish-gray walnut with lots of hills and valleys and different lobes. The lobe most relevant to our conversation is the frontal lobe and a specific area that makes up the bulk of the frontal lobe called the prefrontal cortex. Our prefrontal cortex is what make us unique among all other mammals. It enables us to learn and use language, think abstractly, make rational decisions, plan, and solve problems, etc. It also houses our personality and allows us to restrain ourselves when we are tempted to act inappropriately or say something we may regret. You might know an older friend or relative with dementia who has "lost their filter." They very likely have degenerative damage in the prefrontal area of their brain. This area also allows us to understand the feelings of another person even if we do not have the same experiences. The ability to feel someone else's pain is called empathy, and it allows us to engage with others in socially meaningful ways. A healthy prefrontal cortex is important for congenial interpersonal relations. In the context of our conversation, it is important to know that the prefrontal cortex is very important in damping the limbic system's 5F stress response if it is not appropriate; however, the more intense the input from the limbic system, the less capacity our prefrontal cortex has to dampen it.

Let's think about the brain like a home security system.

The motion sensor outside your front door, for example, is designed to pick up movement and notify you and emergency services (9-1-1). In our illustration, you can think of the thalamus as the part of the system that detects movement.

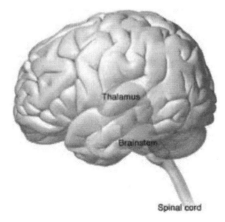

Remember, the thalamus is constantly scanning for input from the outside world via your body's five senses, and in the case of the home security system, we're specifically talking about movement. When movement is detected, the motion sensor (thalamus) sends this sensory data to the alarm system (amygdala).

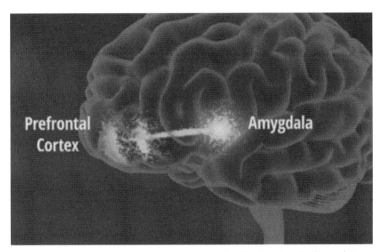

Brain Train Coach (2017)[17]

The alarm system is binary. In other words, it is either "on or off." The amygdala, like the home security alarm, doesn't make decisions about whether or not the threat is valid. It simply sounds the alarm when triggered by information coming in from the sensor. In the case of our home security system, when the alarms sounds, the amygdala is acting as if the sound could be coming from a burglar. But it could also be something as inconsequential as the wind.

Another example would be a smoke detector that could trigger the alarm in the case of smoke from a fire or, if not calibrated correctly, steam from a kettle on the stove.

---

[17] https://braintraincoach.com/amygdala-pfc-connection/

The point is, the alarm sounds without any judgement as to the reason why. The job of the amygdala is simply to alert the person that a potential threat has been detected. This internal alarm sounds, and there is a cascade of events that follow as a result. With our home security system, an incredibly loud sound abruptly begins, which is designed to scare away an intruder and alert the homeowner/neighbor that there is a potential danger, all while the security system alerts 9-1-1. In our body, this alarm triggers a cascade of events that acts on both the hypothalamus and the brainstem to cause our body to be flooded with stress hormones such as cortisol and adrenaline which result in physiological changes to ensure our best chance at survival should there be an actual burglar in the house.

Your body immediately goes on heightened alert. This includes accelerated heart rate, dilated pupils, increased respiratory rate, sweating, etc. In almost an instant, your body makes a decision. Here are a few choices:

1. You could fight and take out this person who has invaded your space.
2. You could run like hell out of your home faster than Usain Bolt.
3. You could freeze in your tracks and hide in your closet as quiet as a mouse.

You get the idea. Your stress response is keeping you alive at this point. This is an appropriate and life-saving response to any life-endangering threat.

But what happens when your home security system alerts you that there is a possible threat, but in reality, it was a false alarm, such as a strong gust of wind that set it off? You investigate, determine there is no threat, and override the alarm by trying to quickly enter your security code. In our brain illustration, in order to override the body's alarm system (amygdala), we must have a healthy prefrontal cortex. Recall that the thalamus receives outside information via the five senses and sends it to the amygdala? Well, it also sends this information to the prefrontal cortex, but does so more slowly. Think of the highway connecting the thalamus to the amygdala as the German Autobahn and the highway from the thalamus to the prefrontal cortex as a 75 mph four-lane highway. You can still make good time, but there is definitely a delay. In brain connectivity, it is measured in milliseconds, but even a small delay can have serious implications.

This results in the amygdala (with a faster "download" speed) responding with an alert signal prior to the prefrontal cortex (slower "upload" speed) reviewing the information and determining whether there is potential threat. Part of the challenge is that we are often in one of the 5F stress responses *prior* to being consciously aware of any possible danger. Let that sink in for a moment, especially as it relates to Cognitive Processing Therapy.

When the slower uploaded information does enter the prefrontal cortex, it enters our consciousness. The prefrontal cortex can be thought of as the Tactical Operations Center (TOC). In this space, you have more data and the ability to integrate the various inputs to decipher the most important and relevant information, including threat risk. You review live camera feeds remotely, assess the threat level, realize there is no threat, and enter the security code, silencing the alarm. This is your prefrontal cortex in action. However, that takes time. Remember, your prefrontal cortex is the part of the brain that allows you to make rational decisions, solve complex problems, think abstractly, plan and restrict your behavior. It is what makes you, *you*.

If we have this amazing TOC in our prefrontal cortex to dampen down our alarm system, then why do many warriors have such a difficult time silencing our alarm and the cascade of events (stress hormones) that follow its trigger? Hold onto that thought as we explain more.

Besides the delayed response and flooding hormones, certain brain structures like the hippocampus and prefrontal cortex can also be affected by pre-trauma experiences. In the most simplistic terms, a history of trauma can lead to misinterpreting a safe situation as dangerous. This is not necessarily a conscious process. Our home security alarm, if not working properly, not calibrated or set too sensitive (because of experiences), can be affected by even the slightest movement such as a leaf being blown by the wind, a loud noise after a waitress drops dishes on the floor, or someone trying to be funny and scare us. This will trigger the alarm, and the cascade of events is in full swing.

There is a saying among neuroscientists that goes, "Neurons that fire together, wire together." Neurons are the primary cells in the brain that speak to each other via electrical conduction. There are 100 billion neurons in the average human brain. *Let that sink in.* This means that neuronal connections are strengthened and reinforced every time they communicate. So, for example, every time you heard an alarm sound in theater that warned of an incoming rocket attack, the neurons that fired together were making stronger connections so that it took much less of a trigger to sound the amygdala's alarm.

When you have experienced trauma, it becomes more difficult to filter out irrelevant information in the prefrontal cortex (TOC). Irrelevant information such as someone pushing in on you in a crowded area, a person walking down the street with an unusual scarf on their head, garbage lying on the side of the road, etc. is more likely to be interpreted as relevant (equating it to a true threat). Remember, your brain's plasticity, or ability to adapt in a theater of war, kept you alive. But now, back home, this adaption has wreaked havoc on your life, mentally and physically. When your brain interprets benign, day-to-day events as scary and potentially life-threatening, your highly stress hormones and 5F stress response get triggered far more than is safe for our bodies. This results not only in a number of false positives but also in a number of health problems (sleepless nights, weight gain, cardiovascular problems, etc.).

At this point, we are convinced that if you wait until you are triggered by something, especially if you wait until you are inundated by the amygdala's alarm system and your body is flooded with stress hormones, it's too late to try to figure out what it was that triggered you. Most likely, you would already be in one of the 5F stress responses. Also, research has shown that some people, during high stress, dissociate. They don't even have access to their frontal lobe to help them sort out what is happening. Instead, we recommend that you work on these issues when you have the cognitive capability and capacity to do so. This means anything that diminishes your cognitive ability needs to be removed (i.e, alcohol consumption, exhaustion, highly stressful experiences, etc.) and resiliency factors put in place (good night's rest, ability to focus and concentrate, good counselor or therapist who can help you see blind spots, healthy relationships, etc).

One specific recommendation is to do the things that help the brain function properly. Following is one such example.

BRAIN-DERIVED NEUROTROPIC FACTOR

There is a protein in your brain called Brain-Derived Neurotrophic Factor (BDNF), which helps you form new nerve connections and improve memory and gives you the ability to develop more options when under stress. The following images demonstrate mouse-brain neurons. The top row, A1–A3, has virtually no BDNF, and in the bottom row, B1–B3, the brain was enriched with BDNF.

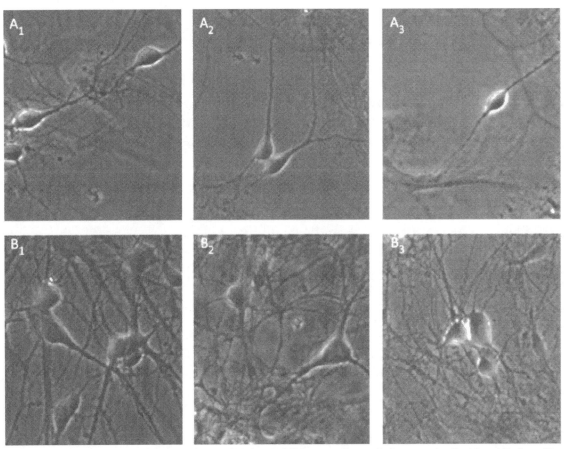

Public domain images: Lalchandani RR, Vicini S. Inhibitory collaterals in genetically identified medium spiny neurons in mouse primary corticostriatal cultures. Psychol. Rep. 2013-11-01 00:00:00 2013;1(6).

You can see how the bottom row of images has a much more robust and dense network of neurons. This is what you want your neuronal pathways to look like!

In patients with PTS(D), we know that they have less BDNF and smaller hippocampi. Think of it as a muscle, and the size of the hippocampus relates to your resilience against stress in life. You have to exercise a muscle for it to get stronger. Well, as it turns out, lifting weights has been shown to help increase BDNF levels—and this is the biological goal of PTS(D) therapy. So, we decided to list out some other things that can strengthen your biological resilience.

Things that increase BDNF:

- Weightlifting
- PTS(D) talk therapy alone (without medications)
- Antidepressant medications
- Meditation
- Whole foods (unprocessed, natural, non-GMO, etc.)
- Employment/contribution to society
- Helping others and serving a purpose greater than self
- Meaningful connections with healthy people

Except for the medications on this list, the rest of these things sound very much like a healthy lifestyle: waking up in the morning, meditating, exercising, going to work/school/volunteer, eating a healthy diet, and talking frankly and positively with someone who cares and understands—now that makes for a good day for PTS(D) recovery. Sometimes even the slightest changes can make a big improvement. Even taking up an exercise program or walking and talking about your day's events with a spouse, significant other or friend (even if on a Bluetooth device) can help tremendously. Some of my best therapy moments are with clients who work on their issues while we go for a walk. Before we know it, we have put three miles of fresh air into our lungs, exercised our legs and started to work things out. What a difference clarity of thought has on problem solving! So, let's ask some very basic questions.

What healthy lifestyle activities are you already doing for yourself?

_____

_____

What healthy lifestyle activities would you consider implementing to help increase BDNF levels?

_____

_____

What benefits would you expect to receive in your life if you started doing these healthy things on a consistent basis?

_____

Is there a connection with someone specifically you would like to have either in person or on the phone while implementing one or more of the above?

_____

_____

Now that you have some idea about what BDNF can do for you, let's talk about another potential solution that has considerable research and support.

MEDITATION

One of the best ways to slow down stress hormones, increase focus and concentration, relax and find peace is to live in the moment with yourself in a quiet area. This can work for folks who are constantly in motion (although challenging at first), people in pain, people who are too busy, nay say'ers, even folks who are spiritual and those who are not. For some folks who are particularly religious/spiritual, it can increase your time with God. We are quickly reminded of the verse that says, "Be still and know that I am God." So, for some of you, even the psalmist figured out that meditation and being quiet is a good thing.[18]

There are many different ways to practice meditation. For the purposes of this book, we will focus on the importance of staying in the moment and calming down the body's stress hormones in the hope that a new homeostasis of relaxation can emerge.

I'm sure you can think of people in your own life who are constantly on edge, irritable, frustrated at even the slightest things, amped up, often use energy drinks in the morning and throughout the day because they get poor sleep, etc. Most people don't want to live like this; they have simply gotten into an unhealthy pattern that needs to be changed for the better. Unfortunately, it's often a sense of frustration because there are usually multiple factors that are causing the problem. Our recommendation is to take one thing at a time and eliminate its unhealthiness. One such example is sleep deprivation. Insomnia is, by far, one of the most challenging issues warriors face. It literally causes a cascade of events, including the use of prescription or over-the-counter medication, alcohol use, or any number of other consequences such as anger outbursts which can contribute to relationship problems, job stress and loss, conflict, etc.

---

[18] Personally, in my prayer time I often find that thoughts enter my mind. Before long, I am thinking about other "things" rather than about my time with God. I have found that using meditation techniques increases my ability to stay focused on connecting with God.

Let's just be real for a moment. I often end up writing books from 2:00 a.m. on because I can't sleep and because it makes it easier on my family because they don't have to see me constantly working. But it has its downfalls. I get easily irritated and angry, have to spend a lot more time and energy thinking about ways not to impulsively say something to my boss when I really want to, have weight gain because I'm up half the night - you get the picture. I also suffer from sleep apnea. I hate CPAP machines because they strangle me and give me a headache. This has been an ongoing "battle," and my dear wife is gentle but an MD and makes clear the toll it takes on my body physically. I know she is right, but I feel stuck. Maybe your issue isn't exactly the same, but something you can to which you can relate. I know what I need to do; I just need to do it.

It's times like this when I slow down and think about what is really happening in my life, in the quiet times when I can be honest with myself and just be. This is the point of meditation. Being with oneself, wholly.

It also has another significant contributing factor. You can't be both relaxed and anxious at the same time. The body just doesn't work like that. So, that being the case, and knowing you can't often be successful in working on issues and problems once the amygdala gets triggered, one ideal time to get centered, relaxed and focused, all while allowing your mind to relax and just be you, is during meditation.

Meditation can also reset your homeostasis. If you are constantly on edge, keyed up, looking for high energy, thrill seeking behaviors to "feel alive", etc., this is where long-term cortisol becomes a significant problem. Not only does it not let you rest and feel refreshed and be in the moment, but it also causes significant long-term health problems. Excess cortisol results in immunosuppression which hinders the body's ability to fight infections, causes a decrease in hippocampal volume and working memory, as well as impaired BNDF functioning and decreased neuroplasticity. Our bodies are not designed to live on cortisol and adrenaline – just like they are not desiged to live on soft drinks, coffee, cigarettes and doughnuts.

One of the keys to getting healthy is to not only do the things we need to get us there, but also to allow our body to readjust to these new healthy habits. In doing them, our prefrontal cortex can help us figure things out and see stressors in an appropriate context of time and space, our hippocampus can help us understand our past experiences in light of current "threats," our lens by which we see the world can change in a more healthy way, the amygdala can recalibrate, and the sensitivity level turned down, and finally the thalamus can get in touch with our five senses and do a better job of deciphering what the body is experiencing.

Hopefully, you have a better understanding after reading this chapter on the neurobiology of PTS(D) and its implications in your life. Feel free to contact us if you need more guidance or an in-depth dialogue about stress, the brain and its impact on the body.

MODULE IV: ADRENALINE ADDICTION AND HIGH-RISK BEHAVIOR

Intent: To help warriors understand that a long-term, high-ops life tempo, along with combat experiences, leads to increased adrenaline, cortisol, and a natural high/euphoria.

Context: One of the challenges of being on deployment is that your body's homeostasis begins to acclimate to your surroundings. Thus, when in war, many unfortunately get attacked by things like RPGs or have to avoid things that are not natural in the civilian world, like IEDs. In Kandahar, we constantly got rocketed by the insurgency. The good news was that if you could hear the whizzing sound over your head, you knew it wasn't going to hit you because you could hear it. However, what you didn't know was whether there was another one on the way. And when you see the devastation that these rockets can cause to the body, ripping it to shreds, you quickly realize that you are not invincible. To mitigate this, you made sure that you hit the ground as soon as there was any indication of danger, whether that was the whizzing of rockets or an alarm indicating incoming fire. Your attention and being "on guard" was a direct result of wanting to stay alive.

This heightened sense of situational awareness and repeated exposure to stress in the AOR leaves a person in an elevated, hyped-up state, which is very similar to that of an adrenaline junkie. Yes, I said it, an adrenaline junkie. Adrenaline kept you alive when you were dodging Indirect Fire (IDF) and Direct Fire (DF). It allowed you to be sensitive to potential threats when you were risking your life on missions. It helped you cope with living in austere conditions while being away from your loved ones. It provided the energy boost necessary to keeping you effectively working 16-hour days during deployment, if not 24-hour days during combat missions. It was imperative to your survival. But you are now beginning to learn what happens to your body when it maintains elevated levels of adrenaline and cortisol over an extended period of time.

 Key Takeaway: **When you cannot relax and recharge due to a threatening environment, you feel the need to stay at an elevated level, and it becomes your new normal.**

People wonder why they cannot sleep when they return home. It's because you are so used to this pace, this adrenaline, including a lack of sleep, and it's very hard to change those patterns back to baseline, especially when a person enjoys feeling very much alive. The rest of the world seems very boring once you've been "in the game." Sitting on the bench or even watching the world at its normal pace is an adrenaline junkie's nightmare. The loss of this thrilling and exciting natural drug produced by the adrenal glands is not something people want to lose. Many warriors actually deploy to a warzone repeatedly just to get the thrill of adrenaline back.

As a matter of fact, we had special ops guys who would come into the USO where I volunteered who played video games until all hours of the day and night. Instead of resting, calming down, and resetting their homeostasis, they and their buddies would stay amped up all the time on video games and power drinks. These same special ops guys actually beat the *Black Ops* video game within four hours of it coming out and walked out saying, "Well, that was easy."

ADRENALINE RUSH

The adrenaline rush is that surge of chemicals into your body that occurs under intense stress. Walter Cannon spoke of this in 1929 when he wrote about the various responses to stress: fight, flight, or freeze. Another name for adrenaline is *epinephrine*, and it's that intense and extremely fast chemical rush that occurs in the body when you are, for example, receiving incoming fire. It also happens when a loud noise goes off, especially when you least expect it. Controlled explosions are a little easier to take, because they usually announce them, and they are, by definition, supposed to be controlled. It's the *uncontrolled* explosions that really trigger our sympathetic nervous system. Just look at what happens when a car back fires near you.

Fill in the blanks in the next several paragraphs with your best guesses. The answers are provided at the end of the chapter.

What typically happens is that this sympathetic system is when (1) _____ floods your system and causes your heart rate to increase, pupils to dilate, and an increase in blood pressure, sweating, intense breathing, etc. It's a great feeling, which is why people enjoy it so much. Assuming that you are safe and make it through the (2) _____.

Adrenaline has at least five benefits:

1. You often have a significant increase in strength (which is why you hear of a mom who lifted a car off her child who was pinned underneath);
2. Diminished feelings of pain (which is why some people can get shot and keep going);
3. Elevated senses (such as seeing, hearing, feeling, and smelling things more intensely, which is also why people are triggered by certain smells that are emotionally attached to the triggering event);
4. Increased (3) _____ (which helps to oxygenate the blood supply); and
5. Significant increase in energy (which can certainly help in times when a person's life is on the line).

When you are in a kill-or-be-killed environment, only the strong survive. In an Area of Responsibility (AOR), when your life is on the line, adrenaline can be your best friend. As a matter of fact, people often feel so good and so intense when they are in this state that they will do anything to keep it, including (4) _____ drinks, (5) staying up _____, and (6) _____/go pills.

Adrenaline junkies will do anything to avoid sleeping. Adrenaline also has the added benefit that, if you don't sleep, you don't have (7) _____ or the problems related to PTS(D). So, it not only makes you feel good, but it also reduces the negative effects of having to reexperience some of your bad feelings.

Unfortunately, there are at least three downsides that accompany this elevated adrenaline-junkie lifestyle.

First, it destroys the body. It's like being on methamphetamine—all the time. The body needs rest, and it has to repair itself, but anyone who has been on a natural high really dislikes having to stop. Eventually, this person not only stops but also usually crashes, which, again, can be a good thing for people with sleeping problems, but it then only trains your body to go, go, go, (8) _____.

I can always recognize warriors with sleeping problems because they almost always have that look of exhaustion in the morning and are drinking some type of energy-boosting beverage or any drink that contains caffeine. They often get into a bad habit of using (9) _____ at night; then they can't sleep, and then they need an upper in the morning. You can see that when the body's normal cycle is interrupted by this drug-seeking behavior, it only complicates things. For example, the body's normal repair process, when interrupted, leaves you in an anxious, jittery state. You just feel on edge, and the slightest things irritate you. The body needs rest to bring back a more normal homeostasis, but this is often interrupted twofold: first by the environment of war and second by your decisions to stay elevated. Welcome to the adrenaline-addiction world.

Second, the mind has to have time to rest to make sense of the world and what you are experiencing. Part of the problem with living at a high adrenaline level or in chronically stressful environments is that areas of your brain responsible for memory (i.e., the hippocampus) and emotional processing (i.e., the amygdala) lose nerve cells (neurons) and connections between these cells (neuronal pathways). Brain imaging studies have shown actual physical changes in size, shape, and connectivity patterns of these pivotal structures. This can be significant because this affects your ability to regulate your emotions, to encode long-term memories, and to make new memories. If you wonder why you have difficulty understanding new concepts or remembering things, it could be that you are experiencing biological changes in your brain. You knew something was wrong, but you may not have known exactly the reasons why. **But it gets better, and these changes can be reversed.**

Third, you don't have to like adrenaline to be exposed to chronically high levels. You may be thinking, "But I'm not an adrenaline junkie." The fact is that exposure to life-threatening situations for a prolonged period of time floods your body (and in turn, your brain) with adrenaline—whether you like it or not. Unfortunately, that's not where the story ends. It also begins to affect a stress hormone called cortisol. Cortisol is typically released in response to a threatening event or situation. Its job is to prepare the body to respond to the threat. However, in combat or disaster relief scenarios, the threat is prolonged for days, weeks, months, and, in some deployments, over a year. Our bodies are not meant to be flooded with cortisol for these extended, long periods of time. This chronic exposure causes the body to adjust to a new "normal," one in which cortisol does not ebb and flow as it does when we are in a normal, non-threatening environment. Instead, the body and brain are flooded with cortisol, leading to biological changes. These biological changes manifest themselves in symptoms that you are most likely familiar with, including memory problems, insomnia, weight gain, a weakened immune system, trouble coping, emotional outbursts, and adjustment issues.

Now let's just ask some very basic questions. Answer the following questions:

Yes	No	
		Do you have difficulty concentrating?
		Do you have difficulty remembering things?
		Do you find yourself irritable?
		Do you have difficulty sleeping?
		Have you gained weight since leaving the military?
		Do you find yourself getting sick more often than before?

You may now be seeing the correlation between adrenaline, cortisol, and some of your problems. Much of this is biological. What does this mean for you? It means that your body is a magnificent vehicle that can adjust. And just as it adapted to develop life-saving strategies, it can be adjusted back with some of the tools and support in this workbook and through seeking out complementary treatment with a trusted, licensed therapist.

On a practical level, let's talk about what happens at night when you need the healthy systems to actually dream and not have nightmares. Nighttime is often a time when you run through the day's events and try to bring some sense of normalcy to it, but there is no "normal" in war. Trying to make sense of why people get killed, why certain decisions are being made, why we are there in the first place, missing home—you name it—is going to increase emotional responses and decrease ability to sleep. This process is interrupted mostly due to your elevated threat interpretation, which directly affects your amygdala, which, in turn, secretes more adrenaline into the bloodstream. This can then translate from normal, healthy dreams to nightmares, and this is the last thing a person wants to experience. As a matter of fact, they will do whatever they can to avoid nightmares, including purposeful sleep deprivation.

A direct correlation exists biologically between sleep deprivation and the effects of both adrenaline and cortisol. Unfortunately, through previous Stanford studies, we know that when someone goes without sleep long enough, the person can actually become psychotic. And by psychotic, we mean they can experience a break from objective reality. Do you want a combat veteran who is sleep-deprived, confused, and might become psychotic in the AOR when your life is on the line?

To be honest, you don't want an impulsive troop, especially if they have sociopathic tendencies. These are the men who take unnecessary risks that can put people's lives in danger. They are the hotheads who think they know better than everyone else. They are the first to jump up and take lead, even abandoning the mission's plans, including the commander's intent, just because they are looking for action. You can imagine this person coming back from deployment—highly anxious, sleep-deprived, angry, irritable, looking for a fight, engaging in high-risk behavior, feeling that everything is a threat, cannot get along with people, loses jobs, etc. Sound like anyone you know?

A great example of living like this is found in LTC Brad Holland.[19] You may not know the name, but he is the guy who was infamous for living on the edge. As an adrenaline junkie, he enjoyed pushing things to the extreme. Unfortunately, Brad attempted a high-risk maneuver that pushed his B-52 bomber beyond the limits of its capacity to fly. In preparation for an air show, he lost airspeed in a high-banking maneuver, which created an unrecoverable crash and subsequent explosion. The event, caught on camera,[20] is often used to illustrate how high-risk behavior can cost people their lives. His copilot, the only guy who would copilot with him, and two other crew members died that day.

COMING HOME

If any of these symptoms sound familiar to you, you may be an adrenaline junkie. Let's be clear: it has its benefits, but it also has its pitfalls. People often talk about going to substance abuse counseling, but when was the last time you ever heard of a debriefing on being an adrenaline addict? Let's take a little test to see how you would rate.

ADRENALINE ADDICTION TEST

Yes	No	
		I drink power drinks or coffee or take stimulants to maintain energy.
		I seek out exciting, outdoor, high-risk behavior to keep me happy.
		I feel anxious/jittery.

---

[19] http://www.historylink.org/File/8716

[20] https://www.youtube.com/watch?v=OSwWf07SDdc

		I wait until the last minute to do things and then rush to get them done.
		I feel that the rest of the world is boring.
		Others tell me that I overreact to situations, or I can sense they want to tell me but won't.
		I am always in the "on" position; "off" is best illustrated by exhaustion.
		I am easily startled by things.
		I find that when I'm not in control, things really bother me.
		I hardly ever feel a sense of calm, relaxation, or peace.
		I believe that losing is not an option and winning is correlated to effort; others don't try hard enough, and they easily frustrate me.
		I walk around a lot, and taking tests is a waste of my time.
		I am easily agitated by other people's driving habits.
		Being on time is not an option because I'm hardly ever on time.
		I am a firm believer that others simply want an easy life; they have no idea how vulnerable they are, and they would be easily killed by a terrorist.
		Finances are always a challenge because I spend money as soon as I get it.
		Focus and concentration are great as long as I'm being asked to focus on something I'm excited about; if not, you have my attention for about five minutes, and then I'm off in my head.
		Go, go, go is a motto; hurry up and wait is a stupid concept.
		When people are talking, I've already tuned them out.
		I sometimes have pressured speech because I have so much to say that I can't even get out what my brain is thinking.
		Racing thoughts occur at night when I'm trying to go to bed.
		I wonder if people think I'm crazy.
		Motorcycles, rock climbing, skydiving, and bungee jumping are things I would do in a heartbeat.
		My legs are jumping while taking this test.
		I have a very high sex drive.
		These are stupid questions; get on with it.

Although this is not a standardized test, let's see how you did. Add up your *yes* answers and see the scoring chart below.

Scoring key
1–5: minimal adrenaline
6–10: moderate adrenaline
11 or higher: Let's just not go there, as your irritability may surface.

CONSEQUENCES

Unfortunately, people do not often change their behavior until consequences force them to. For example, you may not have sought treatment had it not been for loved ones or friends who basically indicated you needed help. They may not have known what to do, but they did know that something was wrong. Unfortunately, too many times we are thrown into a situation where we are forced to change because of consequences, which can be due to legal issues, marital/relationship issues, suicidal/homicidal ideation, mental health challenges, or a series of other reasons. Whatever the reason, we are glad you are reading this workbook.

The best way to change the addiction to adrenaline is to:

- **First, realize what it is doing to your body**. You have to be convinced that adrenaline and high-risk behavior are not good for you. Adrenaline causes heart palpitations, tachycardia (racing heart), arrhythmia (irregular heart beat), anxiety, panic attacks, headaches, tremors, hypertension, strokes, heart attacks, kidney damage, and acute pulmonary edema. None of these symptoms are enjoyable to live with, and over a long period of time, some can actually kill you. *Isn't it interesting that, once again, the same thing that kept you alive in a theater may eventually kill you if not treated properly?*

  Between 5-10% of all visits to U.S. Emergency Departments are patients feeling as if they are having a heart attack. After thorough evaluation, they find out their heart is fine and that the effects of adrenaline are causing the anxiety/panic attacks. You won't die, but you have to learn how to control your anxiety.

  Growing up, I was taught the art of moderation. The idea is that a person who is addicted to adrenaline is, unfortunately, off the chart regarding moderation. The consequences of this high adrenaline create many of the same symptoms we are trying to mitigate.

- **Second, adrenaline affects memory consolidation.** Adrenaline affects retrograde (past) memories to where they consolidate at a higher rate. During highly emotionally, stressful times, adrenaline creates a strong bond between intense emotional states, such as fear and memory consolidation. This is exactly why people with PTS(D) often remember their negative experiences in vivid detail. It is also common for people to try to use avoidance to not remember, but their own biology makes it almost impossible. For most of us, it doesn't take much, such as a particular smell or sound, to trigger us into a reflective moment called a flashback. We certainly don't teach ourselves to do this; it is a biological response that the brain has created. Remember that the brain's intent is to keep you alive, and it did; otherwise, you wouldn't be reading this. However, you are also no longer in a war zone, and it's time to get you back.

- **Third, we need to retrain your brain that not everything is a threat.** Since we were taught risk assessment, this is where we actually need to use it. What is important at this juncture is to understand that there is a clear biological reason why you interpret situations and people as a threat, even if they have no ill intent. This topic is so vital that we wrote a complete module to address it. "Module IX: Possibility vs. Probability" specifically focuses on threat assessment and risk mitigation.

- **Fourth, we will never forget.** I can only speculate that Adam and Eve had nightmares after Cain killed Abel. Do you think for one second that they could ever forget what happened? NO! I'm sure they even blamed themselves and their parenting skills. Instead, we have to find a way to resolve our grief/loss and other issues, which is why we created the following modules: moral injury, survival guilt, and perspective.

- **Fifth, increasing one's resiliency factor and finding resolution is key.** Let me explain it this way. When Chris Kyle, the highly decorated American sniper, was asked if he ever had regrets for killing so many people, he could have said, "Well, I was brought up in church and taught to not kill. I also believe in the Ten Commandments. So, yes, these memories haunt me, and I can never get away from them. I see the faces of the people I killed, and at night I cannot forget them. I feel as if I will be in hell for what I did. I do not deserve forgiveness." But that is not what he said. He had resolved the killings in his mind, and, although paraphrased, his comment sounded something like this: "I only regret that I could not have killed more of our enemies so that more of our guys could have lived." Now that is a person who has resolved in his mind a potential internal conflict. In psychological terms, he is ego-syntonic with his thoughts, because, in the end, he was protecting our men by his actions. What our intent will be is to help you become ego-syntonic with your thoughts and actions to the point of resiliency and resolution.

THE ANSWER

In part, the answer to our addiction to adrenaline is to deal with the previous five issues: understand that they are killing us, deal with the consequences of adrenaline, reduce our interpretations of threats, resolve grief and loss issues, and then create resolution.

Coming off adrenaline will not only be a challenge, but it's also probably not something you want to do. What you are doing, though, is slowly killing yourself, and I would hope that is not why you joined the military. We need to intentionally shift the pendulum of adrenaline back towards where adrenaline is only used when there is a valid threat. We convince ourselves of the existence of high-threat environments, even when one doesn't exist. We cannot continue to believe that someone is going to come into a theater or into our favorite restaurant and start shooting people. We have to recognize our thought patterns and use our possibility vs. probability thinking. Trust me, when it comes to risk assessment and threat mitigation when there is a valid threat, your training WILL take over. Your issue is the opposite, seeing threats when they truly do not exist.

Here are some key points to consider:

1. Not everything is a threat. Remember, most of what we experience in life is due to our interpretation of situations and our experiences. If we continue to think that everything is a threat, eventually, we will prove that to be true, but that will not negate the 100 other times that it didn't happen. We can actually create a scenario where others feel threatened and then feel they need to defend themselves, thus creating a threat environment. And although you may attempt to justify it by saying, "See, there was a threat," there wouldn't have been had you not created it. Remember, in a real threat situation, your training will take over. You don't need to create "drama" or threats when there isn't one.

2. There are pros and cons to believing that bad things can happen at any moment. We are taught in the military to have situational awareness at all times, mostly due to the fact we have been at war where people were trying to kill us. That being said, we have to consider our context. For example, think of your favorite restaurant. When was the last time that someone entered that restaurant and starting shooting people? It probably hasn't happened. Does it mean it can't? No. It can, but this takes us to the issue of possibility versus probability. What is certain is that this leaves a person constantly on edge and thinking that terrorism could occur around every corner. At that point, you are accepting that the world is unsafe, even in your own neighborhood. And this is exactly what terrorism tries to do. **We do not want terrorism winning inside your head**. We will elaborate a lot more about this in Module IX: Possibility vs. Probability.

3. Don't bring it home. Don't bring terrorism home. We fought to protect this land and our families. We also need to protect our minds. If certain things trigger a negative response in you, get away from them. Did you know that the guy who bought the Segway company actually died when he was riding a Segway near the edge of a cliff? The point is clear: stay away from things that can cause you more grief. Here are prime examples: Do you get triggered by watching the news? If so, why do you continue that practice? You can find out that something has happened to someone halfway around the world just by watching or listening to the news, but you have no ability to do anything about it. We have to limit our exposure.

4. We actually believe that we have the power to change what happened by going through our mind's different scenarios and saying, "What if...?" What if I had made a different decision? What if my leadership would have not forced us to go on that convoy—what if, and the thoughts will not stop. Here's the truth: if you knew, for example, when a thief was going to break into your home, you would stay up all night and eliminate the threat. Therein lies the problem. You do not have this perfect intel *all the time*. In reality, the only person who could have that intel would have to be omniscient, and yet our expectation is that we somehow take on the characteristics which only God has. Furthermore, it is not your job to be omniscient, omnipresent, and omnipotent. There is only one who is, and you are not it. So, don't expect that to be your job. You will not be able to figure out the next terrorist act and where, when, or how it will occur. If you could, I'm sure the President would like to talk with you personally. As a matter of fact, it's time to stop and let others take on the responsibility for safety. It's time to let others who are just as highly trained do their job. I know you don't believe that, but there really are people who can thwart terrorism that are as trained as you. Right now, your mission is to get healthy. What you may also find, despite your personally held beliefs about civilians, is that people are very resilient as well. They can actually take care of themselves. Chances are that your spouse or loved ones didn't die while you were gone. We have to account for their human capabilities as well.

5. Take a frustration/irritability meter test and measure how you are doing. As an author, my mantra to you will continue: if you find yourself triggered by certain things, then don't continue to put yourself in positions where you are forced to encounter those things. It isn't healthy.

6. Challenge your mind-reading capabilities. Although you may be correct some of the time, the problem is that none of us is a great mind reader. Even as a well-trained psychologist, I don't even try to read my wife's mind. It's futile. People have their own issues, insecurities, and challenges, and they may have nothing to do with us.

7. Take a close look in the mirror. Are you happy with what you see and what you have become? If not, why? As long as you are not six feet under, you still have the ability, no matter what, to make choices. What you can do is get back to when you felt like you had value, a purpose, and a mission. Most warriors feel a sense of loss when they leave the military. They lost their sense of mission. I encourage you to ask yourself if you have lost this as well. If so, make it a priority to focus in on one thing you can do to feel as if you are making an impact. You need a New Mission!

8. Challenge your personal narcissism. Do you really believe that someone in Somalia or another country really thinks that you are such a threat to their survival that they are going to come here and kill you? The probability is quite high that you are not on their high-value target list.

9. Assess where you are in life. Are you succeeding at your life's goals? If not, what is getting in the way? Actually, it may be important to figure out which emotion is driving your behavior. Is it fear, anxiety, or the need for control? As you determine these driving forces, it will be easier to recognize them and then decide how you wish to respond.

10. Are you living by a set of positive influences in life rather than negative? Let's consider the following list below and see how you are doing with each one. Give yourself a rating on a scale of 1–10 with 1 being *poor* and 10 being *excellent*. Assess each word in relation to how you feel you are accomplishing that emotion or state in your personal life.

A. Love –
B. Joy –
C. Peace –
D. Patience –
E. Kindness –

F. Goodness –
G. Faithfulness –
H. Gentleness –
I. Self-Control   –

If all you did was live by these nine guiding principles, can you imagine how your life would change? Maybe it's time to get back to the simpler things in life that make us happy.

We actually put this list, the fruits of the Spirit, on my children's wall. It's amazing when something goes awry because I will ask, "So, Joshua, were you being kind when that happened?" "Or faithful, or gentle, or patient?" "Did you exert self-control?" "Do you feel as if you gave love?" It may be a parent-child thing, but to be honest, if God believes these are important, why don't we? It may be helpful to take a moment and reflect on these nine key words. Remember when you felt love—true, genuine love? When was the last time you experienced joy and peace in your life? Were you once a more patient person? Did you show kindness and believe there was still good in people? How about being faithful? When was the last time you had a gentle spirit? How much self-control do you believe you truly have? If this were the test of your life, how would you be rated by others? That can be a sobering reality. You may want to write down a few of these that you want to focus on in the next few months.

_____

_____

_____

_____

There is something calming about these words when we strive toward them. And when we implement them, it can create a clean conscience and healthy living. I encourage you to not only resolve the negative things in your life but also to take time to think about the positive things that God thinks are important. I would hypothesize that, when we do these things, it starts the process of allowing adrenaline and cortisol to fall back into a more normal, healthy range. As a visual, it's like a pendulum. In psychology, there is this thing called "regression towards the mean." The normal tendency is that over time things wax and wane but eventually slowly move toward the middle. Let's stop giving adrenaline momentum and let our minds and our bodies heal.

Answer key for this chapter:

1. adrenaline
2. threat
3. breathing
4. power
5. all night
6. caffeine
7. nightmares
8. crash
9. downers

MODULE V: YOU CAN'T HANDLE THE TRUTH

Intent: To help warriors find close, personal, human interactions in which to talk about traumatic experiences from war.

Context: Historically, warriors in general have not shared much of what happened to them in war. Just ask a Vietnam or WWII veteran, and oftentimes their family doesn't even know details of what they experienced. Even though my own brother and I are in the military (he was in Vietnam, and I was in Afghanistan), he has never disclosed what he experienced. He was even hesitant after 60 years to apply for any Veterans Affairs disability, saying that two of his best friends had been killed, and he didn't feel he had earned any benefits. He, after all, still has his life. Only time will tell if today's veterans are more forthcoming with what happened to them. There are at least five key issues one needs to focus on regarding disclosure of traumatic events.

- First, reactions by the listener must be helpful. The responsiveness of the person you are sharing your experiences with is key. One thing is certain. If you decide to share the experiences of war, the person you disclose to has to be able to have enough ego strength to listen and not get triggered or respond in such a way that tells you that they are uncomfortable, and, thus, you need to stop talking. I have, unfortunately, witnessed this inability to tolerate listening to warriors' experiences on many occasions. The veteran wants to share, but the person they are disclosing to often responds in a manner that signifies to the veteran that, "You need to stop talking." Either the person becomes so emotionally involved that they start to cry (which is a nonverbal request to please stop), or they give a judgmental verbal or nonverbal response. There are, of course, other responses that tell the person that they are uncomfortable. Either way, the warrior interprets this as a stop sign and shuts down.

- Second, warriors have to trust and be confident that the information they share will remain confidential This is especially true when war crimes have occurred. The whole point of getting help is to actually get help—not to expose oneself to legal vulnerability.

- Third, ensure that security clearance issues have been addressed. Many warriors feel that disclosing certain information would be breaking the law or their commitment to the service. The last thing a person who is seeking help wants is to get into trouble by disclosing secret/top secret information. A way around this is to find a therapist who has a higher security clearance.

- Fourth, moral injury and survivor guilt issues have to be discussed. These issues are so intense that we created separate modules for each one.

- Fifth, confidence that the person to whom they are disclosing can somehow help them—dealing with their symptoms, being a listening ear and offering empathy and compassion, allowing them to get the "weight off their chest" or finding resolution, etc. This is especially true once you begin to get healthy and help other warriors through their own crises.

 Key Takeaway: Family members do not have to have all the answers, but they do have to care.

When warriors are asking questions—especially very difficult ones such as, "Why are we even here?" or "I don't believe in killing, so why did I do it?"—there is an automatic sense of responsibility that one has to actually know the answer. Sometimes, someone is asking a rhetorical question. That person doesn't know the answer, and they are emoting and trying to determine why they did some of the things they did. It is not your responsibility to take this on. As a matter of fact, you may even say, "I don't know why, but I do know that I love you and care about you, and we can find answers to your questions together." Warriors, more than anything, need to be assured of the following:

1. They are not alone.
2. They are not evil.
3. That if they feel they need forgiveness, it is attainable.
4. That you will not leave them.
5. That there is hope, and they will get through this.

When you think of the people in your life that you can trust to handle what you have to share, who comes to mind? _____

Who in your life do you wish you could share with but are hesitant to?

_____

What would it take to help the person deal with their own issues so that they could be a support to you?

_____

One of the benefits of talking to a professional is that they provide great support, can keep confidentiality, do not need anything from you, and are there to help you with blind spots and figure out solutions. Not all therapists, however, have the same training and experience or understand military culture. When you think of the criteria for someone who could help you work through these issues, is there a name that comes to mind? If so, who? _____ If not, do you have someone that you can ask who can give you a good referral? _____

Is there anything that stops you from using them? If so, what could you do to eliminate this problem? _____

REACTIONS

When you think about different reactions that you have seen from people, what was their reaction when you began to disclose information, and what thoughts went through your mind?

_____

_____

_____

THE DIFFERENCE IN PERSONALITY TYPES

One of the key differences in people, especially as it relates to sharing information, is the difference between an introvert and an extrovert.

Introverts typically have very few friends, but the friendships they have are close and intimate, built on depth. Extroverts, on the other hand, may have many more friends, but their friendships can often seem more superficial. These are relationships built on breadth. When you think about your own personality type, which one would you lean toward?

_____

Knowing that information, how do you think this will affect your ability to share your experiences of what happened in war?

_____

_____

Sometimes, people have a difficult time talking directly about certain events that happened in war. One recommendation, based on a Harvard study, is to actually participate in an activity while you are talking. Although it may sound crazy, even playing basketball while you talk can really be very therapeutic. You could even take a walk and talk at the same time. It can get the body moving and help decrease anxiety.

Key Takeaway: Actively doing something (like walking, playing a sport, etc.) can actually decrease one's defenses and increase trust and confidence to share personal information.

Some people find Eye Movement Desensitization Reprogramming (EMDR) helpful. EMDR is a type of therapy in which they have you follow a series of lights that go back and forth. You can also use hand vibrations or sounds that alternate back and forth. Although the mechanism by which EMDR works is not known, speculation is that it distracts you so that you can better get in touch with feelings and thoughts.

If you had your choice of doing something to help you talk about what happened in theater, what from the list that we just discussed would you choose?

_____

Since we have established that people are not very good at reading minds, one of the best things you can do is communicate your needs directly. This would be a great opportunity for doing just that. Remember early on in the book where we asked you to list out one person that you trust? What would it take for you to share with that person what you are going through while going for a walk? It may just surprise you how much more you are able to share while doing something else at the same time. In reality, what is happening is that it increases trust and decreases defense mechanisms so that you can actually talk about things without sitting directly face-to-face with someone. I believe it's always best to come along side someone. And watching out for the guy next to you is a concept with which we are very familiar.

MODULE VI: PTS(D) VS. COMBAT OPERATIONAL STRESS REACTION

Intent: To help warriors understand the difference between PTS(D) and what the military calls Combat Operational Stress Reaction (COSR).

Context: When we are listening to briefings in the military, we are given certain information about what to expect in war. Sometimes, we call it "death by PowerPoint," but this particular talk is vitally important to understand the question, "Can PTS(D) be cured?"

Example: Richard is a 68-year-old Vietnam combat veteran, and his birthday is in two weeks. He comes to PTS(D) treatment, "because I'm tired of dealing with this stuff. I want a cure." Depending on your provider and/or other veterans, what is the answer? What do you think? Can Richard be cured? Yes or no?

What do you believe about this issue?

_____

_____

_____

_____

_____

The true answer: IT DEPENDS. Depends on what, you may ask. It depends on at least three things:

1. What does Richard mean by a *cure*?
2. What do the experts who created the DSM-5 (I explain what this is on the next page) mean by a *cure*?
3. What would YOU mean by a *cure*?

When I was attending Air Command and Staff College in-residence in Montgomery, AL, after ten months of intense reading, I derived a two-word answer for every question proposed by the faculty. The answer: "IT DEPENDS." It didn't matter what the question was; the answer was almost always, "It depends." I stated this twice because sometimes, when we're reading, we skim and miss things. It's that important.

 Key Takeaway: Life is very complex, and answers depend on intel. The more we know about a situation, the more precise our answers can be. When asked a question, I often follow up with, "Please tell me precisely what in your question you want me to answer." Surprisingly, people are very good at giving you exactly the question they want answered.

The answer to the three questions above about "Is there a cure?" DEPENDS on who you ask AND on your definition of a cure. At this point, the best way to proceed is to define PTS(D) and COSR and why there are two different acronyms in the first place.

PTS(D) vs. COSR

Post	Traumatic	Stress	Disorder
After the trauma	Trauma		A significant problem area in your life that will most likely require professional intervention
Combat	**Operational**	**Stress**	**Reaction**
When in war	vs. strategic; actually occurring as compared to just training for war		"A normal reaction to an abnormal situation" (i.e., WAR)

I'm not sure if you realize this, but WHO you speak with to discuss a particular problem will already tell you in general what the answer will be. For example, if you have a back problem, who do you go to? IT DEPENDS. Do you want symptom relief through medications, or do you want symptom relief from an adjustment? If you want medication, you would go to a medical provider. Based on probability, that person would prescribe a medication. On the other hand, if you want an adjustment to solve your problems, you will most likely go to a chiropractor. Sounds simple, right? But things aren't always simple. For example, when the chiropractor takes X-rays and interviews you based on symptoms, he may feel that you have a problem that may require medication or surgical intervention and direct you to a physician. Or a physician might recognize that you may find better relief from an adjustment. On top of all this, you think you had the answer when others had different answers, but that is why we pay for expert opinions, such as the opinions of people like those who created the "bible" for psychiatric disorders, called the *Diagnostic and Statistical Manual, Fifth Edition* (DSM-5). The reason the DSM-5 is important is because this is where a licensed professional goes to review and verify criteria for diagnosis. And, of course, the diagnosis of PTS(D) is listed.

What I learned from my wife, who is an MD, is that a DO (Doctor of Osteopath) is actually a physician trained in the art and science of physical manipulation/adjustment. However, they often don't do it after training, because it is not as lucrative and takes more time, and, trust me, with managed (or mangled) care, they now have to listen to your concerns, list your symptoms, be cordial, do an assessment, give a diagnosis, write their orders, and electronically send them to your pharmacist, all in 15 minutes! Even though a DO is trained in both physical manipulation and medication intervention, which do you think is the path of least resistance and makes them more money? Simple: prescribing a medication. Otherwise, adjustments take time and often require repeat visits (which they don't have time for).

Key Takeaway: Regarding the question about getting symptom relief, it depends on *who* you ask *and* your beliefs about whether or not symptom relief is even possible.

When we put all of this together regarding whether or not there is a cure for our symptoms, it depends on how we view it. Two of the most important questions to ask yourself are:

1. Do I have PTS(D), or do I have COSR? If so,
2. How bad is it?

For the first question, I suspect a diagnosis has already been done. If not, seek a professional who can do a thorough assessment. Second, for assessing the severity of symptoms (or how bad it is), this is where psychological testing can come in handy.

Various tests are used to determine the severity of symptoms. Here are a few:

1. PTSD Checklist for DSM-5 (PCL-5)[21]
2. Structured Clinical Interview for DSM-5(SCID-5)[22]
3. Clinician-Administered PTSD Scale for DSM-5 (CAPS-5)[23]

WHAT IS POST-TRAUMATIC STRESS DISORDER (PTSD)?

---

[21] http://www.ptsd.va.gov/professional/assessment/adult-sr/ptsd-checklist.asp
[22] http://www.scid4.org
[23] http://www.ptsd.va.gov/professional/assessment/adult-int/caps.asp

DEFINITION: According to the DSM-5, PTS(D) is a mental health condition that's triggered by a terrifying event—either experiencing it or witnessing it. Symptoms may include flashbacks, nightmares and severe anxiety, and uncontrollable thoughts about the event.

SYMPTOMS: PTS(D) symptoms are generally grouped into four types: intrusive memories, avoidance, negative changes in thinking and mood, or changes in emotional reactions.

Intrusive memories
Symptoms of intrusive memories may include:
- Recurrent, unwanted, distressing memories of the traumatic event;
- Reliving the traumatic event as if it were happening again (flashbacks);
- Upsetting dreams about the traumatic event, or
- Severe emotional distress or physical reactions to something that reminds you of the event.

Avoidance
Symptoms of avoidance may include:
- Trying to avoid thinking or talking about the traumatic event, or
- Avoiding places, activities, or people that remind you of the traumatic event.

Negative changes in thinking and mood
Symptoms of negative changes in thinking and mood may include:
- Negative feelings about yourself or other people;
- Inability to experience positive emotions;
- Feeling emotionally numb;
- Lack of interest in activities you once enjoyed;
- Hopelessness about the future;
- Memory problems, including not remembering important aspects of the traumatic event, or
- Difficulty maintaining close relationships.

Changes in emotional reactions
Symptoms of changes in emotional reactions (also called arousal symptoms) may include:
- Irritability, angry outbursts, or aggressive behavior;
- Always being on guard for danger;
- Overwhelming guilt or shame;
- Self-destructive behavior, such as drinking too much or driving too fast;
- Trouble concentrating;
- Trouble sleeping, or
- Being easily startled or frightened.

Also, these symptoms have to be persistent beyond 30 days and cause you problems in functioning, such as in your interpersonal relationships, your job, school, etc.

COSR, on the other hand, is often viewed through the lens of what a warrior who has been to war goes through. Again, the military's perspective is that "It's a normal reaction to an abnormal situation." It is expected that a large number of warriors will experience a stress reaction during periods of heavy combat intensity or high ops tempo. Combat Operational Stress Control teams are put together to minimize stress and determine if distressed warriors can return to full duty within three days or if they need to transferred out of the AOR for mental health care. In essence, the military is trying to normalize your reactions to what you have experienced in war. Stress is due to combat and is a reaction to what you have seen. Thus, one has to ask the question, "Are my reactions normal?"

This is an excellent time to *not* try to answer your own question because of blind spots. We highly recommend that this is exactly the time to talk to those around you and ask them the question. Why? Because they, and other warriors, are much better at seeing your blind spots than you are.

It is not unusual to be in a group of warriors and a person talks about their nodal points and issues, only to have other warriors look at them and wonder why in the world they "blame" themselves. You see, it's always easier to see the splinter in someone else's eye than it is to see the plank in your own.

Truly, the biggest challenge that warriors deal with is a sense of responsibility and forgiveness. They often feel responsible for what happened when, in reality, they couldn't stop it. So, they want to go back in time and try to change reality by saying, "What if I had only _____?" Or they question others and their decisions. Reality dictates, and being responsible for our brothers and sisters in the field is something we take personally. Unfortunately, we cannot get around the two rules of war:

1. People die in war.
2. We cannot change Rule #1.

Sometimes people blame themselves so intensely that they end up suicidal. I would be acting unethically if I did not do everything possible to stop the onslaught of veterans dying. That being the case, I am sharing the following for you or others that may need it.

If you or someone you know is having suicidal thoughts, get help right away through one or more of these resources:
- Reach out to a close friend or loved one.
- Contact a minister, a spiritual leader, or someone in your faith community.
- Call a suicide hotline number. In the United States, call the National Suicide Prevention Lifeline at 800-273-TALK (800-273-8255) to reach a trained counselor. Use that same number and press 1 to reach the Veterans Crisis Line.
- Make an appointment with your doctor, mental health provider, or other health care professional.

CAN PTS(D)/COSR BE CURED?

We asked previously if PTS(D)/COSR can be "cured." The response I often get to this question by most warriors is *NO*, but then I do get responses that indicate it can be "managed."

 Key Takeaway: **Whatever your beliefs may be about PTS(D) being curable or not, ultimately, the question has to be answered: can PTS(D) at least be "managed"?**

Most warriors will say, *YES* it can be managed, but I would argue that you have only so much energy you can expend in one day. If you are having significant sleep problems, that already puts you at a disadvantage. To then have to "manage" PTS(D) symptoms takes even more energy throughout the day that could be used for other things, and then we wonder why we are exhausted all the time. The reason is simple: we are constantly working to either suppress or manage symptoms. Where is the time in that plan to enjoy family, friends and the peace that you fought for?

What is the solution? The solution is RESOLUTION. You have to *resolve* trauma to the point that you do not have to expend as much energy as you would "normally."

Example: Let's say you have just purchased a house and you are doing some repairs. You have to spend $30,000 to get it where you want it. The problem is that you only have $24,000 in the bank. This is an unresolved financial problem that will most likely be on your mind constantly and keep you up at night. The energy you could be spending working on other projects is stolen by this constant challenge. How do you "manage" it? If you manage it by selling a TV, borrowing some money from a friend, or perhaps taking out a short-term loan, you are only borrowing a short amount of time, only to have the problem resurface later, which means that you have to "manage" it by remembering to pay back your friend (a little at a time) or the short-term banker (with high interest), etc. This managing costs you the two things you cannot afford to lose: time and money.

Resolution is a long-term solution. You resolve this example by taking out a low-interest, long-term loan that you can afford to pay back and that comes out of your bank account automatically (assuming you can afford this in the first place). This way, it's *resolved*. Do you still remember it? Of course you do, but you don't have to keep it in the back of your mind because it's already been resolved. In like manner, trauma is NEVER forgotten, but it, too, can be resolved. Put another way, the frontal lobe of your brain leverages your intelligence to override the primitive amygdala so you can stop being so distracted by the issue.

Finally, some may wonder why we can't find a way to just never remember our traumas. Is there any memory dump, surgery, or a magic pill—something to make it all go away? Let's look at it from a different perspective.

THE BLESSINGS OF PAIN

Can you think of any blessings of experiencing pain? If so, list at least three:

1. _____

_____

2. _____

_____

3. _____

_____

Final analogy: Did you know that some people cannot feel pain? It's called Congenital Insensitivity to Pain with Anhidrosis (CIPA). It is a rare disorder that one is born with, and the person cannot feel pain or temperature. Most of our opiate addicts would love this disorder (finally, relief from pain), but here's the issue: without pain, the person cannot detect when they are hurt. Can you imagine cooking something and finding out later that you burned your hand severely and had no idea you burned it? Or you tried to play a sport and broke your leg and did not even realize it? A simple cut could become infected and kill you. Most people with CIPA have to live an incredibly sheltered life because when doing any activity, they risk life-threatening injuries that they wouldn't be aware of. Even worse, can you imagine having a burst appendix, but not being able to feel it? They call it the **Gift of Pain**. Depending on your perspective, pain can be a gift or a curse. Of course, the ideal is somewhere in the middle. We don't want to *not* have pain, but we don't want it to debilitate us either.

The same logic applies to trauma. We need a little pain in our lives to appreciate such things as love and care. A great example is having your heart broken when you were younger. It hurts, but without it, you cannot fully appreciate love when you find it.

Although pain hurts, it gives us a foundation by which we can appreciate life. For those who have experienced tremendous pain, it helps us to readjust our threshold. People who have not experienced trauma simply don't "get it." They don't have that baseline by which to judge things. They don't understand the incredible pain one goes through. However, if all you do is focus on the pain, for example, of losing a friend to an IED, and you want revenge, that becomes your new mission. And that new mission can lead you to ultimate destruction.

An alternative healthy view is to appreciate your experiences and remember. In remembering, we HONOR those who have fallen or been severely injured. I never want to forget those friends who died in this war. The best way I can honor them is to NEVER FORGET, and that is why many Americans have this as a motto!

 Key Takeaway: Honoring the fallen by never forgetting can also mean creating a new mission.

A mission is one that members of the military understand quite well. We go on missions all the time. The problem is that when we lose our military position, we often lose our identity. We don't know who we are anymore. We were once told where to go, what to do, how to do it, what to wear, etc. We had a target, a job to do, a focus. Then we leave, and that is lost—and sometimes we are lost, too.

Creating a new mission helps you put purpose back into your life. People have to have a mission, a purpose, a meaning in life. In the Bible, God says it this way: "My people perish because of a lack of vision. (Proverbs 29:18)" What is your vision? What is your passion?

HONORING THE FALLEN

By honoring the fallen, you can have a new mission in taking care of those left behind. This may include other warriors, the families of the fallen, etc. There is a distinct reason why nonprofit organizations (NPOs) are created. Think about it. Project Healing Heroes, Disabled Veterans of America, Veterans of Foreign Wars, Project Sanctuary—you name them—were all started by someone who felt the pain of warriors and wanted to do something productive with their lives. They created their new mission in life and have impacted millions.

What is your new mission in life? Do you have one? You need one. We all need one. Take some time out of your life to be productive. Take some of that energy, resolve these issues, and give yourself a new mission, and write it down. This can coincide with your End State, but think about the things that you want in your life, and out of your life, and be sure to write them down.

Homework: Create your new mission in life. My new mission:

_____

_____

_____

_____

_____

BIBLIOTHERAPY: *Painless* by S.A. Harazin (2015), and *Pain: The Gift Nobody Wants - Memoirs of the World's Leading Leprosy Surgeon.*

MODULE VII: IT'S NOT ROCKET SCIENCE; IT'S CLASSICAL CONDITIONING

Intent: To help warriors understand the importance of classical conditioning as it relates directly to PTS(D) symptoms and resiliency factors.

Context: Most Evidenced-Based Treatments (EBT) for PTS(D) came out of research based upon female trauma survivors of sexual assault. Although some commonalities with combat trauma exist (e.g., fear of one's safety), they are very distinct—so much so that the EBT is a square hole, and combat PTS(D) is a round peg, and the experts have tried to force them together. Any warrior knows, however, that what they have experienced is very different from what a sexual trauma survivor has experienced. Unless of course the trauma was Military Sexual Trauma (MST). It does make sense that Cognitive Processing Therapy (CPT) would make intimacy one of their top five issues, especially if you have been raped, but in our experience, this is not one of the top five issues for warriors. Relationship issues can be a significant problem, but intimacy of the type described in CPT is not what we see. A critique of Prolonged Exposure (PE), which again is based on female sexual assault, is that it focuses on one specific index trauma. Combat veterans may have one incident that stands out, but for the most part, the trauma comes from numerous occasions when a person's life was in danger and is further compounded by the chronic adrenaline and cortisol flooding their system that has persisted for weeks, months, or years because of the length of deployment. On top of that, PE expects you to work on your most intense trauma, and this can be completely overwhelming for some veterans. We need real research into the effectiveness of therapeutic interventions that are made specifically for combat veterans.

WHAT HAPPENS IN THEATER DOESN'T STAY IN THEATER

What often happens in theater is that combat veterans are in a high ops tempo. We have a mission to do, and that is our only focus. We don't have time to focus on ourselves. In reality, not only is there very little time to mentally process what happens in theater, but we're so focused on mission-essential issues, which can change constantly, that it's not something we even consider.

As time in the AOR progresses, it's not unusual for a person's resiliency factors to be taxed. The more a person sees trauma in combat and has to determine what to do with it, without actually trying to process it, the more the body starts responding accordingly. First, sleep is affected. Then the consequences of sleep deprivation occur: irritability, low frustration tolerance, weight gain, anger outbursts—and all this is occurring with the risk of injury or death by Indirect Fire (IDF) or Direct Fire (DF).

Most therapists will tell you that one of the most important things in therapy is feeling safe and creating a therapeutic alliance. Most of the time, neither one of these two criteria is met in theater. One is constantly at risk of being killed at any moment, thus resulting in heightened situational awareness and hypervigilance. And very few mental health providers are available in the field. In order to meet these two criteria, one would have to go where those are provided, and most of the time it is *not* in the AOR. The consequence of not having these resources easily available as well as having a mission to do, high ops tempo, sleep deprivation, and even some denial, of course, makes it nearly impossible to do any type of healthy processing in the AOR.

 Key Takeaway: **The only time to actually process traumas that one has experienced is when one leaves the AOR.**

DOWN TRAINING—WHAT DOWN TRAINING?

I applaud the military for doing its best to prepare us for war. We train, train some more, and sometimes perhaps overtrain. Even though you cannot simulate real war, the military works hard at doing everything they can to prepare you. The up training is some of the best in the world. For example, most of the service academies spend about $400,000 per cadet. The expense of pilots is well over $1 million. And every troop receives yearly training. This does not even include training every time a troop increases in rank as well as specialized training in one's MOS[24] or AFSC.[25] However, there is little-to-no down training, and therein lies the problem.

How are you supposed to *not* continue doing what you have been trained to do repeatedly if there is no down training? You will simply continue to do what you have been trained to do. It would be akin to spending years on training a military dog to sniff out drugs and then, when he comes home, getting mad at him for not stopping. Yelling at the dog, making him feel stupid, telling him he's not the same, or even calling him a "bad dog" doesn't make any sense. He is simply doing exactly what he has been trained to do.

When I was in the AOR, I suffered a spinal cord illness. I completed my tour of duty in spite of my worsening health and near inability to walk. I was the medical advisor and did not want to leave theater. After all, I was being treated by a fantastic Navy neurologist at Kandahar Airfield. It wasn't until 18 of our service members were seriously injured by an IED that I flew from Kandahar to Ramstein and ended up at Landstuhl Regional Medical Center (LRMC). At Landstuhl, I received some of the best

---

[24] Military Occupational Specialty
[25] Air Force Specialty Code

medical care in the world. Within 24 hours of landing, I had two escorts and a checklist of every test and lab work imaginable: MRI, CAT scan, everything. And all this wasn't just ordered; it was completed.

Think about what happened during your deployment or even post-deployment. There are significant events—**nodal points**—that happened when you probably said something like, "You can't make this stuff up." Sometimes, it helps to write it down. If many nodal points are involved, which could very well be the case, it is sufficient to just write a sentence or two about the event as a marker for use later. Please take time to think back and write down any significant events that you experienced.

1. _____

_____

_____

2. _____

_____

_____

3. _____

_____

_____

4. _____

_____

_____

When you came back from the AOR, it would be interesting to evaluate what down training you received. When I ask combat veterans this question, they often ask, "What down training?" Can you imagine the following scenario? You are taking post-deployment tests, and the Tech Sergeant states, "By the way, if you indicate any issues on this form, you will have to stay here for two weeks so we can assess you." You may think, "Are you kidding me? I haven't seen my family in over a year, and all I want to do is go home and spend time with them." Very few combat veterans at that point would mention a single problem or issue, especially if doing so would cost them time with their family. It is not surprising that warriors are not forthcoming. Especially if it can affect their security clearance.

Then, about two–three months post deployment, after the honeymoon phase of being back home is over and at the most critical time, cracks in our resiliency start to show. Our ability to deny what happened in theater begins to take a backseat to our symptoms. We now have time to think and deal with problems, but the resources we were "offered" are not present. Sleeping problems, nightmares, night terrors, irritability—hyper-everything—all come out. We know we have problems and issues, but what resources are available to us? Talk to our spouse/significant other? We went to war to ensure we didn't have to deal with this back home. That is the whole point. I specifically address this issue in our blog entitled, "Home or Away Game," at www.ProjectHealingHeroes.org. Plus, some of the people in our support network do not have the resiliency factors to handle what we would tell them. This is covered in "Module V: You Can't Handle the Truth."

That "down training" that we were offered—gone. But who can blame us? The military would have kept us from our families had we mentioned any issues. So, we are stuck, trying to deal with all our deployment experiences and very few, if any, resources are available to help us do so. **It's a setup for failure, and that's why combat veterans are suffering.**

CLASSICAL CONDITIONING DOWN TRAINING

It appears that if research on this topic were done, we might logically find that the best way to deal with the problem of classical conditioning is threefold for combat warriors.

First, allow service members to be with their families. They have been gone a long time, and that is the most important thing on their minds. The honeymoon phase will most likely last a couple of months, and then symptomatology begins to reveal itself, and one's resiliency factors begin to become readily apparent. So, why not plan accordingly? It seems like we've had plenty of service members come back from deployment – surely we could easily measure this effectively.

Second, the military should complete a follow-up mental health screening a few months post-deployment. Once a person settles into their new "routine," one would have a much clearer picture of the challenges they are facing. Time has a way of revealing this information.

Third, in theater we were trained to respond to threats. It's very simple. If you've ever had a Psychology 101 class, you may have heard of Pavlov and his dog. Pavlov wanted to test a theory about whether or not he could get his dog to salivate, not only to food, but to a bell. His experiment went like this: it is natural for a dog, or even a person, to salivate when they see food. So, Pavlov would continually give his dog food, and the dog would salivate. Then, Pavlov tested his hypothesis by ringing a bell and then immediately presenting the food, which, of course, was a trigger for his dog to salivate. Pavlov did this over and over and over again.

Bell, food, salivate. Bell, food, salivate.

Eventually, the dog, through classical conditioning, started pairing up the bell with the food. Over and over again, this was repeated, until Pavlov rang the bell but did not give the dog food. And you can guess what happened. Pavlov's dog, upon hearing the bell, was prepared to eat and, in so doing, would salivate. But there was no food. Still, the end result was that when Pavlov would ring the bell, the dog would salivate. This, in essence, is the basis of classical conditioning.

SO, WHAT DOES CLASSICAL CONDITIONING HAVE TO DO WITH PTS(D)?

Let me explain by using an example from the AOR. We, too, are trained in the military to respond to sounds, just like Pavlov's dog. If you have experienced rocket attacks, and you are on an FOB[26] that actually has an early warning system, you attempt to mitigate risk through none other than a warning sound. A siren will (hopefully) go off before the rocket hits, thus giving personnel enough time to react and hit the ground, or take cover, thus minimizing the risk of getting hit with shrapnel.

This is repeated over and over again as the enemy launches attacks against us, and it happened every day at Kandahar Airfield. A Chinese 107 rocket would be fired at us; the early warning system would detect it (most of the time); the alarm would sound, and we'd hit the ground. We had over 300 rockets launched at us during my tour of duty. Think about it. When you see the consequences of what shrapnel can do to a body, you seriously think about following orders and getting on the ground when the alarm sounds.

This is classical conditioning. A behavior is trained by pairing it with a stimulus (and in this illustration, it was a sound, which happened to be a 1950s British siren, just like a bell), and you hit the ground (response). Every day:

Sound, ground. Sound, ground.

Back in the day, parents would call their children to come to dinner or come inside by ringing a bell. When the kids would hear the bell, they paired this with their parents wanting them to come home—even though the parents never said a word.

Now, think about other ways in which we were trained in the military in this manner. What happens when a colonel or general enters the room? What is your response?

_____

_____

---

[26] Forward Operating Base

What do you do when you walk past a higher-ranking enlisted person or officer? There are actually two answers to this one, depending on context:

1. _____

_____

2. _____

_____

What are we called to do (response) when a person is hit with an IED (stimulus)?

_____

_____

Every day we carry and strap on weapons. What happens when we leave the AOR and put on civilian clothes for the first time?

_____

_____

I think you can see how a stimulus (some siren, sound, or explosion) happens and our reaction (response) occurs. When you do this repeatedly in the AOR, it becomes second nature. Now that your body has been trained in theater to respond to certain stimuli, and we do not untrain this, you can imagine what happens. The body will continue to respond the same way until this is unpaired. But when did we get the down training to unpair these paired responses? It doesn't happen.

I will use an analogy to further illustrate. Consider a Bluetooth headset for your phone. Once you pair it, it stays paired and will pick up the signal every time it is within range of your phone. Your headset doesn't "think about it;" it is wired that way—just as you are now wired to respond to certain stimuli. What we are expecting is that we will become unpaired without doing the work to unpair the stimulus. That's like expecting your Bluetooth to not respond when it gets near the phone. It's trained and wired to connect. Of course, it's going to do so. To not do this makes no sense. So, why then do we expect a different response when we get back home, other than what we have been doing repeatedly and over a long period of time? Yes, it's that simple.

Key Takeaway: The answer to classical conditioning is to unpair the stimulus. Again, when did that happen when you redeployed? I'm betting it didn't.

Now, think about how you have been trained to respond in the AOR.

1. High ops tempo: It is wired into us to have situational awareness, hypervigilance, and hyperarousal to stay alive. In this case, Darwin had it correct, although luck also has a voice. When you left theater, who untrained (unpaired) you to go back to homeostasis (baseline)—i.e., relax? I'm betting it didn't happen. Guess what your body does then when it is triggered or experiences a stimulus, such as seeing a burqa or something in the middle of the road while driving?

    _____

    _____

2. Adrenaline and cortisol (stress hormone): A high ops tempo trains you to be ready all the time. At what point did you *untrain* this? I assume it hasn't happened. Keeping this high going, we seek out high-risk behaviors, because it keeps the adrenaline flowing. So, what behaviors do you exhibit that keep your adrenaline pumping? Just for fun, is your leg jumping as you read this?

    _____

    _____

3. Life and death: We are around it all the time in the Area of Responsibility (AOR) or, for first responders, in our own backyard. As a matter of fact, it may have been that at your base, Contingency Operating Base (COB) or FOB, the flags were at half-mast *all the time.* That is because people died every day. I looked forward to the day when the flags were raised all the way. It never happened. Let's say you cannot even get a hot shower for days on end; it may frustrate you, but in light of a person not coming home alive, it's not important. Your frame of reference has changed, especially when it comes to what's important and what is not, and then it happens: you redeploy and, on the flight home, someone starts to make a complaint about something trivial. What is your response?

    _____

    _____

I am confident that you are seeing the pattern of CLASSICAL CONDITIONING and how it plays out in our lives. Simply put, we have paired our response to the stimulus, and it is not unpaired. We keep responding to sights, sound, and smells as if we were still in the AOR, because we were not trained on how to unpair them. Using our analogy, are we going to blame the Bluetooth for not unpairing itself? NO! It's doing its job. To think otherwise is crazy. We aren't crazy; we simply can't expect a different response than that for which we have been trained.

KEEPING A STIMULUS-REPONSE LOG

At this point, it is important to try to determine why you keep responding the way you do. If you put it into the framework of classical conditioning (stimulus, and response), you will probably be able to look at your life and write down what is happening. Start with your symptoms, and work your way to the stimulus.

For example, if you get angry all the time, ask yourself why you are so angry. It's likely that something bothered you to the point that you wanted to explode. Exploding is one answer, but another answer is thinking critically and realizing you're not crazy but only responding in this manner because that's how you've been trained. What is good, though, about ALL this is that, if you've been trained (or paired), you can become untrained (unpaired).

In your LOG, write down the stimulus and your response. If you find this difficult to do, try writing the response first and then writing down your stimulus. Either way, you have to make the connection between the two. Do this for at least five, if not ten, of the issues you struggle with. A great one to start with is insomnia.

1. STIMULUS: _____

    RESPONSE: _____

2. STIMULUS: _____

    RESPONSE: _____

3. STIMULUS: _____

    RESPONSE: _____

4. STIMULUS: _____

    RESPONSE: _____

5. STIMULUS: _____

RESPONSE: _____

Unpairing the stimulus from the response not only deals with how you got into this situation (classical conditioning), but also, as you can see, unpairing it is how you can get out of it.

Since we have already spoken about Pavlov and his dog in Psych 101, let's find out how Pavlov reversed this behavior. You can imagine, if you were Pavlov's dog, that when he would ring a bell and you got food, it would make you happy. However, Pavlov then decided to retrain him ***not*** to respond to the bell. How did he do this? It's simple: he did the same thing in reverse. He simply rang a bell but did not give him food. The dog, in preparation for the food, would salivate, but then there would be no food. Pavlov repeated this over and over and over again. Eventually, Pavlov *extinguished* (or stopped) the dog's behavior, or salivating with the bell, because the bell, over time, never produced the desired effect—food. When this happens enough times, the response to the bell will stop. In this case, the bell would ring, but Pavlov's dog eventually gave up thinking he would ever get food, so he just quit responding to the bell (i.e., no salivation). Pavlov literally "unpaired" his dog's response to the bell.

This unpairing of conditioned responses increases resiliency formation. You actually become more resilient because you recognize what the problem is and create a plan of attack (unpairing) on how to stop it. As you can see, this isn't rocket since; it's classical conditioning.

Some people may have a hard time with unpairing a stimulus and don't know exactly how to do it. If that is the case, you might want to contact a trained provider in combat trauma to help facilitate this transition. Take your STIMULUS LOG with you and show the therapist what exactly you are trying to unpair. You can do this in various ways, but, in the end, this is what you want to do. You want a stimulus with minimal response.

Example #1: Instead of reacting to incredibly loud noises, you train yourself not to react as strongly, especially when they come upon you unexpectedly.

Example #2: When you smell a certain smell that takes you back in time, you have to unpair the smell and the flashback. Otherwise, it will just continue.

Example #3: You see blood and begin to experience dissociation, which is how the body protects itself in a threatened situation. You can use mindfulness to remind yourself that you are no longer in the AOR. You are in a safe place, and you can begin unpairing these issues.

As you continue, you will find that your resiliency formation increases and your symptoms decrease, which is exactly the direction we are looking for.

People often ask, "OK, Doc, how long do you think this will take?" My response is, "Probably as long as it took you to get there." Then they seem depressed. In reality, the more you work at this, the more it speeds up the process, so there is no reason to delay.

HOMEWORK

1. Create your STIMULUS–RESPONSE LOG, and notice the patterns.
2. Ask yourself, "Can I, on my own, unpair these two issues?"
3. If yes, keep working on it. If not, there is no shame in asking others to help you and/or to reveal your blind spots.
4. Repeat the unpairing until you can tolerate the stimulus with whatever response you have been able to achieve. If you can tolerate it, you are successful. If not, more unpairing is required.
5. Tell others in your group about your STIMULUS–RESPONSE and what you are doing to mitigate it. Other warriors need to be encouraged about this process and want to seek success.

MODULE VIII: DRONES AND GUNNERS—HOW PERSPECTIVE CHANGES THINGS

Intent: To help warriors understand the importance of perception, and how *the way* you see things influences your beliefs about reality. This interpretation includes significant nodal points—points that you will never forget and mark a turning point in your life. These experiences become deeply embedded in your brain, so deep that the beliefs you adopted as a result of them may not even be obvious to you. In turn, beliefs also influence how you perceive the world, creating a feedback loop. Significant events affect memory when tied to an intense emotion.

Context: When you begin to look at the areas in which you are stuck, you quickly realize (or become defensive about the idea) that how you perceive things is based not only on what you experience, but also on how you interpret it. Many of us come to situations with a particular background, or *lens*, through which we see things differently than other people. As a matter of fact, these preconceived ideas, thoughts, and emotions often influence our reality that we experienced in theater more than the reality itself. How we interpret what happened to us can actually make us more resilient or entrench us even more in a particular belief system.

Example: Take a look at the picture below.

What do you see?

1. _____

2. _____

3. _____

This picture was used on a German postcard in the nineteenth century and represents what is called "projection" in psychology. You project from past experience onto the picture what you perceive it to be, based on experience. The shading, lines, image, and sometimes color all come together, and you form an "answer" in your mind as to what you think it represents. These are called constructs. In essence, your mind is constructing an answer from the inputs you received. The same thing happens in war, but before we move on to that topic, you probably would like to know the three answers.

1. A young woman
2. An old woman
3. Nothing; only two are present. Whatever you came up with was a complete projection and a construct that most people don't agree on.

> Note: If you have a hard time seeing the "reality" of both images, here is the solution. For the young woman, she is facing to the left away from you, has a very small nose, and her ear is actually the eye of the old woman. The old woman is facing directly left, and her mouth and chin are actually the young woman's neck.

Next is an example to show how this plays out in reality. Let's say that you are driving to work, and the car in front of you swerves and almost hits another car. In your brain, you interpret the driver as a jerk who is probably late to work, and it ignites anger in you. You have this intense, concrete view of right and wrong, and this person clearly needs to stop his actions immediately. He then runs a red light, and you slam on your brakes. Still angry, you decide you had better not run a red light, so you call the police and report him. Your elevated response continues to fuel you, and you continue on to work but don't say a word. Your peers can tell that something is wrong but leave you alone because they know you are a warrior.

Your boss says something about a job you did yesterday, and clearly he isn't all too happy about something. Instead of getting furious and saying the thoughts that run through your head, you walk away, and the last words he hears are, "I quit!" That was your third job in as many months—all because some jerk decided to start your day off by putting people's lives in jeopardy.

You get home, drink a beer, shake your head, and think to yourself, "I'd rather be back in the military where I didn't have to deal with civilians." As you kick back in your chair and watch the news, you see that same car from the perspective of a police camera. Your eyes focus on the TV, and you cannot believe what you are seeing. Instead of pulling this jerk over, the police car pulls alongside and then in front of him. You turn up the volume on your TV to hear the news anchor say, "Today, due to a tip from a 911 call, this man was escorted to the local hospital after his nine-year-old son suffered a life-threatening injury. The heroic efforts and coordination of the police and the hospital saved this child, as time was extremely critical. Although the boy is still in critical condition after surgery, they expect a complete recovery. The parents want to know the whereabouts of the hero that called 911. More on this story at 10:00 tonight."

You are flooded with so many emotions, but two things are clear. First, your interpretation of the event that happened couldn't have been more incorrect. You drew a conclusion that, because of the way this guy was driving, he was a "jerk." Clearly, other alternative thoughts could have emerged; however, none of those alternative thoughts were explored. In the end, your interpretation was wrong. This is part of what we will work on—specifically, how you interpret other people's actions. Second, you will never forget that situation and your part in it because it is now tied to an emotion. From now on, you never assume negative things about bad drivers. These are called nodal points, and you don't forget them because of the encoding of the hippocampus (long-term memory) as it relates to emotions (amygdala).

Now, the following question arises: Do you have the capacity to learn brain flexibility when it comes to interpreting situations and possibly other people's actions? It's challenging because we may not know the "whole" story. Warriors who are struggling with PTS(D) often take a negative view regarding situations and motives. So, we fill it in, just like the pictures. In this case, instead of assigning the word "jerk," we insert "panicked father." If you are a dad and consider what you would do if it were your son, it changes everything.

 Key Takeaway: Brain flexibility is a key component of **Resiliency Formation. For example, the more flexible you are in situations to "see things" or interpret things differently, the more resilient you become. The Air Force has a saying, "Flexibility is the key to air power." The Army, "Adapt and Overcome." Adapt means to be able to be flexible enough to change tactics when the enemy makes a move.**

What negative views of life are you aware of? Hopefully, your blind spots are not so severe that you cannot recognize them, especially if others bring them to your attention. Think about this question, and write about it in relation to your view of the intelligence of people, their motives, how you see the world, whether you trust people, whether you feel the world is safe, etc. Finish the sentence based on the key phrase below.

1.   I believe the world is... _____

_____.

2.   When it comes to people, I believe... _____

_____.

3.   For the most part, safety is... _____

_____.

4.   When it comes to trust, I... _____

_____.

5.   My relationships with people... _____

_____.

6.   Only other veterans... _____

_____.

7.   Civilians are... _____

_____.

8.   When people ask me about the military, I would tell them... _____

_____.

9.   I believe the government... _____

_____.

10. The only people I trust in my life are... _____

_____.

I doubt that anything you wrote down surprises you, but think about what you wrote (above) and how that affects your life. Did you write your answers from a positive perspective? For example, "I want to have positive relationships with my wife," versus, "I want us to stop fighting." If so, put a plus next to the number above. Or, did you write things from a negative perspective? If so, please put a minus next to the number. Now is the moment of truth. Is it possible that your actions have made you jaded, and this has completely affected your perspective on life?

This is what I have heard from other warriors when they complete this exercise: we tell ourselves, "They are civilians. They will never get it." "The world is evil. I know, because I've seen it, and you are just sheltered—mostly because of people like me who do the dirty work." "If you've been where I've been and seen what I've seen, you would buy a weapon and carry it, too." "Of course, I don't trust people. They lie, cheat, steal, and kill." "I don't have a problem; it's the people who didn't go to war that have the problem. Just wait until these terrorist groups start pulling this crap on our soil." "You can't handle the truth." "Pain is just weakness leaving the body, and you are a pain in my ass." "In another context, you would be thanking me for carrying a weapon. Who do you think you are going to turn to when chaos breaks loose?" Do any of these thoughts sound familiar?

Before we "solve" this problem, here are a few more examples that may help us. What do you see in this picture?

Answer: First, right in the middle is a person with a hat on with the back facing us, and to the left of the person is a tree with branches going overhead. A stump that has been cut down is directly below the person. Second, there is a bearded man's face. The eyes are placed directly to the left and right of the previous person's hat. The eyes are turned a little to the right. The person's bottom is the tip of the bearded man's nose. Can you see it? How fast can you flip back and forth with the images? This is the beginning of learning how to create brain flexibility.

What you see in this picture depends entirely on your perspective and thought processes.

Finally, look at the below series of lines.

Follow these ROEs[27]:

1. You must make the number nine out of these six lines.
2. You must add five straight lines.
3. You can pick up your pencil or pen to accomplish the task.

---

[27] Rules of Engagement

The Answer:

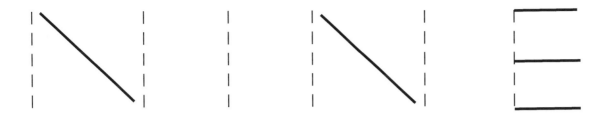

Now, let's put this exercise together with how we interpret the experiences in theater that we have had. How we look at our trauma history has just as much to do with our past and how we perceive things. Most warriors make their frame of reference the trauma. It is the basis for their symptoms. It is what they have nightmares about, and it is what they focus on, but just like trying to lose weight, as soon as you make a decision to do that, you realize how hungry you are. So, how do we fix this?

We must understand that our perception influences how we perceive things. Our resiliency formation must take into account perception and how we "see the world."

I encourage people to focus on the future instead of always looking at the past. We certainly have to resolve the issues of the past, but sometimes we get so focused on the past that we have difficulty with the present and the future. This hindsight bias is very much like driving a car. You have to know what's behind you, especially if you've ever been hit from behind, but if you drive with your eyes focused on the rearview mirror instead of the windshield, you will eventually crash.

GAINING AN ESCHATOLOGICAL (END TIMES) VIEWPOINT

Neither of the lead authors shies away from any resource available to help warriors, including spirituality. Many of the issues surrounding what happens are related to guilt, remorse, forgiveness, and justice issues. We often hear, "Well, it just isn't fair." I would speculate that over half of the warriors I have dealt with have issues related to these topics. Either they feel guilty about their actions (like running over a child in a convoy) or angry with other people who made decisions that got people killed. From there, they often blame God. Why? Because He is the only one who can stop the madness of war. He is the only one, for example, who is omniscient (all-knowing), omnipotent (all-powerful), and omnipresent (always present). It makes perfect sense that we would then turn to the One who has the power and authority to stop the chaos, but no matter how hard we try to change things, we cannot control God. We can't help but think that He *should* have changed the outcome. Could He? Yes. Did He? No. Why is that? I don't know, but I do know that God allows us to have free will, and war is a war of wills.

Finally, we often forget that, no matter what we experience, feel, think, etc., the enemy has a voice. For some reason, warriors completely disregard this vital piece of information, but it is so important that we dedicate a whole module to the topic later in this workbook. Let's now focus on what we *can* control.

YOUR PERSPECTIVE MATTERS

In the end, it's your perspective that matters and how you view the world. Whether that be seing the world as safe, unsafe, just, unjust, disregarded by an ungrateful military, overwhelmed by symptoms or have gotten to the point that you no longer want to feel or do anything. In response, you may self-medicate and isolate.

Let's postulate the difference in perspective between a drone pilot and a gunner on a .50 cal. The guy on the .50 cal. has no choice but to deal with what is directly in front of and around him. Threats are less than 100 meters away, hopefully in the forward position. His buddies count on his ability to pull the trigger, fire repeatedly, and take out threats so that they can live for another day. We do not put someone in that position who has a hard time making decisions, has Attention Deficit Disorder (ADD), doesn't have good hand/eye coordination, is passive, doesn't follow orders, or becomes aimless. The gunner is almost always on high alert (which creates the hypervigilance upon returning home) because it kept him and his buddies alive at war. I tell people that what kept you alive now keeps you up at night. The hypervigilance brought you home, but now it's keeping you from *feeling* that you're home.

In contrast, the drone pilot sees the "BIG PICTURE." He has to. He has to cover hundreds of miles of land or sea until there is a threat or a target that has to be mitigated or eliminated. He cannot afford to become complacent, because it could cost people their lives. They call it overwatch for a reason, and if you aren't watching, that's a major problem. What happens is similar to a camera lens. The aperture has to be widened so that we can fully see all threats.

When I ask warriors to raise their hands if they have experienced the following, almost all do. As I list these different issues, ask yourself, "Do I experience that too?" I'm going to bet you say *yes* to at least five out of the seven questions.

- ☐ Sleeping problems – check
- ☐ Irritability – check
- ☐ Anger outbursts – check
- ☐ Isolation – check
- ☐ High-risk behaviors – check
- ☐ Self-medication – check
- ☐ Prescribed medication – check

How did you do? Are you like most warriors, saying *check*? If so, almost all warriors are saying *yes* to these questions, and if the majority are saying *yes*, isn't this the definition of normal? If we are all doing it, is this not considered a normal response? Well, it is for those of us who have been in combat. But then, why do people say that I am acting differently when I come home or that I am not myself? It's because it's based again on their frame of reference—their perspective. These symptoms are normal, given what we've been through in war, but they're not considered normal in the civilian world, and we shouldn't want them to be. When we bring home nightmares, sleeping difficulties, inability to talk about issues (or when we do, people don't want to listen), anger outbursts, interpretation of threats around every corner, inability to go into restaurants or other places until seeing all of the exits, expectation of someone walking in and shooting so that we think about what we would do first, and the need to check and recheck everything, we are letting terrorism win.

 Key Takeaway: Terrorism wins when we change our lifestyle.

WE CANNOT AFFORD TO LET TERRORISM WIN!

You need to evaluate why we went to war and ask yourself if you have paid and are paying the price of freedom in your own life. If you are experiencing the above symptoms, are stuck and cannot get out, live in your own isolated world, have to take medications for significant symptoms, avoid things, feel numb, check out, even dissociate, experience flashbacks, etc., are you not experiencing the consequences of war? Please remember that the purpose of terrorism is to cause exactly some of the same things you are reporting. Create chaos and fear and a place where you no longer feel safe—where you have to mitigate situations, where you are constantly thinking about safety and security, even to the point that you cannot sleep. It creates hypervigilance and hyperarousal and alienates you from others. At that point, if this is happening, then we are letting terrorism win. I say *letting* because you do have a choice. As terrorism has a voice in the matter, you do, too!

Create a "situational log" this week and place a special emphasis on how you interpret various situations. Think not only about the situation but also, more importantly, how you perceive it. What are your thoughts? Did you interpret things in a negative manner? Did you interpret that people had ill intent? Sometimes they do, but most times they do not. Remember the story we started out with—about the jerk who was driving recklessly? If brain flexibility had allowed for a different interpretation, things in our warrior's life would have turned out differently. In this case, he probably wouldn't have quit yet another job. Instead, the news media may have been talking about how he helped this little boy by contacting 911 and the importance of getting involved.

At this point, asking you to do this may be difficult if not unfair. It's hard to see things differently, especially when you have core beliefs about the world, people's motives, etc. Think about whom you trust, for example. Why do you trust their motives? It's probably because they have proven themselves, which means that you come to the table with a viewpoint that people have to earn your trust. Most likely, it's because it's a form of protection from earlier distrust where people lied or hurt you, but if you continue with this interpretation, it creates a barrier and isolation, as you will have very few friends. Instead, think of coming to the table and trusting people until they prove otherwise. The difference could be significant in your life. Can you do it? If yes, that's great; if no, then make that your *New Mission.*

While completing your situational log, also focus on your "interpretations." Do your best to think about how you perceive your world and your reality. Unfortunately, sometimes we can't see these interpretations easily, because we are blind to them (what some refer to as blind spots). The best way to see blind spots is to ask someone you trust. Ask them to read this chapter and give you feedback on what they see you doing. This type of honest feedback is immeasurably helpful. Or, if they don't know the answer, start seeing a professional who can help you put together a pattern of these interpretations. An intelligent expert in this field can help you see things you may have never seen before. It is truly eye-opening and can change your life.

At this point, start listing situations where you interpreted things in a negative manner, and write them below. Then, assuming you want to get better, think about other alternatives, such as the perspectives we've been working with in this chapter. Sometimes, in this situation, there is not a clear right and wrong but instead your interpretation of the information. This exercise will definitely affect your life, your mood, your energy, and your perspective.

Interpretation Log:

_____

_____

_____

_____

_____

_____

_____

_____

_____

_____

MODULE IX: POSSIBILITY VS. PROBABILITY

Intent: To help warriors understand the difference between what *can* happen versus what will *most likely* happen.

Context: To engage the logical, frontal lobe and the hindbrain, which interprets threat assessment.

ATTENTION BIAS

Have you ever wanted to go to Las Vegas and gamble, hoping to become a millionaire almost instantly? You know, grab a few friends, hop on a plane, take in the windowless buildings with millions of brilliant lights, and stay up way too late? Las Vegas offers extreme stimulation—all intentionally designed so that you have no idea what time it is. More specifically, it is designed to keep you awake and keep you gambling.

You aren't the only one who wants to be an instant winner overnight. The government bets on this and sells scratch-off tickets by the thousands. At the time of this writing, the Powerball is up to $1.5 BILLION. As they say about the lottery, "You can't win if you don't play," so somebody's got to win it, right? It's the same concept: high-risk, high-reward.

Many military members are naturally inclined to risk-taking. We like high-risk, high-reward. It feeds into our need for an adrenaline rush and gives us instant hope for a future that may seem bleak at times. Just think what you would do with $1.5 BILLION! (Actually, that's $750 million, because you know the government will take half.) Would you buy a new sports car, buy a cool house, go on vacation to exotic places, and maybe give some away to a parent who has sacrificed all of their life for you? Go ahead and just do it. Spend that dollar or ten or even twenty. Your chances go up exponentially the more you risk! Right?

No matter what your views are on gambling, one thing is true: it is based on a calculated risk. Very similar to the military, people who run the gambling industry are betting on you! They are betting that if they can get enough people to bet by actually giving away some of their earnings, all on the hope that it "could be you," the money will pour into their laps as one big pile of cash. In reality, it's based on math and psychology. Do you know what psychologists call this type of behavior? [28]

---

[28] Intermittent Reinforcement Schedule

INTERMITTENT REINFORCEMENT SCHEDULE

Consider all those wonderful slot machines where you see people lined up in a row with lights galore, sounds going off, people smoking, and the occasional "winner, winner, winner" flashing—someone just won! Oh, more money, more money, as you put in more cash and pull the lever and hit the buttons. The intermittent reinforcement is that for every 1,000 pulls (for example) of a slot machine, you win! The challenge is when will that lucky time be? Well, it's a crapshoot, no pun intended. The point is that you are hoping for and expecting it to happen when you pull that lever. Otherwise, you wouldn't do it, and you justify your behavior in your head: "It's got to be somebody who wins, right?" Occasionally, that is exactly what happens, and the reinforcement of a belief that you will be that lucky one propels you to keep spending money. It's intermittent, and it gets you hooked.

Reality, however, sometimes hits us right smack in the face when we put in a lot of money, expecting a high-risk reward, only to get nothing. Our expectation of being that one big winner fails. High-risk, high-reward . . . at least you tried. Gambling is what I call a government donation, because the odds of your winning the Powerball are less than the odds of your getting hit by lightning.

Why do we as military members play high-risk, high-reward games, expecting to hit it big? It not only feeds our need for feeling alive (e.g., "Module IV: Adrenaline Addiction and High-Risk Behavior"), which is what often happens when we come out of a war zone, but we also truly believe that it can happen to us.

The same thinking applies regarding terrorism! You say, "What? I don't expect something bad to happen all the time." Are you sure? Let's look at this questionnaire. Circle either *Yes* or *No* to the following questions:

		Question
Yes	No	1. Do you feel the need to own a weapon?
Yes	No	2. Do you feel the need to have cameras at your home?
Yes	No	3. Do you often use situational awareness when it comes to going out to a place where there are a lot of people?
Yes	No	4. Do you just happen to "notice" exits and scan for threats?
Yes	No	5. Do you get easily startled?
Yes	No	6. Do you get anxious when thinking about going out to places?
Yes	No	7. Have you changed when you go to places, such as going grocery shopping at night when there are fewer people out?
Yes	No	8. Do you isolate?
Yes	No	9. Do you watch television and the news and get irritated or angry?
Yes	No	10. Do you believe you could be a target of terrorism?
Yes	No	11. Do you believe in sleeper cells in America?
Yes	No	12. Are you on medication for sleeping problems and/or anxiety?

		Question
Yes	No	13. Do you have nightmares or night terrors about people trying to harm, kill, or destroy people, places, or things?
Yes	No	14. Do you believe in always being prepared in case something happens?
Yes	No	15. Do others tell you that you seem distracted or tense when you go out to places?
Yes	No	16. Do you feel the world to be an unsafe place?
Yes	No	17. Do you worry about your kids or what the world will be like for them in the next generation?
Yes	No	18. Do you get angry, frustrated, intense, or opinionated when it comes to political issues?
Yes	No	19. When you watch the news or listen to the radio and hear of another situation where somebody has killed someone, do you feel as if you need to be prepared at all costs?
Yes	No	20. Do people tell you that they just want the old you back?

If you answered *yes* to five or more of these questions, you have probably been significantly impacted by your deployment. I often interpret this as a feeling in which the world is unsafe. Trauma experiences don't just happen in the military. Some of us come into the military already having experienced trauma.

PRE-MILITARY TRAUMA EXPERIENCES

In my work with warriors with PTS(D), I discovered that over a quarter of them had some form of traumatic experience even before they joined the military. They had experienced death or loss, witnessed horrible acts of abuse, were in foster care or verbally abused, etc. They go into the military hoping for a safe environment and a change from what they have already experienced as a child. Then something happens when they are deployed, such as death and destruction, which only reinforces the belief that the world is an unsafe place. What does this have to do with being stuck in a particular mindset? It's the impact of a phenomenon known as **attention bias**.

ATTENTION BIAS

If you have ever been to the VHA and just recently received your disability rating from the VBA and happen to have decided to get DV license plates, you just might start seeing them everywhere. Or, if you want to buy a new car and you finally decide on a particular model, all of a sudden you start seeing them all over the place. In psychology, this is called attention bias. You actually start "seeing" things you hadn't noticed before. Simply put, your attention goes toward a particular thing when previously you hadn't noticed it. Another example is if you want to lose weight, and you decide to eat less, and suddenly you start noticing how hungry you are all the time. You only think about food and what you can/can't have. Your attention is now focused on calories, and you see the world through very attentive eyes of "How many calories are in that?" Before you know it, instead of thinking about what you normally think about, everything you think about is focused on food. It clearly has your attention!

 Key Takeaway: In attention bias, when you become aware of something, your attention goes toward that which you previously hadn't noticed.

Let's return to Las Vegas. You are sitting there, and your attention is on the lights, people, and lure of money. You want to win, and you notice every person who ends up being that one winner—the one every thousand times that they pull that lever (or whatever it's set to, to let someone win). Of course it is by chance, or so it seems.

Let's put this all together: high-risk, high-reward, the chance that you might be the big winner, attention bias toward things that reinforce winning, such as lights and sounds and that big "winner" sign, etc. Now you are into it, and Vegas is excited.

What is the probability that you will win? It depends, but remember that you tell yourself that it could be you. The same belief systems with intermittent reinforcement occur regarding our beliefs about terrorism when we come home.

WATCHING THE NEWS

The news is about sensationalism. You see, the people who make the news have a vested interest, just like everyone else. As a matter of fact, the higher the ratings, the more they can charge for advertising, and the more money they make. So, just like classical conditioning, their interest is tied to money. And how do they pair it? They sensationalize anything to gain your attention, which increases their ratings. Where does that leave us then? Well, it should then not be surprising that we would hear about a bus being blown up or a lone gunman on a college campus or the next terror organization beheading someone halfway around the world.

Out of eight billion people, something tragic is going to happen, but the media makes it out as if something is happening every day, almost every hour, and that it could happen in our own back yard. Because, remember, based on what we learned from Maslow and his hierarchy of needs, if something threatens your safety and/or security, you *will* pay attention to it. And both the national and local news make sure that you pay attention. Have you ever noticed that news focuses on people getting injured, stabbed, or shot, or a house on fire or a burglary—you name it. And then our own reinforcement of this belief comes into play when we start making arguments in our heads about the fact that it *can* happen. So, you begin to list examples:

1. Ft. Hood shooting (twice)

2. 9/11
3. *S.S. Cole* bombing
4. Numerous college campus shootings
5. Branch Davidians in Texas
6. Khobar towers
7. ISIS beheadings
8. Orlando night club bombing
9. Police shootings
10. _____

The list goes on and on, and people wonder if we live in a safe world?

These events, combined with our experiences in war, are why we believe the possibility of life-threatening danger is so real that we ensure that we, as warriors, have situational awareness at all times, carry a concealed weapon, have cameras installed, and only go to certain places at certain times (or don't go out at all). We make sure that we have an exit plan and strategy for every location. We constantly scan and monitor our surroundings and keep our sense of awareness heightened. All of this, by the way, leads to elevated blood pressure, anxiety, worry, arousal, startle reflex, etc. When we just come back from deployments, where all of this is "normal" anyway, we continue to feed it, even when we have the chance to lower our adrenaline and subsequent cortisol.

WELCOME HOME, TEXAS ROADHOUSE STYLE

While I was Active Duty at Air Command and Staff College, Maxwell AFB, my wife decided to join the Air Force. Upon my return from Afghanistan, she left for Commissioned Officer Training (COT). We were celebrating her accomplishments at Texas Roadhouse when *it* happened.

In Kandahar, Afghanistan, we used a 1945 British siren sound whenever a rocket was inbound. The idea was to hear the siren, hit the ground (so as to not get hit with the rocket or, more likely, shrapnel), and then head to shelter (in case multiple rockets were inbound). We were enjoying our dinner at the restaurant when someone's phone went off, and the ring sound they chose just happened to be the same one that we would use for incoming rockets. What were the chances of that?

In my hurried state, I couldn't decide if I was going to grab my wife and kids on the way down to the floor, so I ended up hitting the floor, all while looking at my loved ones' faces on the way down. I then flipped over and took a prone position with my face on the ground. There I was, lying on the floor of Texas Roadhouse—just me and the peanuts. When I realized what I had done, I turned over and sat up. Everyone was just looking at me—actually staring at me! I thought I was immune to PTS(D)-like symptoms. I have a doctorate in psychology and three master's degrees, have worked two years at a level-one trauma center, am well-versed in the signs and symptoms of PTS(D) and taught on it for years, and yet, there I was, lying on the floor. It was a reaction that was completely unexpected but normal, as I had been doing it for my whole tour of duty. It was at that nodal point that I realized, "Ah... So this is how PTS(D) symptoms happen."

Have you had a similar experience after coming home? If so, what was it?

_____

_____

_____

_____

I'll share with you the rest of my story. While I laid there, I looked up, and my kind wife quietly asked, "Honey, are you OK?" I replied, "Yes." She asked, "May I ask what you are doing down there?" I'm sure she could see at first the panic on my face that was quickly covered up by embarrassment and confusion. "Well, I thought I would just come hang out with the peanuts for a while," was the only thing I could think to say. I brushed myself off, got up, and sat down. Nobody said anything. They just tried to act normal. This was my new normal. In theater, my actions could have saved my life. In Texas Roadhouse in Montgomery, AL, I looked like an idiot. Somebody, please tell my body I'm back home. PLEASE.

Later, my wife whispered to me, "Honey, what happened?" I said, "I'll tell you later, but I'm OK. Thanks for caring." Time passed. Later that night, I explained to her what we would normally do in the AOR when a rocket came in, based on the stimulus of the alarm, and that was to hit the ground so as not to get killed. She felt so bad for me. Although she was being empathetic, my attention was focused on my emotions. I cried and sat there, wondering what was wrong with me. I'm emotional; I'm confused; and I'm exhausted all the time. I think about all that I've been through, and it runs like an incredibly up-close-and-personal movie in my head. Any little trigger takes me back there in an instant, and I replay the movie as if it were in high definition. Every moment, every second, every sound, even feeling the ground is as if I were lying on the rocky soil in Afghanistan.

I can remember exactly where I was, what was happening, and who was around me when rockets would come in. On one particular night, I was on the phone with the Office of Special Counsel and just said, "I have to go now!" as I hung up the phone. That day, three people died from an incoming rocket, and I identified them, as usual. It was my job. When I finally returned the phone call to the investigator, he asked what had happened. I explained it to him. He became very quiet, and then finally said, "Please be careful." Uh, yeah, I'm trying, but I don't control the rockets. I do, however, control what I do when the siren goes off. So, I'm trying. This is now my new normal.

Referring back to attention bias, after our experiences in theater, we focus on everything that could possibly go wrong. Why? Situational awareness, safety, and a sense of control. As military members, we are trained—trained to be ready at all times, for all situations, for all threats. So, what's the problem?

The problem is that you cannot relax and enjoy life. If you constantly have your attention focused on the possibility of threats and conflict, you will see them everywhere, just like our attention bias toward Disabled Veteran (DV) plates. What you look for you will see, and sometimes what you look for you *create*.

POSSIBILITY VS. PROBABILITY

The reality is this: Is it *possible* that terrorism can happen? Yes. So, you do everything you can to mitigate it, but the question is when will it occur? Just like the possibility of winning the lottery, you have no idea, so you stay "ON" all the time. It's possible that something bad is going to happen, and you tell yourself that you have to be prepared; however, you have no idea when something will happen, so you have no choice other than to be ready ALL THE TIME.

The problem with always being "ON" is that you can never "SHUT OFF." You can never truly relax and just enjoy life. Your spouse (if you still have one) says you can't relax and just *be present*. You are constantly scanning for threats, and they notice. Instead of going out and having a relaxing evening, you have to sit with your back to the wall and create an escape plan in your mind, JUST IN CASE something happens. You try to pay attention to your wife, but your mind goes to the guy who looks as if he is up to something, and you plan your first move and the next and so on and so on. It's impossible to relax and enjoy your evening when you feel as if your life is threatened.

Is it possible that something can happen? YES, but what are the chances of a gunman coming into your favorite restaurant in your town on that particular evening? One in 80 million? Yet you list examples of when it did happen. Remember our list we created? You can't deny it. It happened, but what is the chance it will happen in your hometown, on your date night, at that moment? That is what we are after.

What *is* guaranteed is that you are not going to connect with your loved one, and they know it. You are stuck—stuck between wanting to have a good time and feel normal again, and yet having to be prepared, like a good Boy Scout, in case something happens. You are betting, like in Vegas, that something is going to happen.

Let's deal with a little reality though. When was the last time you were in a restaurant and someone pulled a gun out and started shooting at you? Think of your favorite restaurant. Has it ever happened in your town, on your date night? Probably not, but you change your whole experience by expecting something to happen, just in case. Have you ever wondered why some people think that you have changed? You have. You are no longer the same. We think differently, act differently, and convince ourselves that civilians will all be dead because they are not prepared.

Based on this logic, you have to be:

1. at a heightened state of being alert;
2. always looking for risk and risk mitigation;
3. hoping nothing happens but prepared in case it does;
4. spending a lot of your thinking time strategizing about your next move;
5. spending enormous energy looking for threats;
6. wondering who or where or when something might happen;
7. telling yourself that threats are right here, right now, and you must be ready; plus,
8. you startle easily because you have attention bias toward everything.

You get the point. And people wonder why we cannot relax. *As long as we are willing to let this continue, terrorism is winning in our personal lives.*

So, based on the .0000008 possibility that something may happen, we spend 100% of our energy trying to stop it. However, nothing happens—no gunman, no terrorism, nothing. The night is over, and your loved one looks at you and thinks, "I wonder what they would be like if they could just relax," or, "When will you go back to being you again?" or even, "Is there any hope this will ever change?" You take a deep breath and sigh because you can read minds, and you know you are no longer that same person. You know it, and they know it.

You have convinced yourself that something bad is going to happen because it is *possible* that something bad could happen. You even expect it, and you have changed your whole life because of it.

Think about this for a second. What are the goals of terrorism? What do terrorists hope to instill?

1. _____

_____

2. _____

_____

3. _____

_____

4. _____

_____

5. _____

_____

6. _____

_____

7. _____

_____

8. _____

_____

9. _____

_____

Based on what you wrote above, has terrorism then affected your life? If so, to what degree? If you believe that it has, only one conclusion remains: terrorism just won! I repeat: TERRORISM just won! That statement may upset some of you, but the question is this – is it true?

By definition, terrorism tries to do the following:

1. Create fear, worry, or a belief that you are unsafe.
2. Create a belief that it's going to happen to you or someone you love.
3. Make you think about what you would do if something bad were to happen—all the time.
4. Attempt to get you to think about and see (attention bias) that someone is out to get you (hypervigilance).
5. Create a feeling that anything could happen at any time, leaving you in an alert, anxious State (hyperarousal).
6. Get you to change your lifestyle.
7. Cause you to change thoughts and beliefs about the world and the expectation that something bad could happen at any time.
8. Cause sleepless nights and create nightmares and night terrors.
9. The list goes on and on.

At this point, we are allowing terror into our lives, and it must stop. We didn't join the military to be in therapy, to have PTS(D) symptoms, to deal with this constantly, to feel that the world is unsafe and people are out to kill us around every corner. We did the opposite. We joined to stop terrorism, for people to feel safe, to enjoy life, yet here we are, letting terrorism create destruction in our own personal lives. We brought it home. Is that what you want for your life? I hope not.

This leaves us with probability. Is it possible that something bad could happen? YES. The same is true about a meteor streaking across the sky when I step outside and hitting me in the head. It is possible, but is it PROBABLE?

The problem is that because it's possible, we think it's probable. This is how we got ourselves into this mess of PTS(D) symptoms. Yet, the reality of it happening to you is that .0000008 chance. Possible, yes; probable, no. But we allow terrorism to win 100% of the time, because we are worried about the possibility.

Here's how terrorism wins on a daily basis:

1. It takes away our security and safety.
2. It takes away our thoughts because we never know when it can happen (hypervigilance).
3. It takes away innocence.
4. It takes away our ability to sleep, relax, and enjoy life (hyperarousal).
5. It takes away our joy and steals our future.
6. It causes physiological problems (consequences of cortisol and adrenaline), and that is how we end up with weight gain, PTS(D) symptoms, heart attacks, and our bodies deteriorating at a very high rate compared with the general population.
7. It destroys our relationships.
8. It causes us to seek relief in such things as high-risk behaviors, drugs/alcohol.
9. It causes financial problems because we can't keep a job, because we often don't trust people,
10. especially those over us or in leadership.
11. It causes us to lose serenity and peace.

 Key Takeaway: We lose to terrorism when we live our lives based on possibility, not probability!

Key belief: My nine-year-old son is afraid of the dark and will not go certain places in the house because he believes there is a threat. Nothing has ever happened to him, though, and no bogeyman has tried to kill him, but the FEAR that it may happen leaves him immobile. He will not go into a dark room. As his dad, I know nothing will happen, but until he experiences this for himself at some point, he will not trust it. Are you like my son Joshua? Are you changing your life based on fear? If so, terrorism wins. Don't let terrorism win.

Homework: Ask yourself if you live your life believing that something bad could happen anyplace, anytime, and if you have adjusted your life accordingly. Think about how you have bought into the lie that something is possible vs. probable. Let us decide to take back our lives and not let terrorism win.

This is your challenge: to be accurate in your risk assessment and stop thinking that something bad is going to happen every time you step outside. You have to start somewhere, whether that may be changing your beliefs about terrorism or stopping yourself from believing that bad things are probable vs. possible and getting your life back. At this point, take a few minutes to think about the thoughts, beliefs, and behaviors that allow terrorism to win in your life. Then consider how you might challenge and ultimately change those beliefs in an effort to create a new, safer reality. It's time to list practical changes in your thoughts and behaviors that you can make. If you have blind spots about these issues, just ask your family, fellow veterans, and professional counselors what they see in you. If they are honest, they will tell you, even if they are concerned about how you might respond.

List thinking and behavioral changes you need to make to stop terrorism from winning in your own life. What are the recurring thoughts or behaviors that you do that let terrorism win? Please write them down.

THOUGHTS:

1. _____

_____

2. _____

_____

3. _____

_____

4. _____

_____

5. _____

_____

BEHAVIORS:

1. _____

_____

2. _____

_____

3. _____

_____

4. _____

_____

5. _____

_____

Ultimately, this leaves us with one question: do you want terrorism to have this much of an effect on your life? I certainly hope not. We need to readjust back to our "normal" way of living instead of superimposing our negative thoughts and reactions back onto our previous life. This is part of how we "get back" to being ourselves. Certainly, we can justify our actions, but that will not help us become more resilient. Our task is not only to recognize the signs and symptoms but also to begin the process of increasing our resiliency.

MODULE X: SURVIVOR GUILT

Context: Military members who make it home without their fellow combat veterans often experience what some have called survivor guilt, which is the guilt one has about being alive when others are not. It strikes at the core of our being—guilt often based on a sense of responsibility. As American military members, we carry a heavy burden of responsibility to make sure everyone comes home alive. We deploy with friends, and we know their families. Or we make good friends in theater to the point that we would even be willing to put our lives in their hands and vice versa. We know the pain of coming home, knowing they didn't, and that their families may blame us, even inadvertently or overtly, based on their intense loss. We may mind read and superimpose our thoughts onto them. We may think they hold us responsible for our failure of not keeping our promise "to bring everyone home safe." We may even think they hate us.

If we could make a deal with God, we would bring them back alive, even if it meant we had to die, but we cannot. We are left with this huge, gaping hole inside us that desperately needs to be filled with something. Unfortunately, this hole is often filled with things that distract us temporarily, such as alcohol, drugs, or high-risk behavior. Inevitably, we are left with long-term consequences that are often worse than anything we could ever imagine. Yes, the price of freedom is quite high!

Example: Thomas was a 28-year-old Army infantry soldier deployed to Afghanistan. His company was on foot patrol in the Kandahar Province when the point inadvertently stepped on an IED and was instantly killed. Looking around, there was chaos, and Thomas, in full battle gear, adrenaline pumping, ran to another buddy and could see that he, too, was seriously injured with one leg completely missing. He yelled for the medic, and his friend was later Medevac'd out. Unfortunately, his friend, Brian, didn't make it.

When he redeployed back home, there was cheering and crowds and family members and signs of appreciation and sacrifice—and heartache. Brian wasn't with them. Brian died in combat. With tears in his eyes, Thomas knew the emotion of happiness to be home and an intense dread of the wounds of war. Brian's family wasn't there. He later saw them, and the first time Brian's widow's eyes met his, he couldn't stand the pain. What could he possibly say? What could he have done differently? What about Brian's family, especially his children? How could he face them? Feelings of failure came over him. Guilt, remorse, and responsibility all hounded him. On one hand, he wanted to tell Brian's wife what had happened but felt he couldn't for many reasons: security issues, fear, failure, tears, flashbacks—he felt them all, and his worst nightmare was before him.

One of the most significant issues that can help build resilience is reminding ourselves of why we joined the military in the first place. The military heavily emphasizes the issue of *intent*. I'm writing this during an evening at the Air Force Academy. The one thing the Commandant of Cadets asks repeatedly when the cadets do something wrong is, "What is the evidence of their intent?" For it is in understanding one's intent that one may find forgiveness, or at least a more balanced, healthy perspective.

 Key Takeaway: A person's intent may be good, even if the outcome isn't.

YOUR INTENT

Why did you join the military?

_____

_____

_____

Intent: Thomas's intent was to join the Army to bring about peace and security and safety in this world. He watched as 9/11 happened and felt helpless. He saw people jumping from the buildings rather than being burned alive, the firefighters and police officers and the sacrifice that was made, the crowds running from the buildings and then white ash covering everything, people covering their mouths, trying not to breathe in the toxic air. He couldn't stand by and do nothing. He joined the Army because he wanted to run *toward* evil, not away from it. Unfortunately, what he came back with was remorse, guilt, and regret. What would you say to Thomas?

_____

_____

_____

_____

Collateral Damage and the Consequences of War: It's Personal

It has been said that there are two rules of war:

Rule #1: People die in war.
Rule #2: You cannot change rule #1.

Let that sink in. There is nothing you can do about people dying in war—NOTHING. You are not in charge; you are not in control; and you cannot change the rules of war. It's like playing chess, and not one scenario will stop a pawn from being taken—not one. On the ground, it feels as if we are pawns in a chess match. We get angry with those above us who put us into situations where we have few, if any, options, and the consequences can be severe. When we deploy, we often become very close to those around us. As a matter of fact, we often aren't thinking about the bigger End State that we will read about in Module XV about why we are there. It's now personal. We are actually fighting for the brother or sister next to us.

We know they have our backs, and we have theirs. We will not only live for our country, but we will also die for it. We say that, but when it happens, when someone dies, it stops us in our tracks. TIME STOPS! It becomes very personal. Feelings of time simply stop, and you look around at your surroundings and the hell that is occurring. Others may feel an intense sense of wanting revenge, which is the emotion I hear about most. People will redeploy many times in an attempt to get revenge, even if that means dying. Some even want to die in the process of getting revenge just to get away from the internal pain that haunts them. *For some, it is easier to risk one's life than it is to feel the intense survivor guilt one carries.*

For warriors with PTS(D), the mental processing of all these past events doesn't stop. Then you flash back to reality when you are standing in front of the person's widow, and you wonder what just happened to time. It's called dissociation. You simply do NOT mentally associate with the here and now. You have so many thoughts and memories, so much pain and guilt that you go backward in time and relive what you experienced in light of your current surroundings (triggers) and wonder what's wrong with you.

When I came back from deployment, I actually had someone tell me, "You can't take war personal." If you could have measured my internal anger at that time and actually heard the thoughts in my head, you would have put me in a very safe place, very far away where I could not hurt that person. If most of us are honest, the internal thoughts we have at times of harming others or ourselves would have us put away. We know it because we know what we are capable of doing. We are not trained killers who want to hurt others for ill intent, but when you have suffered such incredible loss, looked death in the face, and then have someone who chooses not to serve their country say such a foolish thing, you do your best to control your raging thoughts.

Have you experienced anything similar to flashbacks and dissociation? If so, what do you usually think about?

_____

_____

_____

_____

In asking, "Is there anything wrong with you?" the answer is a resounding, *NO!* There is *nothing* wrong with you. Your brain is trying to make sense of all of this. It's confusing and scary, and your emotions can be intense at one moment and then completely cease to where you feel nothing. Your brain has not resolved this portion of your deployment. Unresolved issues do not go away. If you don't believe that, just ask any WWII or Vietnam veteran. It's not time that heals. It's what you *do* with the time that heals!

GETTING TO RESOLUTION: GETTING TO WIN-WIN

There are at least three types of scenarios in which a person will "negotiate" with another person (and in like manner, themselves psychologically).

Example: Going to buy a car.

1. Lose-Lose: This is when neither party gets what they want. You negotiate the sale of a car, and you want it for $25,000. The sticker price is $36,000. The car salesman states that he will sell it for $32,000, but that is his final offer. You cannot afford $32,000, so you say you can afford $28,000. The answer is *no*. The deal is off, and neither side wins: lose-lose.

2. Win-Lose: In this scenario, one person wins, and the other person loses. Using the example above, you plan to buy the car and have $28,000 ready to go. The car salesman is pressured because it is at the end of the year to sell cars. He knows that he has to sell the car at $32,000 but decides to go ahead and make the deal at $28,000 because of the pressure to sell the car. His fear is that if he doesn't, he will lose his job. He feels as if he is in a no-win situation. This is another example of Lose-Lose. Since he must sell this car but cannot get the price he needs, he makes the decision to sell it. In the end, he gets fired for his decision. You get the car for $28,000 and win; he loses his job: win-lose.

3. Win-Win: You plan to buy the car, and you offer $28,000. The salesman says he cannot do any less than $32,000. How do you get to win-win? In this scenario, both players have a need—one to buy and one to sell. You stick with your End State at all times and keep

referring back to it. We both want the same thing—one to buy and one to sell. Do not let anything get in the way of your End State. You look at possible options, including trade-in, financing, and bartering—anything. The salesman must sell due to the end of the year, so a rebate is thrown in. We are now at a price of $30,000. You have literally a piece-of-junk car worth $500, but you offer it up, and he then has "wiggle room" to make it worth $1,000, with his boss' permission: $29,000. You can do $28,000 but no more. So close, but you keep your End State in mind. Finally, the car dealer is in need of a contractor to do what you are good at, so you offer for the next two weekends to come in and do the work. Deal DONE! You both win: win-win.

Unfortunately, in survivor guilt, nobody feels as if they win. You are upset, feel responsible, have horrible guilt (lose), and the widow has lost her husband (lose). Remember the two rules: 1. people die in war, and 2. you cannot change rule #1. You feel very stuck!

This often occurs when people cannot see a way out. You say such things as:

1. "I cannot bring them back."
2. "I did everything I could, but it wasn't good enough."
3. "I am a failure. I promised their family I would bring them home safe. They were my responsibility."

What are the things that you say to yourself? Don't just look at the lines. Write what you actually say in your head.

1. _____

_____

2. _____

_____

3. _____

_____

4. _____

_____

5. _____

_____

How do we get to win-win (if it is even possible)?

First, you have to completely shift your frame of reference. You already know the facts. You cannot bring people back to life, you cannot change the game, and you cannot change other people. What you are left with is reality and what is in your head. Since we cannot change reality, we go with what we can change.

RESOLUTION OF THE MIND

Remember the reasons that you decided to join the military? Was it for financial reasons? To serve and protect our way of life? Was it to get revenge after 9/11 and the injustice of innocent people dying? Was it to serve God and country? Because it's tradition in your family to serve?

From my experience, even if people join the military for financial gain, it's because they are trying to be responsible citizens and do it through hard work. Otherwise, they would have simply been a bank robber.

Unless you are a sadomasochist, you served for honorable reasons. You have done your job, and you served when others would not. You went, you fought, you sacrificed, and your family did as well. You wrote a blank check to the U.S. government, up to and including the price of your life. YOU did this. If you are reading this, there is a reason why they call us the "less than one percenters." Less than one percent of the U.S. population now serves in the military. You are it. Without you, someone else would have to go. You may not feel it, but you did this. That is what America refers to as a warrior. You may balk at the notion of being a hero, but society often has a broad definition of what it takes to be a hero. If the definition of a hero is someone who goes when others will not, then you are a hero because you went. At the very least, you are a warrior, because you were a part of trying to stop extremism in some form or another. You have defeated terrorism by going against your own mortality and fear and went halfway around the world to fight for the things you listed above. You are a winner, and America should be and is grateful—WIN.

 Key Takeaway: Some of you may have heard this for the first time. Let me say it again. You are a winner—a warrior, survivor, a servant, a hero. WIN.

In the chess game analogy, we often feel the total opposite and that we are PAWNS—pawns promulgated by invested interest. Instead, God sees us as KINGS—warriors who served valiantly, and my prayer is that your friends who died did not die in vain. They are in heaven now: their mission is complete.

I wonder what they would say to us if they could communicate. It was worth it? I did my duty? I served my country? I did not want to die, but I knew the risk? I raised my hand, just like you, and was willing to die for it all? They cannot and SHOULD NOT be forgotten. This would be the worst-case scenario, so your pain and suffering serve as a reminder to be honest and that they are not forgotten. Let that sink in for a moment. The memory of them means they are not forgotten.

The price of freedom is not only paid in their sacrifice but also your memory. Let's now think about what they would say to YOU if the roles were reversed.

You did your job. You were willing to sign up, not hoping to die but willing if it happened. You died serving our country. People die in war, and nothing can or will change that, which is why we are the last people in this world who want to fight a war! Why? We pay the price, and it is personal.

Your friend did not die in vain. He will NOT be forgotten. You will not let it happen, and, depending on your theological viewpoint, he WON. He did exactly what he set out to do, and that was to serve and fight at all costs, even if that means to the death. He did it. He completed his mission. He did not fail; he did not falter. He WON. It can be extremely devastating when one of our own dies, but think about this question for a second: which is harder to do—live or die? You only die once. To live is a daily activity.

REMEMBERING AND HONORING THE FALLEN

One of the very best ways to honor those who have died is to continue serving. Terror and evil try to take things away from us. The best way to combat terror is to give. Give back to those left behind. This may mean answering questions that the fallen's widow may have. It may mean giving time to play with their son or daughter in baseball, soccer, football, cheerleading, or another sport. It may mean giving money to their college fund. What would your friend do for you? Fall apart, drink, or use drugs to deal with the guilt? If so, then terrorism is winning.

Or do you want to do the opposite and invest—invest in love, joy, peace, patience, kindness, gentleness, and self-control? Do not let them be forgotten. Honor them with your time, your energy, and your money, but make it personal. Personally get involved with others who feel the same way. Join a not-for-profit organization that has the same passion as you do, and if there isn't one, create one. How do you think 501(c)(3) nonprofits came about in the first place? Every single one of these organizations has a founder who wanted to do something. So, do something to win.

FAILURE OR FORGIVENESS?

One of the biggest things survivor guilt does is weigh us down to the point that terror wins. I have actually had warriors who stated it this way: "There is no heaven." When pressed regarding how they come to this belief, they say, "Because if there is a heaven, then there is a God, and if there is a God, then there is a hell, and if there is a hell, then that's where I am going, so there is no heaven." Wow! We do crazy things to deal with survivor guilt and pain.

Alternative decision:

1. There is a God, and he can help me deal with my pain.
2. God is personal, and he cares about me.
3. I need to resolve my guilt and find a purpose and a passion for life again.

But what do I do with my guilt?

GUILT QUESTIONNAIRE

1. Do you believe anyone blames you for letting your buddy die? Yes or No? If so, who?

_____

2. Do you blame yourself? Yes or No?

3. Does God blame you? Yes or No?

If you can and feel it necessary to go to the widow and ask for forgiveness, even though you did nothing wrong, do it. Go and ask for forgiveness for not being able to stop evil. Ask for forgiveness for not being all-powerful, all-knowing, and all-present. You couldn't be everywhere at all times. You couldn't have known the enemy's mind (all-knowing) because, if you could have known their intent, you would have stopped it. You couldn't be everywhere (all-present), including where your buddy who died was. Otherwise, you would have changed the game. We try to change reality, but the problem is that you are not omniscient (all knowing), omnipresent (everywhere), or omnipotent (all powerful). Simply put, you are not God.

You cannot stop evil by yourself, and when evil had a voice, it used it in killing your friend. It was the enemy that killed him. Although we do our best to stop the enemy, the enemy did just that. So, what is there to forgive? Asking for forgiveness for the enemy choosing to kill? We don't ask for forgiveness for others. We ask for forgiveness for ourselves and only when it is warranted. Maybe seeking out a spiritual leader can be helpful at such times, or a friend who can relate. Remember that resilient people aren't made of stone. They are made of clay. They aren't stagnant. They are flexible and pliable. They can mold to the situation. They adapt, and they overcome.

What do you need to ask forgiveness for specifically?

_____

_____

If you wrote anything at all, then ask God for forgiveness. Why? Because God makes it very clear. I John 1:9: "When we ask, He is faithful and just to forgive us and cleanse us from all unrighteousness." God is in the business of forgiveness. If you feel you need it, it is granted.

God explains it this way: He expects perfection. Heaven is perfect, and anything that enters it must be perfect. Without perfection, you infiltrate perfection with impurity, and then it is no longer perfect. God has two choices: maintain heaven's perfection or let things in that aren't perfect and you no longer have heaven (by definition). God actually illustrates sin through archery. When you shoot your arrow at the target, do you know what they called it when you missed the mark?

They called anything less than a perfect shot "sin." That's what they called it. Sin was simply missing the mark. I've missed the mark many times. I have now, by definition, joined the imperfect human race. Heaven is perfect, and I am not. But God provided a solution, as He always does. It's called Grace. **Grace is unmerited favor**. We don't deserve it, and that's the point, but He gives it anyway. Grace is getting something we don't deserve. Heaven's requirements are met: PERFECTION. Grace meets the requirements of payment for perfection. You are not perfect, but God's grace pays the price.

FORGIVEN, BUT I DON'T FEEL IT

What do you do then when you don't feel forgiven? This is why we don't base our beliefs on feelings. We base beliefs on facts: the fact that God has forgiven us and that He has paid the price. We base it on the cross. Literally, Jesus paid the price. You just have to receive it. But it's not a gift if you don't take it. It's being handed to you. Do you accept the gift, the gift of forgiveness? This is what life comes down to.

So, what do I do when I cannot forgive myself? This is easy—easy when you know the answer. First, accept the fact that God expects perfection and that Grace has paid the price. Second, realize that when you don't forgive yourself, you are basically saying this: *God's expectation is perfection, but my expectation requirement of myself is actually higher than God's.* We set our standards higher than God's when we cannot and do not forgive ourselves. REALLY? Yes, really. Did we really just say that? Yes, my expectations are higher than God's. NO! God's standards for perfection have been met, and we cannot set our standards higher than God's, can we? If you can, then you are bigger than God. Let that sink in. Do you really want to make an argument that your standards are higher than God's? No. God has forgiven you, and now it's time to forgive yourself. In so doing, this is how you can resolve survivor guilt—through *forgiveness.*

BIBLIOTHERAPY: *Soul Repair: Recovering from Moral Injury after War* by Rita Brock

MODULE XI: THE ENEMY HAS A VOICE

Intent: To help warriors understand that, even though we can create the best operational "O" plan possible, the enemy can force us to change it based on their decisions.

Context: One of the biggest challenges that warriors have to deal with is death. We somehow think that if we had done things differently, had more intel, had more weapons, not gone on that route, leadership made a different decision, etc., then the outcome would have been different. The reality is that even though you can create the best plan of attack, all hell can break loose once the first shot is fired. In reality, if things went as planned, we would never suffer a single casualty. No one would ever die in war. Why? Because people don't write O plans that specifically lay out casualties. Today, casualties aren't tolerated.

In contrast to previous wars, I wonder what the O plan would have been for D-Day. They knew the only way to win the war was to take the beach at Normandy, a piece of land that our enemy occupied, and the only option to take it was to take it by brute force, unfortunately, creating heavy casualties. There was no other Courses of Action (COAs) chosen. There may have been options, but that was the only COA that was implemented. That was the O plan. In today's world, we create O plans that leadership knows may be a high risk for casualties, but we often talk about mitigating those to the point that casualties are nonexistent. For the persons on the ground, however, their point of view may be of a distant leadership that is making decisions that could get them killed. So, they often do not follow the plan. They change it on the battlefield. Some military personnel on the ground often see it with an "us vs. them" mentality, and the "them" is leadership. In this dichotomous[29] thinking, the blame for people dying is often placed on those in the leadership role. What is often neglected in our blame is the **enemy**. When something goes wrong or not according to plan and people die, we often blame either those in power or ourselves.

My argument lies in the fact that we have to attribute some responsibility, whatever that may be, to the person who killed our buddies/friends. Unfortunately, we often negate the impact and responsibility that our enemy has.

WHO IS RESPONSIBLE?

---

[29] two things that are sharply opposed to each other

When we talk about war, we cannot deny that some rules cannot be ignored. Do you recall the two basic rules of war?

Rule #1: _____

Rule #2: _____

If you don't remember, here they are:

    Rule #1: People die in war.
    Rule #2: You cannot change rule #1.

Unfortunately, these rules are true, but it doesn't change the fact that when it is someone you know, someone you care about, you want to change the rules of war—or, at least, change the situation so that the person didn't end up dying.

I believe other rules of war also apply, but I'd like you to give this some serious thought. If you were writing other rules in war, what would they be?

Rule #3: _____

Rule #4: _____

Rule #5: _____

Rule #6: _____

Now that you have contemplated a list of other possible rules of war, let's talk about COAs. Each time a commander is given a challenge or a serious problem, that commander needs solutions. They don't need people who only come to them with problems. Anyone can complain; in the military, we find answers. As a leader in the military, I love it when people not only come to me with problems but also have given the problems serious thought and have some potential solutions on how to fix them. Nothing is more frustrating for a person who has a problem than not having any answers, and nothing is more frustrating for a leader who is responsible for people's lives to only hear of problems but have no immediate possible solutions. We are all after the same End State.

In this context, it is increasing our Resiliency Factor. That being the case, let's look at the intent of COAs. By definition, a COA is a possible mitigating solution to a problem. It's that simple. In the military, we are about mitigating risk. Of course, there is going to be an inherent risk in any decision, but anything that you can do to mitigate it, or lessen the impact, is a good thing. Let's talk about how you go about doing that specifically.

Most commanders would like to have at least three COAs for each problem. For example, if I say that Rule #3 (above) is that the *enemy has a voice*, then how would we go about mitigating that? Let's list them. If you were a commander or a person going up against an enemy that has a voice in what they are going to do, how would you go about stopping or mitigating them? Even though we are not listing any particular scenario, there are some general things that one might do to mitigate an enemy attack. Can you think of three possible mitigating factors?

COA #1: _____

COA #2: _____

COA #3: _____

If you had continued your military career, chances are that the higher you were promoted, the more you would have been challenged to think like a military commander. Having the opportunity to be in charge, make decisions, and come up with COAs is someone's job. Why not make that yours? This is especially true as we relate these concepts to our own lives now.

Now that *you* get to be the deciding factor, take a look at the COAs and think about the pros and cons involved. For example, it's not that one is the right answer because most likely all three answers have pros and cons. What you have to do in decision-making is consider the pros and cons of each COA and make the best decision possible based on the information you have **at the time.** The reason this is so important is that in war we don't always have the best intel. Time is also limited, and decisions must be made.

You can begin to see the inherent challenges in this process. You can also see the importance of having good, if not great, intelligence. All of a sudden, making decisions, especially if you take into consideration the weight of responsibility, makes for a lot of thinking and strategy. Can you imagine having to be the person making the decision about Normandy in World War II? You know for a fact that a lot of American lives will be lost, but what choices do you have? That's what the COAs are designed to be—alternatives—but, at some point, you have to make a decision, and in doing so you take on the inherent pros and cons of the decision.

Please take a moment to either write down COAs for each of the rules you created, or, if you are in a group, discuss them.

I went ahead and created a few rules that I believe apply in a war zone as well as some based on my own experiences and talking with other combat veterans. Take a look, and then use the following Likert scale to judge them.

Circle your response to each of the following statements:

Rule #3: You cannot go back and change reality.

Completely False	Possible	Maybe	Somewhat Possible	Completely True

Rule #4: The enemy has a voice.

Completely False	Possible	Maybe	Somewhat Possible	Completely True

Rule #5: You will never forget.

Completely False	Possible	Maybe	Somewhat Possible	Completely True

As we deal with different rules of war that most likely cannot be changed, we see why it is that we often feel stuck. Nothing is more frustrating than being involved in something where you have responsibility without authority. Even when you are blessed to have both responsibility and authority, you still face the stubborn rules of war.

You can come up with the best COAs to mitigate Rule #4, that the enemy has a voice, but what do you do when the enemy kills one of your soldiers? Here's what typically happens:

WE TAKE ON THE SENSE OF RESPONSIBILITY AND CONTINUE TO CARRY IT.

Because of the way we are raised in this culture, we value human life. We take it seriously when someone, especially someone who has been under our command or our responsibility, dies, even if that means they deployed with us, and we had nothing to do with it.

We often feel a sense of responsibility. We say things in our minds, such as, "If only..."—you finish the sentence. Do you carry any "If only..." statements around in your head? Let's list them (if so), and add how that affects you.

"If only _____,
then _____."

"If only _____,
then _____."

"If only _____,
then _____."

We often take responsibility for outcomes for various reasons. It could be due to culture, spirituality, family upbringing—a host of reasons.

Let's talk about why we feel a sense of responsibility and where it comes from. I personally was influenced heavily by my parents and attending church. We were taught the Ten Commandments, one of them being, "Thou shalt not kill." If I take God seriously, and this made his Top Ten, then I better take it seriously. What other influences in your life bring about a sense of responsibility? List them (for example, church, school, athletics) and then what you were taught, such as, "Thou shalt not kill."

1. _____   –   _____

2. _____   –   _____

3. _____   –   _____

If you have trouble with this task, think about how you were raised. What did your parents, grandparents, church, Boy/Girl Scouts, etc., instill in you? In the military, we are taught, "Never leave your Wingman." This is specific to the Air Force, but the other services have similar beliefs. List them.

_____

_____

_____

Hopefully, this will encourage you to think of other influencing factors on your moral code. If you think of others, either go back and fill in the information or write them down. The point is that all of this helps formulate our moral code.

MORAL CODE

Just like any COA, your moral code can be either helpful or make things more difficult for you psychologically. As a matter of fact, this is usually where people begin to realize they have internal conflicts. On one hand, they believe in serving valiantly in the military. On the other hand, they may be faced with the ugliness of war in which they had to kill someone. This creates an inherent moral dilemma. **We talk a lot about Resiliency Formation, and this is where it all comes together.**

We've already talked about how our moral code is instilled in us. We have also talked about the enemy having a voice and our COAs, but what happens when things do not go as planned? When our friends die and we feel a sense of responsibility? What then?

121

www.ProjectHealingHeroes.org

EGO-SYNTONIC VS. EGO-DYSTONIC

Ego-dystonic is a word that describes a dilemma in your moral code that you cannot resolve, for example, "Thou shalt not steal," and you steal something. If you cannot resolve this in your mind, you are ego-dystonic.

If you are ego-syntonic, you have this moral dilemma in your mind, but you have found a way to resolve it or a way in which you view or interpret it neutrally or positively. It does not bother you or cause you symptoms.

Remember the movie *American Sniper*? When asked if he had any regrets for killing over 100 of the enemy, Chris Kyle said, in essence, "No, my only regret is not killing more of the enemy so that more American lives would have been saved." Would you say he is ego-syntonic or ego-dystonic?

He would be ego-syntonic. He has resolved this in his mind. He has few, if any, regrets, and this belief system has a direct impact on his feelings. This lessens the weight significantly.

WHERE DOES THAT LEAVE YOU?

If you have moral dilemmas or issues with others that remain unresolved, the best way to determine what to do is to actually list them. Hopefully, you are not blind to them, but if you are, just ask someone close to you what they see as your internal conflicts. They cannot read your mind, but they can see the consequences of your internal conflicts in your actions and your behavior. If you ask those who care about you, chances are they will be honest. Don't get defensive when you hear what they have to say.

Let's now actually do the hard work. You may need a small break before continuing. Either way, this is one of the most important parts of therapy, so let's give this our best effort.

WHAT KEEPS ME UP AT NIGHT?

When you think about what has happened to you and what you think about, most likely it is unresolved. You struggle because you have not yet found resolution. Let's list possible dilemmas: moral injury, guilt, remorse—anything that affects you. If you can, list your Top Five. Then, after listing them, if you have a mantra (something that you tell yourself), what is it?

1. _____

_____

_____

2. _____

_____

_____

3. _____

_____

_____

4. _____

_____

_____

5. _____

_____

_____

Now that you have listed these, let's talk about our sense of responsibility. What were you specifically responsible for? What did you do, or not do, that continues to keep you feeling stuck? Chances are it's something that you regret. For example, look at what you said for number 1. After rereading it, write down specifically what it is that you regret, feel guilty about, feel impacts your life, etc.

_____

_____

_____

_____

_____

_____

No matter what you wrote, this is the core issue that needs to be discussed. To increase your resiliency formation, how you resolve this dilemma will be key. Obviously, people would like to change what happened. The problem is that we are not God. We cannot bring people back from the dead. We cannot change the outcome. We cannot go back and do things differently or wish others would. This is simply a rule.

Focusing on what we cannot do is futile and leaves us stuck. What we can do, however, is work with what we do have, so let's talk about what we can change.

When you think about what you can change, what comes to mind? Anything? Again, it's natural for the mind to think about what we cannot change, but what can we do with this situation? The one thing we can do, instead of beating ourselves up over something, is give fair weight to what has really happened. Let's do it this way. What weight of responsibility do you place on the following? Put a percentage next to it on a scale from 0–100.

I blame:

_____ – _____ %

_____ – _____ %

_____ – _____ %

Does it equal 100 percent? If not, go back, and change your percentages.

The topic of this Module is "The Enemy Has a Voice." That being the case, did you list the enemy? If so, what percentage did you assign them? If you didn't list them, why not? The reason is often that we focus on what we did and what our leadership has done. We minimize any impact that the enemy may have had, but, if we take into account that the enemy decided to fire, and they decided to use the element of surprise, and they killed our soldiers, are they not the enemy after all? Are they not to bear some part of the responsibility?

 Key Takeaway: Even though we take it personally when one of our friends dies in theater, the Enemy has a voice, and we cannot minimize their responsibility. We cannot simply blame ourselves. In order to change reality, we would have to be omniscient, omnipotent, and omnipresent, and we are none of these three things.

To be honest with ourselves, we need to realize that our enemy is the one who did the killing. Decisions may have been made that made it easier for them, but ultimately, they had a voice. They fired a weapon or did something to cause serious injury or death. As a matter of fact, without an enemy, we wouldn't have been there in the first place. We don't often correlate the AOR with a vacation. It's not usually our top destination spot to visit and just hang out. We are there for a reason, a purpose, and often it is to mitigate the evil intent of others and to get closer to our End State. You cannot change Rule #4, The Enemy Has a Voice. They use it. Since this is the case, rate this again to include the enemy.

I blame:

_____ – _____%

_____ – _____%

_____THE ENEMY_____ – _____%

Did your numbers change at all? They did if they have to add up to 100 percent, especially if you did not include the enemy in your first calculations.

WHAT DOES IT MATTER?

Ultimately, the person who was with you in the AOR is still dead. You cannot bring that person back, but you can work on not blaming yourself 100% and actually realizing that you need compassion just as much as the family members of the one who died. You are worthy of grace and mercy. In reality, it is very likely that you blame yourself and will not forgive yourself in an attempt to somehow ensure that the person's memory is not forgotten. You may be acting like if you beat yourself up enough, it will somehow make you feel better. Well, as a psychologist, I can tell you, beating yourself up for the purpose of penance or somehow trying to make yourself feel better never works. Even if you were the one who caused the death (which most often is not the case), you deserve compassion, grace and mercy. Remember, there is only one who was perfect, and you are not Him. Another key component other than the importance of shifting blame from oneself is actually accepting loss and doing grief work. Grief work is something that is vitally important in getting you closer to resiliency. We highly recommend that you seek out a grief counselor, pastor, spiritual advisor, therapist, whomever you trust that can help free you from the burden and weight of guilt.

Blaming yourself or others is never going to change the outcome. It's not the outcome we are trying to change, though, because we cannot change reality; rather, it's ourselves. I always tell our warriors that they are only six inches away from being healthy. Typically, that's the distance between your thumb and your index finger when you place them across your forehead. It's the mind or the size of the brain. What you carry around with you is in your head, and you are only six inches away from being healthy. To get there, however, we have to work on our resiliency formation, and to do that we must accept the following:

1. There are rules of war that we cannot change.

2. One of them is that the enemy has a voice.
3. We need to resolve moral and ethical dilemmas in our heads and in our hearts.
4. We need to place appropriate responsibility onto the situation.
5. We cannot change the past, but we can change how we deal with the future.
6. We will NEVER FORGET. We are the ones who are left with the memories, and how we resolve these will impact how we move forward.
7. Forgiveness about our percentage of responsibility is attainable.
8. We often take on more responsibility than we should.

Finally, let's focus on the aspect of honoring the fallen. Sometimes warriors blame themselves so much that they develop an attitude of apathy because it all seems so senseless. They are left with more questions than answers. In essence, why did this person have to die? Was that death in vain?

Many veterans who fought the intense battles of Fallujah and other (since lost) locations, have expressed this sentiment. The whole intent of this workbook isn't to create different COAs or ROEs, or to change reality. It's to help individuals process their emotions, grief, and beliefs and help them move forward into the next chapter of their lives in a more resilient manner. Veterans are mentally trapped and having a hard time seeing the reality that it was not their fault and yet feeling a strong sense of responsibility.

In order to break free, sometimes we have to see things from a totally different perspective—a more realistic perspective. If you are having a hard time forgiving yourself, consider the following letter, written by a veteran, to the person who died.

Dear _____,

It's been a long time since I've seen you, buddy, and I want you to know that I think about you every single day. I've been thinking a lot about what happened, playing it over and over in my mind. Please know that if I could have done anything to save your life, I would have gladly died in your place to do it. I not only think about you every day, it has impacted my life in ways I cannot even begin to explain. People tell me to move on, get over it, but they don't understand.

I've been thinking about how I am going to go on, given what happened and all. I know you would want me to go on. I know you wouldn't want me to stay down and depressed forever. You were always so funny and light-hearted. You had such passion for life, a mission, a purpose. I've lost mine. I no longer feel as if I'm even a good person. Not only to others, but myself.

I decided that I want to live in a way that honors you—I want to get back the old me. I will NEVER forget what happened and how much you mean to me. I finally realized that moving on with my life doesn't mean that I have forgotten you. It means you saved me, and I don't want to let you down. Godspeed; until we meet again at the big battle in the sky.

Yours forever,

———————————————————

One of the healthiest things we can do to let this all sink in is to think about how we would respond to the people we deployed with if *we* were the one who had died. I know it's hard to think about, but what if you were the one who had been killed? I came very close to death during my deployment, so this isn't a strange concept for me. Let's do one final challenge.

HOMEWORK ASSIGNMENT

I want you to write a letter to the person or people who have died as if they were the ones living and you had died. Would you blame them? Would you be angry? What would you tell them? What would you do about their guilt, remorse, and forgiveness? What would you tell them about where you are now? How would you describe your life after death? What would you tell them to do until it is their time? If you quickly ran through those questions, please reconsider your answers to them and add whatever questions you feel are important.

It's time to write a response letter. Even if you only do this for yourself and never give it to anyone, it will help bring about healing. It will also be one of the hardest things you will ever do, but I guarantee that it will help you to become more resilient by resolving some of these issues.

Your new mission is now upon you. Chances are you received very little, if any, outbriefs on how to deal with these issues. **Now is your time.** Think about what you would say, how you would answer the questions I posed to you, etc. Remember to keep in mind why they may have joined the military in the first place. We all raised our hands and vowed to live and die for this country. Unfortunately, some people pay the ultimate price, but what if it were you that died? What if they were struggling with these issues—what would you tell them to do to move on? They are no different from you. We are all human.

Take the time to write your letter and give it to your therapist or others, if you are in a group setting, once complete. Then debrief on what you were feeling when you wrote it and any new challenges that you came up with. We have found this exercise to be one of the most therapeutic things you can do, so let's get on with the healing process.

If I had died instead, I would tell those left behind... (address the issues related to grief, loss, futility, the future, how it impacts the family, etc).

———————————————————————————————————————

———————————————————————————————————————

———————————————————————————————————————

_____

_____

_____

_____

_____

_____

MODULE XII: MORAL INJURY

Intent: To help you address the psychological wounds of war that pit your core beliefs against what you have seen and sometimes what you have done. To some, because you may feel as if there is <u>no</u> answer to what you have done, it seems hopeless. We believe otherwise.

Context: If PTS(D) is the signature wound of the invisible war, moral injury is the infection.

WHAT IS MORAL INJURY?

Moral injury, at its most core, is an offense in some manner against humanity that goes against one's core beliefs and/or values. According to a research article published by Litz et al. (2009), moral injury is "perpetrating, failing to prevent, or bearing witness to acts that transgress deeply held moral beliefs and expectations." These transgressions, or wrongdoings, can occur when we do things we shouldn't (i.e., lie, steal) or choose not to do something when we should (i.e., My Lai – where people began killing everyone in the Vietnam village, including women and children and no one stopped them).

Moral injury occurs when you are experiencing conflict in your head and in your heart over something you believe to be inherently wrong. Cognitive dissonance is the stress you feel when you have to choose to do something that you believe in your gut is wrong. Moral injury is the result of following through with that action (or inaction). Due to either internal or external forces, you make a willful decision to engage or not engage in something that you consider to be wrong. A transgression is an act that goes against a law, a rule, and/or a code of conduct. Military members are all too familiar with a code of conduct. A violation of this code has its consequences in the Uniform Code of Military Justice (UCMJ). This is often why people are afraid to say what's going on. To confess means possible imprisonment, while non-disclosure has the same effect. You feel imprisoned by these conflicting thoughts and emotions.

Moral injury's sting is that it leaves you feeling judged, either by yourself, others, or by God. Depending upon where you are in the process, our hope is that you end up being made whole, either through resolving the issues you feel in your heart and in your head or through forgiveness by God, others or self.

MORAL INJURY AFFECTS YOUR PHYSICAL WELL-BEING

Moral injury goes beyond our individual internal conflicts. It's a hurt so deep that it takes your breath away. Anyone who has suffered devastating news to the point they cannot even breathe will understand this. Warriors and first responders may experience a lack of oxygen to the extent they experience a panic attack. You literally cannot catch your breath. It is a hurt that goes beyond the moral transgressions of beliefs and actions, it penetrates your soul. If not addressed, it can literally extinguish your breath for living (it could lead to suicide).

TARGETING MORAL INJURY

You may not be familiar with ancient archery, but when you would aim your arrow at a target and miss the bull's-eye, they would call out one word: sin.

Sin is the reason why so many of our warriors are devastated by haunting memories of what they have witnessed, caused, or experienced firsthand. It is impossible to escape that which pierces your soul. We hold a core belief about right and wrong, about how things should be. And then along comes war, and the reality of what we live and experience. These deeply held beliefs go beyond morality. Morality is about right and wrong. Soul injury affects not only morality, but also speaks to the essence of the person at the core of their being.

HOW DID WE GET HERE?

Some people have witnessed, experienced, or caused something so awful that they feel unworthy of getting better. How did we get to this point? I think we can only answer that question by giving some examples of real world, warrior situations. Although your personal moral injury may be different, the concepts will be the same. You will have a chance to write down and process your specific moral injury.

Decision Points in War

You may have heard of times in war when warriors in combat will say, "something just doesn't feel right about this." Many times, they will make decisions based not on intel or command, but on instinct. Sometimes when on convoys, you receive orders and there is something that tells you that this is a bad idea. Your command tells you one thing, and your gut tells you something else. It is the old brain versus gut argument. So, how do you predict or determine what choice a person will make? Do you listen to command, or listen to that still, small voice inside you, that gives you a competing message? In war, people listen to both. It's impossible to know which one may have been the right decision, until after everything unfolds. But even then, you don't know what would have happened had you made the other choice. You cannot prove a negative. It's a dilemma which most warriors have faced in their career. GO, NO GO. This route, or an alternative route. Turn down this street, or take another path. Shoot, don't shoot. Either way, a decision is forced upon us.

Sometimes there is no easy answer, nor a good answer when we are at war. Remember, Rule #1: people die in war, and Rule #2: you can't change rule #1.

I was trying to teach my son Joshua that there are certain questions in life to which you cannot give a yes or no answer. For example, if someone asks you, "Have you *stopped* stealing?"

If you answer YES, it says that you are confessing you were stealing, but you've stopped now.

If you answer NO, it says that you haven't stopped and are still continuing to steal.

Neither answer has a good outcome.

This is an analogy similar to what it is like to make some very difficult decisions in the heat of battle. Sometimes, no matter what you would have chosen, there was not going to be a good outcome. <u>Some of you need to hear that today.</u>

 Key Takeaway: One of the biggest challenges that US military members face is the concept of responsibility. "It is my fault." We place more responsibility on ourselves than anyone should ever carry. If everything we do in the military is to be done as a unit, why is it we often blame no one but ourselves?

We are in this fight together. Even though you may have been a catalyst, you did not end up where you did on your own. A series of events had to occur in order for you to be at that place, at that time, with that decision.

Burden of Responsibility

 Unfortunately, we have been trained at an early age, in boot camp and throughout our military career, that we are responsible for those on our left and on our right, and that being responsible is a good thing. But there can be too much of a good thing, and we can become our own worst enemy.

We took on the personal responsibility to ensure that "all will come home alive." Unfortunately, in war, this is sometimes unattainable. Why? Because people die in war.

It is ingrained in our belief system that we are the ones responsible for bringing everyone home alive. We carry this, despite the fact that the outcome in some firefights is not going to be good either way. You are caught in a dilemma of making a decision in which there is simply no good answer.

If you are like me, you don't like playing games you can't win. In reality, if it is a game I can't win, I don't play. But war isn't a game, and we aren't playing around. It's a matter of life and death. Sometimes the decisions we have to make have consequences that we had no intention of causing. Oftentimes in war, decisions lead to life or death, whether that death is that of one of our own warriors, a child, even a terrorist.

WHY MORAL INJURY HAPPENS

1. In the military we are trained to demonize our enemy because it's easier to kill someone who is evil. So, killing the enemy is not wrong, we're told. Yet, you may feel in your gut that killing anyone is wrong. Or, you may have to kill someone who is not a confirmed enemy, but just a threat. This causes moral injury.

2. We have power. We have authority. When given power and authority, we may do things we wouldn't normally do on our own. In the Stanford Prison studies college students were separated into groups in a mock prison. Some were guards, and others were prisoners. The guards became incredibly abusive. They encouraged each other to psychologically abuse the prisoners to keep control over them much like what really happened at Abu Ghraib. Moral injury occurs when we act from a place of power and authority that does not agree with our sense of right and wrong.

3. We're placed in situations where we have to make incredibly difficult, life-ending decisions in mere seconds.

A Moral Injury Example

I have heard many times people give the example that they have been trained over and over and over again to never, under any circumstances, stop a convoy. Why? Because that is when you and everyone else around you become vulnerable. We have to mitigate this risk at all costs, which means you are trained that you DO NOT STOP for anything. It doesn't matter what the "IT" is. You DO NOT STOP. Period. You train and train and train, experience scenarios, and train some more. But at all costs, you DO NOT STOP that convoy.

Fast forward to Iraq or Afghanistan in which we were in combat operations. It's a war zone. People are trying to kill you. This may be your first experience, or you are a seasoned professional. Either way, the hairs on the back of your neck stand straight up. You grip the steering wheel of a massive piece of machinery that weighs over five tons, and your job is to get from point A to point B with your men, women, and your convoy of assets. You have a mission to do, and nothing is to get in the way of you accomplishing that mission. You may have even gotten together to pray before you headed out because, well, we want God on our side, especially if our mission could mean the difference between life and death. Music is blaring before you get into your truck, and you're pumped and ready to go.

En route, it happens. There is a crowd on both sides of the street as you drive by, and you are vulnerable. You are looking around to see where the enemy may be lurking. Your breathing changes, your heart is pounding, and there is a lot of information coming at you. Remember: your brain suppresses, or inhibits, 99% of what it senses, but when this is happening, it allows more information in than normal. Your senses become keenly aware of your surroundings as your brain quickly processes the most important information. You use your situational awareness and keep intensely focused. If you do not, it could mean the difference between life and death. You remember what you have been trained to do, and the military mantra instilled in you: DO NOT STOP at all costs, and get everyone through this alive.

Then out of nowhere, a child is pushed in front of your truck. You see her face. She's very young. She is lying in front of you, looking directly at you. You have a split second to make a decision. You are trained DO NOT STOP at all costs. Your brain is trying desperately to process this decision and its consequences. It happens so fast that you are completely stuck in the moment, looking at her, trying to make a decision about what to do. If only you had the time to come up with the best decision, but there is no good outcome.

For those of you who have experienced this, you probably need to take a break because you might have a flashback. You need to take a break and come back to it. There will be no need for more details.

Outcome Option #1: If you stop and make her life the priority, you put everyone else at risk, including yourself. This is what the enemy wants you to do. That is why they chose this time, this place, this child.

In this case, they use our own moral beliefs against us. They create a moral dilemma that will affect our actions. We either stop, or we don't. There are no other options. Remember, we don't like playing games we can't win. In this situation, it's not only that we can't win, we can't even find a good alternative. There are no good outcomes.

So, you decide. Your brain decides to stop the truck, which in effect, halts the convoy. Now all of your buddies are at risk. At that split second, you hear, "DON'T STOP. DON'T STOP! We're going to get killed. Get us out of here, damn it!" Then out of the corner of your eye one of the enemy pops up with an RPG. You are hit. The truck is blasted onto its side and on fire. Everyone behind you can't move. People are screaming on the comms. In pain, a call is shouted out, "Medic, medic!" You made your decision. You did the unthinkable. You stopped the convoy. The enemy was hoping for this decision. They set the stage. They were prepared. They wanted and needed you to make that decision. They used your own moral belief system against you. You discover you are bleeding and the ringing in your ears will not stop. Dazed and confused, you try to get your bearings. Chaos is everywhere as the firefight ensues. You hear the rounds from an AK47 going off and people returning fire with a 50 Cal, M9s and a 9MM. Another RPG. Another explosion. And you go unconscious thinking, knowing, your decision was the pivotal one... you STOPPED.

You wake up in a hospital bed a few days later from a moderate Traumatic Brain Injury (mTBI). Your arm is broken. Your leg is shattered. But you are alive. As you awaken, your brain hurts, but you remember small details of what happened. You go through in your mind the events as best you can. You see that girl's face that triggered all of this. You see her eyes as she laid there on the ground looking up. That is when you remember doing the unthinkable, the one thing you were trained not to do. You stopped the convoy. Emotions overwhelm you. The weight of everyone on your convoy that was killed or injured is on your mind. You tell yourself, I FAILED. I failed at my mission. I failed my brothers and sisters. I failed their families for not bringing them home alive. It was my responsibility, and I failed.

How do you even begin to live with yourself with the weight of the world on your shoulders? This is exactly the type of moral injury that many of our men and women struggle with. The example may be different; you have your own examples, but the concepts are the same. The enemy used what you believe against you. Yet, here you are. You've completely succumbed to your emotions and heavy heart as you blame yourself for your own failure. It was you who made the decision to go against your training. It was you who hit the brakes. It is undeniable. You made a choice, and it cost people, your people, their lives. The weight of their deaths is upon you. You begin to mind-read that their families will blame you. You become depressed and possibly suicidal because you cannot tolerate the weight of this decision. At your very core, you are overcome with grief. You feel you would be better off dead than to make any more decisions in your life that could cost other people.

I've met folks like this. They are depressed and suicidal warriors who will not even make a simple decision. They feel as if their punishment should be death. They do not deserve to live. They have judged themselves and believe they have been judged by others and by God, and they deserve to die. The weight is simply unbearable.

Outcome Option #2: The shouts from your drill sergeant in preparation for your deployment "DO NOT STOP" run constantly in your head. It doesn't matter what the enemy throws at you, <u>DO NOT STOP</u>. So, no matter what happens, you do not, at all costs, take your foot off the gas. As a matter of fact, you push through even harder to get you and your buddies through the situation and out of harm's way. You mitigate risk by getting the hell out of there. You DO NOT STOP.

You see the girl's face in front of you as she is lying on the road after being pushed into harm's way. You may have a daughter similar in age. As this child lies there on the ground looking up at you, you know what you must do. You are committed to the mission. That mission is to ensure you will get the lives entrusted to you from point A to point B. So, you make your decision. While feeling the weight of the truck run over the child, you slightly bow your head down. You know you are the one who killed her.

Your heart is heavy. You are by yourself with your emotions, and you hear on the radio the guys saying, "You did the right thing. You saved us. Let it go." They say this because they think about how they would be feeling if they were in your shoes. They think about the hurt and the pain and the thoughts that will go through your mind. They have empathy.

"Thou shalt not kill." What do you do with that? You didn't join the military to kill a child. You joined to stop evil. and here you are, the killer. You have become, in your mind, the evil one. You conclude that you do not deserve forgiveness. What kind of God would forgive something like this? You keep driving as if you are in a daze. You have that thousand-yard stare, but no one can see it. You are on autopilot. Your training has taken over, and you have no idea what the outcome of stopping would have been. You hear the comms again, "You saved us. Let's get out of here." You took the life of a child, an innocent child. The weight of the world is on your shoulders.

This is moral injury.

In this situation, you were forced to make a moral decision. There was no good outcome either way. The problem is that most of the time you don't even know what the outcome would have been. We can only speculate. And sometimes in our speculation, we are wrong. Simply put, only God knows what the outcome may have been. Other factors may have played out of which we are not even aware. What we do know is that you blame yourself either way you go. It was your decision, after all, your responsibility, your call. By default or not, a decision was made.

We make decisions out of fear. Even though someone is not a confirmed threat, a moral decision is made to kill. Sometimes we do things in the military that if we spoke of them, it would get us imprisoned. We killed even innocent people because we were scared. We were scared of what these folks were capable of. For example, there's a family in a car, driving to a gate, but they didn't stop for whatever reason. Despite our warning efforts and ROEs, they continue. They are interpreted as a threat, and threats have to be stopped. Later, we find out they truly were not a threat, but we didn't know that at the time

We made decisions out of revenge. We were angry. Angry because a buddy had been killed and we took our vengeance out on a person. We didn't have to kill them; they could have been detained. But our anger that seethed inside of us decided to take revenge out on this person, and we annihilated them. There are countless stories of this happening in war. Unfortunately, this is not unusual. It happens more often than we care to admit. To admit this revenge killing means a death sentence or possibly life in prison. Our lives would be over. So, we keep these things to ourselves, and live with the knowledge that we went against our core beliefs about humanity. They are our enemy, but we are the killer. "Thou shalt not kill" becomes a mantra in our brain that we cannot escape. What is left of this moral dilemma? It often leads to condemnation. We condemn ourselves because we have gone against one of God's commandments. We do not deserve to live because we have taken the life of another human. We are evil and unforgiveable. For those of you who can relate, you understand better than anyone else.

So where is the hope? Is there even a future for us? I have no idea what you tell yourself at times like this. But, one thing is for sure, you tell yourself something about what you have done. What is it?

What do you tell yourself?

Don't leave the lines blank. It is important to actually write down what goes on in your head. Burn this book later if you have to. It might even be therapeutic.

For some, the mantra may be negative such as, "I told you that you would never amount to anything. You are a failure. Just wait until people find out what you did."

For others, the mantra may be more positive. The thing that may have popped into your head is, "Our help comes from the Lord." This same God whom we believe would condemn us is the only chance we have.

Whatever thoughts you do have, positive or negative, I can assure you that what you believe in your soul matters. It will affect your behavior. This is why it is so important. There is a saying, "For as he thinketh in his heart, so is he. . ." (Proverbs 23:7). What you believe becomes the essence of who you are.

The answers to these moral and spiritual questions are so vast that it goes beyond the scope of this book. You may want to read *Soul Repair: Recovering from Moral Injury after War* by R. Brock (2013).

You could also use the REACH worksheets in the back of this book to process through these thoughts. However, we highly recommend you do not do this alone. This is where someone in your life who cares deeply about you can be helpful. This may be a spouse, a friend, or another veteran who has worked through it successfully. If not, find a compassionate and understanding therapist. Either way, it is imperative that you process these thoughts.

EGO-SYNTONIC VS. EGO-DYSTONIC THOUGHTS

One processes moral injury in one of two ways:

1. Ego-Syntonic: It means you can live with yourself and the choices you have made. You tell yourself things to make yourself feel better, or you genuinely feel justified in your actions and believe you made the right choice. I think of the example of Chris Kyle who, when asked if he felt guilty about killing so many people, responded by saying that he felt bad for not killing more because that would have meant that more of our guys would have made it home alive.

2. Ego-Dystonic. It simply means that you are in a deadlock, oftentimes between your thoughts and your feelings. These two are opposing each other, and you are not in sync. On one hand, you may believe, "Thou shalt not kill," and on the other, "I killed someone." You can see the internal conflict. It is not unusual that conflict without resolution leads to condemnation.

Warriors often blame themselves for their actions, especially when it does not fit with their core beliefs. At that point, something has to give.

This is the essence of the moral injury. We morally know that what we did and what we believe are in conflict. In this situation, we do not have resolution. Without resolution, it's hard to be resilient. It's the opposite. People become depressed or suicidal over these thoughts and cannot find a way out from under them.

COGNITIVE DISSONANCE

Leon Festinger, who coined the term "cognitive dissonance," believed that a person becomes unstable due to this internal conflict, and they are motivated to find resolution. In the process of this internal conflict, without resolution, they will actively avoid situations and information in order to decrease the distress.[30]

Most warriors can relate to this quandary. Avoidance of situations and triggers is something that you can understand on a daily basis if you continue to remain in conflict. This, I believe, is at the core of insomnia. Insomnia is the number one stated problem of warriors across the country.

Most people have heard of defense mechanisms. These are various thoughts and behaviors people use to deal with things like emotional distress. We use them, literally, as a defense. Unfortunately, during sleep, we no longer have defense mechanisms in our arsenal of weapons against this emotional turmoil. Without a defense, we are left to deal with relentless nightmares and ruminating thoughts that haunt us.

I hope we are beginning to bring clarity into how this all fits together. It's a vicious cycle. Triggers, avoidance, cognitive dissonance, defense mechanisms, insomnia, conflict, exhaustion, medication to solve these problems, side effects, and triggers again. It's time to get off this cycle of destruction.

MORAL INJURY: A SECULAR AND SACRED APPROACH

This is where our book deviates from mainstream psychology. We present both a secular (non-religious) and sacred (religious) approach to resolution. We believe in giving people full disclosure on all options. To not do so, in our opinion, is unethical. We need to be informed consumers, and with due diligence, we provide you with options.

The Secular Approach

The key to solving moral injury from a secular viewpoint is found in resolving cognitive dissonance. This resolution is not something you find; it's something you choose.

---

[30] Festinger, L. (1957). *A Theory of Cognitive Dissonance*. California: Stanford University Press.

Resolution facilitates resiliency. You create resolution by making a willful decision that you will confront head-on the conflicting beliefs, acts, and emotions that are causing distress. Sometimes it is easier to look at what is not resolution, so that we can eliminate these myths.

Resolution of Moral Injury is Not...

1. Resolution of Moral Injury is not accomplished through avoidance and numbing. You cannot avoid if your intent is to resolve.
2. Resolution of Moral Injury is not found in a magic pill. Medications are never a long-term solution. Their effectiveness wears off over time, and one is left either maxing out that dose, or adding another medication, and another, and another. This leads to being on multiple medications, not only for the original problem, but for the side effects these medications cause. Medications have their place in the healing process. Remember the extinction burst in Phase I. When confronting issues, symptoms get worse before they get better. If you are having difficulty tolerating the symptoms as you begin the process of confronting these situations, that is where medications can take the edge off. Unfortunately, some people view medications as the answer. They were never intended for that purpose when it comes to cognitive dissonance. They may be warranted for other reasons, which is why a professional relationship with a psychiatrist should be required. They are the experts at medication decisions and adjustments and should be the first line of defense while working through this material.
3. Resolution of Moral Injury is not relying on defense mechanisms. If all you do is play a defensive game, you can't win. Without an offense, you cannot score, and you cannot win. We are about winning. Defense mechanisms are another form of avoidance through tolerance.
4. Resolution of Moral Injury is not discounting civilians. The "you don't understand, you've never been there" mentality doesn't work. I actually had a warrior give me this argument at one point. He obviously didn't know my background. It was amazing the transformational attitude once he found out what I actually did in the military. Before that, I was discounted. Civilians *can* help you throughout this process.
5. Resolution of Moral Injury is not believing that time will heal. No, it won't. If that were true, neither WWII nor Vietnam veterans would have any PTS(D) issues. It's not time that heals; it's what you do with the time that matters.
6. Resolution of Moral Injury is not using "I have PTS(D)" as an excuse. That is simply the most ridiculous argument one can make. You are not a disorder. You may have a disorder (or not), but you are not defined by it. I may have cancer, but I am not cancer.
7. Resolution of Moral Injury is not a label. Stating that you are a label, such as "I'm a Disabled Vet," only minimizes one's capabilities. That may be true in certain areas of your life where you are no longer able, but what about the areas of your life where you are able. Remember, brain flexibility is the key, and overgeneralizing is not our friend.
8. Resolution of Moral Injury is not working to maintain a diagnosis for financial gain. "I'll lose my disability rating if I get better." We are not the VA. Our motivation is to get you better, not

to increase your disability rating. People can both have a disability and be resilient at the same time.

9. Resolution of Moral Injury is not giving up when your course of life has been altered. Most warriors never counted on being where they are in their life at this place and time. Most people thought they would make the military their retirement. Did you know only about 15 percent of all military members ever make it to their 20th year? Fifteen percent. That leaves 85 percent, the majority, out of the military prior to retirement.

10. Resolution of Moral Injury is not hopeless. We believe you have a new mission and a purpose in your life where you overcome issues related to such things like moral injury and survivor guilt.

There have been books written on how to approach addressing cognitive dissonance and how to resolve this dilemma. Instead of reinventing the wheel, we will instead direct you to Bibliotherapy and Psychotherapy to bring about resolution. Do not do this work alone. You do it with the support, help, and encouragement of those who not only understand (which may mean professional help), but peers who have also "been there."

The Sacred Approach

We would like to present you with a different approach to cognitive dissonance. We believe it goes way beyond cognition. It is more like soul dissonance. It integrates not only cognition (your thoughts), but also your feelings and how you see yourself after experiencing war. You may have even changed at the core of your being, your persona, your personality. This is why we are not the same when we come back. We are changed, that is true. And so would someone else, if they had experienced the same things we have. So, in the nicest way possible, "judge not, lest ye be judged." Only God knows the heart.

The Moral Compass and the Search for a New Paradigm (example)

When dealing with moral issues, you do not want to feel as if you are simply spinning out of control. You want direction, guidance, and instruction on how to resolve these issues. If you could solve it on your own, you would have. There would be no need for resolution or this chapter.

Guilt and shame are two significant concepts in the moral injury arena. You may remember the United States Marine Corp commercial with soldiers running. They are clearly in a desert war zone with an explosion in the distance. Brilliantly, the narrator asks the question, "Which way will you run?" I believe they hit the target on this one. This is the difference between those who run away from danger, and those who run toward it. Which direction will you run? Military members have already made this decision when they joined. Whether that is our nature, or training, we run towards danger. Similarly, so do police, firefighters, and first responders. We are all of the same substance.

It is this directionality that will become pivotal. A compass or azimuth is the horizontal direction of a compass bearing. We have heard that a person may have lost their "moral compass." But what does that really mean? Simply, you've lost your direction in life.

Guilt is when you have concluded that you are responsible; you missed the mark, and you point the finger directly at yourself. You are the one to blame. You made the decision. You made the choice. But it went against your moral values and beliefs and landed you right in the middle of feeling guilty for what you have done.

Shame is when someone else has concluded that you are responsible, you missed the mark and they point the finger directly at you. It is like in a court of law when the prosecuting attorney stands before the jury, making their strongest arguments about why you are guilty, and then points directly at you and says, "You are to blame. It was you that did this." The amount of shame you feel is in direct proportion to how much guilt you accept.

 Key Takeaway: When it comes to moral injury, which direction the finger is pointing in regards to responsibility will determine whether a person will feel guilt or shame.

The problem with the moral compass argument is that it is a two-dimensional answer in a three-dimensional world. Let me explain. The moral compass only points to a direction on the horizontal plane and expects you to move in that direction. This is how we do land navigation. It is two-dimensional. Direction is the X-axis and distance is the Z-axis. Resolution does not involve only finding your direction and moving towards it; it requires a third dimension. For example, what if we were a drone pilot trying to hit a three-dimensional object? You cannot just leave the weapon on an airstrip and point the weapon in that direction and fire. It has to fly there in altitude as well as in direction and distance.

Moral injury involves more than just conflict between beliefs and values. Moral injury has impacted your core being, your soul. And what we do to our soul not only affects ourselves, but it also affects our fellowship with God. This is the third dimension. For sake of example, I will argue that deity is the Y-axis. You are reading this book in two dimensions, but what if the words literally came off the page, and the examples came to real life? This is where moral injury penetrates inwards into your soul. You do not simply look at direction and distance: you look at the core of your being to find resolution. This core is not isolated just to yourself; it is intertwined by its very nature with God. This is why forgiveness becomes such an issue with soul injury.

Soul Restoration

Soul restoration not only looks outward in regards to where you should be heading in life and the time it takes to get there, it also looks inward, examining transgressions. You cannot simply point in a horizontal direction, add time, and find resolution. Time, by itself, doesn't heal the invisible wounds of war. Look at our WWII and Vietnam veterans. They have had plenty of time and direction but are still in internal conflict. You need to think about your soul. You need all three dimensions to find resolution: distance, direction and deity.

I place God right smack in the middle of resolving moral injury. In a world where we have attempted to dismiss God, I see this as the third leg of a stool. Without all three, people become unstable. This is why people seek a solution to moral injury through forgiveness. They know in their innermost being that what they did was wrong. The guilt they experience can be relentless, and their moral compass continues to point right at them. The cognitive dissonance is so strong, they have to do something to alleviate it. So, for those who feel that forgiveness is the only solution, there is good news. Grace can alleviate cognitive dissonance and the moral injury. Grace is unmerited favor from God. It is unmerited because it is not based on your merits. It is based on what God has done. It is His sacrifice that atones for the transgression. Ever wonder why you feel you can't live up to the standard? Because being human means being imperfect. And Grace is perfection personified. For some, you need to spend some time with God and get your cup full of grace. Drink it up, and enjoy the weight being lifted from you. If you need help, seek out a spiritual counselor whom you trust to help you walk that path and not feel alone. God created fellowship with us and with other people for a reason. God is not an Army of One. At that point, if you have found resolution, you can end here in this chapter. Resolution is the goal and if you are there, you need to enjoy this experience.

Deeper Challenge

Do you remember the story in the Bible when the man was born blind and his friends asked, "What sin did he commit?" that caused him to go blind? The answer from Jesus was "none." He did not commit a sin that caused this. He was born blind for a different purpose, but the answer was that he did not cause this, he did not sin.

I now have that very same question I would like to pose to you. What sin did you commit for which you need forgiveness?

Definition of Sin

Let's come full circle. Remember: by definition, sin is missing the mark. Do you feel as if you missed the mark? One of the challenges of judging someone is that you may not know their heart, or what was their intent. Trying to figure out someone's intent is very complicated, but it also speaks directly to the question of "What sin did you commit?" Because without sin, there is no need for forgiveness.

It's About Intent

We are trained over and over again in the military to assess a person's intent to cause or not to cause harm. This is why hypervigilance is such an issue. We try to mitigate risk by figuring out another person's possible intent. This is why some warriors cannot walk into a room without checking the exits, sizing people up and assessing the situation for risk. We may or may not be correct in our assessment, but one thing is for sure, we will not stop assessing. Morgan Luttrell, former Navy Seal, and brother of Marcus Luttrell from *Lone Survivor*, told me once, "Do you know what you call a civilian who doesn't assess risk?" His answer: "A victim."

Your Intent

Only you and God know what your intentions were when the perceived transgression occurred. Only you and God know what was in your heart at the time. If you are guilty of a crime and your intent was to cause harm, yes, forgiveness is required. But if it was not your intent to cause harm, where is the sin or transgression that needs to be forgiven? This could be debated, whether one has sinned or not, but I argue there is no sin.

This leaves us with you and God alone to decide. Was it your intent to cause harm? Or did, for example, a situation present itself where a girl was thrown out in front of you and it was the intent of another person to cause harm? One must assess intent accurately. We are disturbingly good at feeling responsible. We justify it by saying, "But I was the one who killed her." Yes, you were the one driving the truck. Yes, it was the truck that caused her to die. Yes, it was a direct result of your being in the driver's seat. You tell yourself these mantras repeatedly. But <u>NO</u>, it was not your intent for a child to die that day. <u>It was, however, the intent of the insurgents</u> to throw her into harm's way, knowing that she could die, with the ultimate goal of killing you, along with your warrior brothers and sisters. It was their intent to cause a moral dilemma. Without their intent, the child watches the trucks go by, like every other child. Let me repeat, only you and God can accurately know your intent. But in this specific example, where is the transgression? Where is your intent to kill a child? Where is the sin? **There is none!**

Intent to Serve

Most likely, your decision to join the military was multi-faceted. Your intent could have been a strong desire to serve our country. Some people join as an escape from a poor home life, looking to the military to provide opportunities for a bright future they feel they otherwise would not have. Some people join for financial reasons or as a means to obtain an education. Still other people have a strong desire to take out bad guys in an effort to make the world a better place. I joined shortly after 9/11. My intent was to stop people who terrorize others. I had grown up with the belief that "Evil triumphs when good men [or women] do nothing" (Edmund Burke). I can assure you that your intent was very likely to do **good**, not harm.

It was, however, the intent of the insurgent to cause harm, even death. **He is the one who has sinned**. He is the one who transgressed.

If you need forgiveness, then ask. God gives freely. But chances are, it was not your intent to cause harm or, in this situation, to kill a child. Whatever your circumstances, it is between you and God. But whatever you do, use discernment to answer this question correctly and act accordingly. Either ask for forgiveness and receive grace, or understand that you have not transgressed, and there is no need for forgiveness. **Either way, this is resolution**. Resolve yourself today to the truth.

There is one last issue that I have seen combat veterans struggle with, and I will not leave this for you to answer by yourself. Here is the statement...

"GOD CAN FORGIVE, BUT I CAN'T FORGIVE MYSELF."

People often do not question whether God is in the business of forgiveness, but they do question whether or not they deserve forgiveness or can forgive themselves. Sometimes by forgiving ourselves, we feel as if we are off the hook. We need someone to blame for our soldiers getting killed, and by not forgiving, we do not forget. I will argue that forgiveness does not mean forgetting. We will honor the fallen in a way they deserve without condemning ourselves in the process.

Here is how I answer this dilemma: God's standard is complete and total perfection. If you were to put it in terms of a scale of 1-100, God expects 100 every time, an A+. There are no exceptions. When one says that God can forgive but you cannot forgive yourself, you are saying that God's standard isn't good enough or high enough. "I demand more."

There is no higher requirement than God's perfection. It cannot be exceeded, and trying to do so is not only impossible, but also unattainable. We cannot place our expectations above God's perfect standards. So that being the case, God provides a solution to sin which we can either accept or reject.

1 John 1:9: "If we confess our sins, he is faithful and just and will forgive us of all unrighteousness."

RESILIENCE

With forgiveness issues resolved and there being no more guilt, shame or condemnation, where does that leave us? Can you just imagine for a moment how your life would be different if you forgave yourself? How would it affect things like sleep or cognitive dissonance about the experiences you had in war? Does it have the potential to give you a hope and a future?

We believe in giving people a new mission and passion for life. We hope to get you psychologically healthy to the point that you can help others. We want you to lead other veterans who struggle with these issues to this resource so that they, too, can find resolution and resiliency. We hope to get you to a point where you are not self-medicating, but exercising, putting healthy food and nutrients in your body, feeling as if you are making a difference in someone else's life, and are, of all things, forgiven (if necessary). In essence, we hope to help you become once again a whole, caring, compassionate, and purposeful person. Remember, without a target, you are aimless. So, let's get to work on the REACH worksheets to solve moral injuries, get the support and encouragement you need, the friends and peers who care about you involved, and the tenacity to let nothing get in the way of accomplishing your new mission.

We have to apply all of our military training, concepts, brain flexibility, OODA loop (Module XIII), understanding, healthy relationships, REACH sheets, and spiritual guidance to overcome one of the most psychologically, morally and spiritually challenging issues that military men and women face. It is simply not easy, no mission is, but there are answers. Even if you have not resolved these dilemmas, our hope is that you at least better understand how you got to where you are and that there is a way out from under the weight of it.

BIBLIOTHERAPY: From a resource standpoint, we refer you to: *Soul Repair: Recovering from Moral Injury After War* by Rita Brock.

MODULE XIII: THE OODA LOOP

Intent: To help warriors understand how Resiliency Formation Training intentionally uses military concepts, such as those that have been effective in winning war, and integrates them into our lives in order to increase resilience and decrease negative symptoms.

Context: The OODA loop was designed intentionally to help the United States win in war. Four basic concepts are involved: **Observe, Orient, Decide, and Act.** Our purpose is to help military members utilize this strategy in their post-military life.

You may or may not have been exposed to the concept of OODA loops in your military career, but in essence, if you can overwhelm an adversary's OODA loop, you can win in war (at least according to author John Boyd). If this concept is effective for winning a war, or originally, air-to-air combat, it may be a concept worth considering for strengthening our Resiliency Factor for PTS(D). This is what the OODA loop looks like:

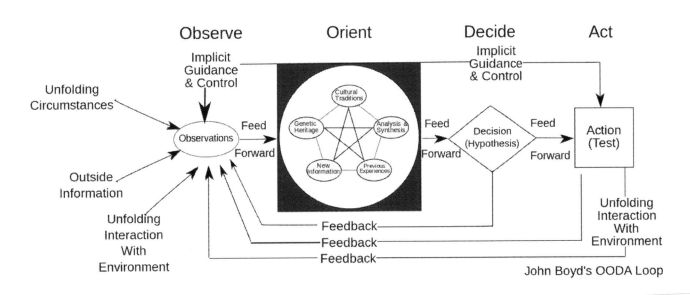

John Boyd's OODA Loop

Former Air Force Colonel John Boyd, at the age of 33, came up with the idea of the OODA loop as a decision-making capability in air combat. Although the Russian MIG-15 was faster and could outmaneuver the American F-86 fighter plane, the F-86 won more dogfights because *the pilots had a superior field of vision.* Simply put, they could see more of the game being played. This clearer picture enabled American pilots to see things more clearly and make quicker decisions.

But what do air combat principles have to do with PTS(D), you may wonder? Well, Boyd concluded that, when our circumstances change, **we often fail to shift our perspective** and instead continue to view the world as we feel it *should* be rather than how it is. And this static inflexibility to grasp a dynamic environment is what creates our rigidity, vulnerability, and ultimate failure.

People who suffer from PTS(D) often interpret their surroundings in a particular way, normally as a threat environment, <u>even when no threats exist</u>. The transition from war, which is a threat environment, to the civilian world, mostly a non-threat environment, would require "untraining" in classical conditioning or what I call "unpairing" of the conditioned response. However, I have yet to talk with a warrior, even those who have been through the Warrior Transition Unit, who actually unpair the stimulus and response that has been created. Using the Bluetooth analogy, it only makes sense that, if you have a paired response between your phone and the Bluetooth device, it will naturally connect the two together. The solution lies in unpairing the stimulus and the response.

For example, if you hear a loud noise that you didn't expect, such as a car backfiring, you may react strongly by experiencing a startle response. Your sympathetic nervous system kicks in, your heart starts pounding, your breathing becomes more intense, your pupils dilate, and you may even start sweating. The sooner you can recognize what is happening and calm yourself down (engaging the parasympathetic nervous system), the faster you can return to a healthier baseline.

The same applies for a fighter pilot in a dogfight: time is critical. If you misinterpret your threat environment and do not open your field of vision and your perception, you will inevitably experience what are called false positives. This simply means you positively identify a threat, but it isn't a true threat. Can you imagine being a fighter pilot, thinking that Surface-to-Air Missiles (SAMs) were being fired at you, only to lay down all of your chaff[31] as a countermeasure, and then find out that it was not a credible threat, and you've used up all of your defenses?

 Key Takeaway: Combat veterans often default to seeing the world through risk mitigation lenses and their environment as a potential threat, even when no such threat exists. Unfortunately, we do not take off these glasses when we return home. By continuing to behave this way in the civilian world, the warrior often ends up often creating consequences for himself/herself they never intended to create. At times, we can become our own worst enemy.

I was once confronted by a combat medic who is now an ICU nurse. It seems that one of this nurse's psych patients, in a psychotic episode, jumped out of a third-story window. Thankfully, the patient landed on the second-floor balcony but was dangling from the catheter and trying to pull it out.

---

[31] Chaff is a countermeasure made of aluminum or plastic as a way of distracting radar-guided missiles from their targets.

The combat medic, without thinking and responding with training, jumped out the third-story window, unhooked the catheter, and brought the patient back to safety.

When the warrior was going through the debriefing with the civilian supervisor, the warrior was asked, "What in the world were you thinking? You jumped out of a third-story window." The only response the person knew to give was, "You apparently haven't read my personnel file, have you?"

This person was a medic in the military, and medics go to any length to solve whatever medical problem is before them, even sacrificing their own lives if necessary. Having the supervisor know the former medic's history was the best way to even attempt an answer to this question. Maybe you have come up against similar experiences in which you acted or responded in a way that others asked, "What in the world were you thinking?"

Allow me to introduce the OODA loop and what we can do to create options for ourselves.

Stage 1: OBSERVE

If you don't have eyes on the current situation and assess a potential threat credibly, how can you have true situational awareness? In the Observe stage, the idea is to be mindful of new information and any unfolding circumstances. This stage is highly correlated to military intelligence. The more accurate the information (i.e., intel), the better you can orient yourself, create a plan, and ultimately multiply Courses of Action (COAs).

Think, for example, if North Korea puts up a communications satellite and we interpret it as a military satellite and destroy it. In so doing, they respond by firing off a weapon of their own, and now we are in a fight with North Korea, all because we interpreted a situation that was later discovered to be inaccurate, thus escalating the situation unnecessarily.

How many times do we become our own worst enemy? We interpret a situation as a threat when there truly isn't one, and, in so doing, *we create the threat*. As combat veterans and first responders, our jobs are to observe and assess situations accurately. We have all been trained in the use of force. But what happens when we interpret everything as a threat which needs a use-of-force response? We are trained, after all, in the art and science of mitigating risk. You can see how the consequences of interpretation and only one COA would become problematic.

A simple illustration may be helpful. You are back home, driving to work when all of a sudden you see trash built up on the side of the road. You swerve hard and almost crash your car for no apparent reason but to get away from it. Why? For those of you who have been involved in experiences with roadside IEDs, insurgents would use trash, dead dogs, anything they could to hide an IED. Before war, you would have never have even given this trash heap a second thought. After war and having situational awareness that kept you alive, swerving is a response in which you have naturally been trained. Remember: what kept you alive in theater may now be a behavior that is causing you significant problems, in this case, a possible panic attack and a car accident.

THE ART OF MINDFULNESS

Right off the bat, we have no choice but to talk about the present, the "here and now." It's impossible to observe situations clearly if you are dissociating or experiencing flashbacks. To observe correctly, you have to be "in the moment" *completely*. This is one of the most significant challenges you may face—trying to stay in the "here and now" at all times. It is often referred to as mindfulness. Yet, this is exactly how to live your life to the fullest. You have to strive to be ever-present, mentally and emotionally.

On a scale of 1–10, with 1 being *none at all* and 10 being *completely in tune with each moment*, how would you rate yourself on being able to stay in the moment? _____

If it is not a 10, what memories steal away your ability to be present?

_____

_____

_____

_____

Let's talk about what can prevent you from living fully in the moment.

First, triggers happen. Some kind of trigger occurs, but it takes a concerted effort, if you struggle with flashbacks, not to let it continue. Commit yourself to living fully in the here and now. You may be amazed at what can happen. One of the best ways to do this is to stop what you are doing and notice what is around you. Notice your breathing, the temperature, the pressure of standing or sitting, light, other sounds, etc. So many times, we do not slow down enough to just breathe and enjoy life. Have you ever been told that you aren't breathing, or to "just breathe"? There is a reason for it, and taking a deep breath can actually help the process.

Second, denial is real. When we have overwhelming feelings or thoughts, sometimes our tendency is to simply shut down. We deny that there is a problem and just "don't go there." We find ways to deny through distraction, avoidance, hyperfocusing on something other than what we are trying not to think about.

Third, you have blind spots. Sometimes we don't even realize what's happening and go from one extreme to the other. From denial (totally ignoring the problems in your life) to distraction (filling a void through high-risk behaviors or alcohol), the problem is the same. How do you deal with a blind spot if you don't even realize that it exists? It's simple: with a family member, friend, or therapist. Chances are they know what problem you are dealing with but may be afraid to tell you because of how you may react or overreact. If you want to correct your problem, you need to be willing to take productive criticism.

In John Boyd's OODA loop, each area of concentration is designed to help you open up your vision to what is really going on. It is constantly attempting to obtain an accurate and reliable situational awareness. This is done through constant feedback with your environment. If, for example, you feel as if when you go to Walmart that people are a threat and there are too many people and exits to keep track of, you may start to avoid it during peak times or altogether. In reality, does a threat exist? A person who believes that threats can come at any point, any place, any time, is interpreting their world through a threat lens. And these "glasses" or perceptions, if nothing else, cause us to alter our behavior and interaction with the world. If you remember the "Possibility versus Probability" chapter, this is where that information comes in to help you make a clearer decision. Just think of it as a set of glasses. If you have ever heard of beer glasses, every person of the opposite sex becomes a lot more attractive with those on. And if you are wearing threat glasses, everywhere you make a decision to go, the world is seen through the lens of risk mitigation, even to the point that you decide not to go anywhere as the ultimate mitigation of risk. Just remember, the more we alter our view through these lenses, the more we have changed.

Let's jump into the first section of Boyd's OODA loop: OBSERVING.

There are four factors involved in the "Observing" phase:

1. Unfolding circumstances
2. Outside information
3. Implicit guidance and control
4. Unfolding interaction with the environment

Let's look at each one of these in detail as it relates to PTS(D) and resiliency, using a common illustration of going into a location where there is a crowd. One of the first things veterans will say is that they look for exits and assess who might be a risk and place themselves in a position where they can mitigate such risk. However, besides those issues, other things come into play.

First, unfolding circumstances:

What happens in a situation in which you interpreted things as being different, out of place or a concern for safety? For example, you see a college student with a backpack come in a place near the door. What is your thought process?

_____

_____

_____

_____

In this example, did you immediately go to interpreting the backpack as a potential threat? Possibly an IED or a bomb? Did you "naturally" interpret this as a threat, even though one may not exist? And if so, why do you think you did this?

_____

_____

_____

_____

Second, outside information:

Did you, for example, look closely at the college student's race, gender, appearance, etc? Would experiences with a certain culture or group make you more alarmed? Yes or no? If so, how?

_____

_____

_____

_____

Third, implicit guidance and control:

When you predict things to come true and use mind reading, how accurate are you? Have you ever been incorrect in your assessment? In essence, how many times have you changed what you do to mitigate risk and then nothing happened?

_____

_____

Fourth, unfolding interaction with the environment:

Give examples of situations where you interpret threats being possible but not probable.

_____

_____

_____

_____

Let's say you are going out on a date with your spouse or a good friend. Although you are there to spend time with that person, how much do you think they know what is going on in your head? Do they know you are working this hard in your mind to figure out exits, threat mitigation, etc.? And how can we be fully in the moment when we are expending so much energy making sure things are safe? In reality, are you doing this so much that you are now on auto-pilot? Do you even do it now without even being cognizant that you are doing it?

_____

_____

_____

Stage 2: ORIENT

The whole point is to know where you are in time and in space. Five components are involved:

1. Cultural traditions
2. Genetic heritage
3. New information
4. Previous experiences
5. Analysis and synthesis

Let's use an example of your coming back home and seeing someone wearing a burqu. Prior to going to a country where we are fighting an enemy that hides behind women and children and that uses schools and mosques as base, etc., was this a trigger?

1.   Cultural traditions: Does someone wearing certain clothing trigger you? What other cultural traditions or practices are a trigger?

_____

_____

_____

2.   Genetic heritage: What about certain people from certain locations around the world? Are they a trigger? If so, what types of people?

_____

_____

_____

3.   New information: As you make your assessment, what types of new information do you consider? What is the context? Are you possibly at someone's wedding where it is their culture to wear certain things? The last time you were in this situation, what was the context?

_____

_____

_____

4.   Previous experiences: What experiences have you had that now make this situation an issue for you?

_____

_____

_____

5.   Analysis and synthesis: As you analyze the information in your current context, as compared to war, and synthesize all of the information, including no longer being in a war zone, how does this change things?

_____

_____

_____

If you actually took the time to think critically about these questions, you are on your way to healing. It is this critical thinking that you didn't have time to do in theater that is part of the key. Most of us didn't have time in theater to process information. But now we have the time. But our temptation is to use avoidance and numbing so as not to have to think about these things. And that does not bring us to resolution. So, let's continue looking at these things with the training we've had so that we can now come fully home and be fully present.

STATIC VS. DYNAMIC INTERPRETATIONS

Mental models or paradigms are designed to help us understand and explain the world in which we live. However, the weakness is that, when we create mental constructs in an attempt to understand, it limits our ability to accurately comprehend very complex things. In essence, we are trying to put something in a pre-made box so that we can see and understand it. A perfect example is our attempt to understand God. As soon as we use an analogy or construct in order to understand God, we limit our perception of Him. But God is not bound by time or space or anything else.

As we begin to orient ourselves to a new situation, we try to explain it with constructs or paradigms we have previously created. Unfortunately, our paradigms of explanation may not be sufficient or accurate. And if they are not constantly changing with the latest intel (or information), we risk using old constructs and paradigms.

For example, back to our illustration with someone who is wearing a burqa. Your previous experience of culture and context may have affected your construct of this person as potentially being a homicide bomber. You begin to then react and respond accordingly, based on this paradigm. Especially if you have had experiences where a burqa was worn by a homicide bomber, you would definitely have a strong reaction to this trigger. But our context has changed.

In context, what if I provide you with new information. What if I told you that you were in your hometown with a good friend of yours who just happened to have met a girl from another country while in college. And in their country, at weddings, it is appropriate for the mother of the bride to wear a burqa as a sign of respect. The person is there to celebrate the new marriage and has no ill intent whatsoever. However, would that matter much to you if you continue with your old construct and do not take into account new information and context?

Boyd would argue that, if you are static (not willing to consider alternatives) in your thinking, you will not be able to interpret the situation dynamically (flexibly) and accurately.

Consider another example as that one may have triggered some folks. If so, you can use that as a barometer to know how difficult this will be to change. But it can change.

Let's imagine that an Army platoon is in enemy territory, and they are cut off from all communication. The last known location of the enemy is directly to the south of their current position. However, that intel is over 20 hours old. The question is, where are they now? They may move forward with their plan to attack from that location, but what is not known is if the enemy has made any tactical changes to their plans and moved to a different location. Without the dynamic capabilities of intelligence, they will continue to respond with what they have previously experienced or known.

A current manufacturing example is Kodak. Kodak was a well-known manufacturer of the original technology that was used in digital cameras. As they continued to focus on their traditional film, they were not dynamic in seeing the digital changes being made and ultimately had to file for bankruptcy.

Both examples illustrate that the key is being dynamic and not static. Thus, in the Air Force, one hears "Flexibility is the key to air power." The Army has their own version: "Adapt and overcome." All military branches understand the importance of living in a dynamic world. As a matter of fact, Boyd's own paradigm for how he saw the world was living with ambiguity. In a world in which we try to maintain power and control, the reality is that things are constantly in motion, constantly changing, and evolving. If we view the world in like manner and are ego-syntonic (good) with it, we expect things to change, and then we adjust accordingly. However, when we become static in our viewpoints and in our paradigms, we lose our flexibility and our ability to dynamically change, and we ultimately lose.

As we orient ourselves to different situations, we have to be dynamic in our approach. We have to continually monitor situations, use the best intel that we have available to us, be mindful of our limitations in our constructs and paradigms, and then utilize feedback loops to once again observe, orient, decide, and act.

BRING THE HAMMER

Can you imagine having a toolbox, and the only tool that you have in it is a hammer? You may have heard the old saying, "If all you have is a hammer, then everything else looks like a nail." No matter if you are trying to screw something in with it, drive something in with it, or bend something with it, you have no choice but to act as if everything is a nail. And if, as a combat veteran or first responder, you see the world through only the lens which perceives things as a threat - well, you get the point.

In RFT, we try to add tools to your toolbox. So, that being the case, let's review a few key concepts:

1. Being dynamic, not static, is key.
2. Paradigms and constructs are helpful but limiting.
3. If you view the world as a threat, you will keep bringing the hammer.
4. Assessment of your toolbox may reveal that all you have is a hammer, and it's time to add more tools to your toolbox.

Stage 3: DECIDE

Boyd believed that decisions were best made by considering various models and constructs while forming a hypothesis. In our context in dealing with PTS(D), the various models which one may consider could include context, motive, background, history, perception, experiences, and goals. Specifically, if you see someone in a burqa, instead of assuming that the only model possible is one of threat, what other alternatives could there be? Getting cues from the environment can help us to consider alternative models and thought processes.

The difficulty in understanding situations so that you can form a good decision is that we have the dilemma of never having precise and accurate intelligence. Very similar to a combat commander who has to make a decision that could cost people their lives, we have to mitigate as many distractions and internal/external threats as possible. We have to make decisions based on the information we have as opposed to the information we do not have. So, in context, when we initially see something that could push us in a particular direction, we have to stop ourselves and ask, "Am I applying a threat model to this situation?" And, if so, "Is it accurate? Are there alternative hypotheses or models that I might want to consider?" "What is the probability of my worst fear coming true?" "Are my actions and thoughts following a fear model?" "What other models could I employ that might be more helpful to myself and my family, given the context?"

The whole point of creating hypotheses is that there are numerous answers we might want to consider. And, in the military world, hypotheses are akin to COAs. But, in order to come up with our COAs, we need to understand the various models/concepts/ perspectives that are influencing our choice of COAs. After challenging one of my clients, my client stated, "You give me a headache." I laughed because that means he's thinking—and seriously thinking. I now consider this a compliment. But think about it. In order to understand how we can approach various subjects with flexibility, we have to come at our situations from various perspectives, hypotheses, and COAs. Otherwise, we'll just keep bringing the hammer, and everything else becomes a nail.

Stage 4: ACT

This is where you make a decision and test your various hypotheses. The reason why it is put in this language is because it will encourage you to *experiment* with different decisions and see which one works best for you. If a hypothesis (COA) is inaccurate or does not solve the problem, move on to your next one. Keep repeating this test until you come up with an answer that does work.

Feedback loops are probably the most important element in effectively using the OODA loop process in the real world. We constantly have to use our intelligence and surveillance systems to monitor our life – yes, I made it personal – to see if our COAs are getting us the desired results. In essence, we are now back to the Observing stage to see the impact of our actions on the target. If the target is not being hit or met, and we judge this through observation, we reorient ourselves, change coordinates, and make a different decision.

This is very similar to smart bombs. The idea is to use coordinates to take out targets. However, solar flares, weather conditions, mechanical failures, etc., can all change the bombs' trajectory and, instead of putting bombs on target, we miss. Do we then just go home and say, "Oh well, we missed. I'm hungry, time to go to the DFAC[32]"? By no means. We observe the situation through continually changing intel, orient ourselves to the situation, come up with another hypothesis about the confounding variables, and then act again. This is repeated until the mission is accomplished.

So, let's make this very, very personal. You have targets that you need to hit. These targets are probably already a part of your End State. They are the things that matter most to you. Let's just say that having a healthy, positive relationship with your spouse/significant other is important to you—so much so that you list it on your End State. This means that you will do whatever is necessary to be successful in your relationship with your spouse. She informs you that there will be a party on Friday night, and she would like to go. You have no desire. So, you contemplate your COAs.

> COA #1: You could say you have to work late.
> COA #2: You could try to talk her out of it.
> COA #3: You could feign illness.
> COA #4: You could say, "Why don't you go ahead, sweetheart. They are your friends. I'll stay home and take care of the kids."

None of these COAs meet *her* need to spend time with you. They do not hit the target. This is where you have to consider all COAs, even if they are not ones which you would truly want to choose.

> COA #5: Spend time with your wife at the party and buy her flowers.

You actually go the extra mile by buying her flowers, and, instead of seeing this as a waste of money, you reframe it (thinking differently) by realizing that the little bit of money you spend on flowers isn't about the flowers; it's thinking about her. These are actual credits in your relationship

---

[32] Dining Facility

bank account—an investment. And if this isn't convincing, just talk to someone who did not invest and has been divorced multiple times. The cost of divorce is much higher than the cost of flowers, I can assure you.

And, ultimately, it may cost you a little time which you would rather spend doing something else. What it does is that it shows your spouse that she is an investment worth your time and energy. When it comes to an investment of time and energy into your relationship, it is well worth it. And how you know if it is or isn't worth it goes back to the feedback loop. Just wait and see the response you will get (feedback), and see if it doesn't reinforce you to continue that sacrifice. If, for some reason, the feedback you receive does not hit the target, remember, don't lock into just one response (static). Think dynamically, and come up with a new COA.

The OODA loop has been successful in war and has been used also in business and myriad other situations. Just think about using the OODA loop in various areas of your life, not just PTS(D). The concept alone can change not only your thinking but also your life.

What are some other areas of life in which you could use the principles of the OODA loop? Think about your job, for example. Are you having difficulties in your job? What would happen if you applied these basic principles to your job situation? Give this some serious thought. Write down just one example in your job, or whatever else you would like to address, and go through the OODA steps. Finally, how will you know if your COA is working or not?

In my job situation (or lack thereof), how could I apply the OODA loop?

1.   Observe

_____

_____

_____

2.   Orient

_____

_____

_____

3.   Decide

_____

_____

_____

4. Act

_____

_____

_____

5. COAs

   a. _____

   b. _____

   c. _____

MODULE XIV: MEDICATIONS FOR PTSD

Intent: To educate warriors on the scope of the help they can expect from medications that treat PTS(D) symptoms.

Context: To take the time to explain how medications can help, how you can get them to work even better, and which ones to avoid.

Example: Too often, warriors are prescribed high-powered sedatives and hypnotics within minutes of talking to a doctor. In one example I've seen, a veteran joined a teleconference with a VA doctor and was prescribed Valium after only five minutes. The veteran was never provided the information about the hefty side effects which would have allowed him to make an informed decision.

BUILDING YOUR SUPERHIGHWAY

As discussed in Module III: The Neurobiology of the Brain, Brain-Derived Neurotrophic Factor (BDNF) is an important protein that increases the connections between brain neurons. BDNF works to build a more robust hippocampus that helps you become more resilient to life's stresses while simultaneously improving memory.

Think of these neural networks in the brain as a superhighway complex, where there are lots of large and small roads with many intersecting and merging lanes, complete with U-turn options. In severe PTS(D) or depression, the amount of BDNF and neural connections in the hippocampus are greatly reduced. Think of this like a country road that hasn't been travelled for a very long time. What happens when you neglect an unpaved, country road for a few years? Weeds, trees, and debris begin to cover it up. It could soon become undriveable, at least in your favorite Tesla.

To begin the process of resetting your life after severe trauma has essentially thrown it off course, you will need to begin forming new habits, thought processes, and behaviors to sustain your growth. If you, for example, decide to start making your bed every morning as soon as you get out of bed (and have never done that before), it will be a challenge to remember it at first. This is sort of like having an overgrown tree on a neglected road overhanging too far and hitting your car, distracting you from what you're doing.

After a time of consistent effort, the road will become clearer in the same way your new, healthy habits become easier. In your brain, the neurons you use to accomplish these healthy behaviors literally build up their chemistry. The neurons recruit their neighbors to help and develop cross-connections, in some cases growing new, complete neurons! And, you guessed it, BDNF is the chemical responsible for all of this brain growth. In Module III, we discussed healthy lifestyle activities that increase BDNF, but we'll focus on the medication approach in this module.

SYNAPTOGENS

"Antidepressant" medication increases the amount of BDNF in the brain to increase neuron connections. For this reason, Dr. Daniel A. Williams coined the term "synaptogens" in his book, *Combat PTSD in America: Toward a Permanent Solution*, because these medications do a lot more than fight depression. (Synapse means the neuron connection, while "gen" means generate or create.) Any substance or activity, such as weightlifting or meditation, which increases BDNF is a synaptogen. Therefore, "antidepressants" work like fertilizer in the brain to support healthy lifestyle choices and a happier mood.

Both psychotherapy and antidepressant medications work together to increase the brain's resilience by increasing BDNF. Mentally, psychotherapy helps patients learn healthier ways of thinking. Biologically, both talk therapy and antidepressants enhance synaptic plasticity to beef up the capacity of the hippocampus.

Here are the medications for PTS(D) that have the most scientific evidence:

Class	Mechanism	Examples	Helps with...
SSRI (serotonin-specific reuptake inhibitor)	Increases serotonin between nerve connections in the brain	Sertraline (Zoloft) Fluoxetine (Prozac) Paroxetine (Paxil)	PTS(D) Depression Anxiety Irritability
SNRI (serotonin and norepinephrine/ adrenaline reuptake inhibitor)	Increases serotonin and adrenaline	Venlafaxine (Effexor)	PTS(D) Depression Anxiety Irritability Concentration/focus Energy
Alpha-2 blockers	Calms down the nervous system by decreasing the effect of adrenaline	Prazosin (Minipress) Propanolol (Inderal)	Nightmares from PTS(D) Anxiety

BAD DRUGS

Benzodiazepines are usually prescribed to treat anxiety or insomnia. Examples include alprazolam (Xanax), clonazepam (Klonopin), eszopiclone (Lunesta), temazepam (Restoril), zaleplon (Sonata), and zolpidem (Ambien). For decades, these medications were prescribed almost without question because they can often be safely used over short periods of time, such as a few weeks. They work on the brain's benzodiazepine receptors just like alcohol, so people can feel their relaxing effect pretty quickly (20–60 minutes). This is why they are one of the most abused medications.

The following medications have been shown to prolong and potentially worsen PTS(D) symptoms:

Class	Mechanism	Examples	Worsens...
Benzodiazepines	Inhibits the GABA receptor in the central nervous system, like alcohol	Alprazolam (Xanax) Clonazepam (Klonopin) Lorazepam (Ativan)	PTS(D) Memory Sleep Intelligence Addictions Doubles the risk of dementia
Non-benzodiazepine benzodiazepine receptor agonists	Inhibits the GABA receptor in the central nervous system, like alcohol	Eszopiclone (Lunesta) Temazepam (Restoril) Zaleplon (Sonata) Zolpidem (Ambien)	PTS(D) Memory Sleep Intelligence Addictions Doubles the risk of dementia

Unfortunately, recent scientific evidence is uncovering some long-term risks associated with these medications that were previously unknown. When used for years at "moderate" doses, benzodiazepines can cause serious **problems with concentration and memory**. A review of many studies looked at patients who had been on moderate doses for years and then stopped the medicine. A few months later, the patients could think much more clearly and remember better. Overall, their IQs improved about nine points.[33]

When used to treat insomnia, benzodiazepines and related medicines can also cause major problems with concentration and memory. One study found that, for patients aged 50–65, using just 30 or more doses a year for three years **doubled the risk of becoming demented**.[34]

---

[33] Barker MJ, Greenwood K, Jackson M, Crowe S. "Persistence of cognitive effects after withdrawal from long-term benzodiazepine use: a meta-analysis." Archives of Clinical Neuropsychology 2004; 19:437–454.

[34] Chen PL, Lee WJ, Sun WZ, Oyang YJ, Fuh JL. "Risk of dementia in patients with insomnia and long-term use of hypnotics: a

When used to treat insomnia, these medicines are not as effective as most people would think. A review of studies found that, early in a course of treatment, these medications improved sleep only an average of 48 minutes per night.[35] One study found that, when patients used one of the benzodiazepine-related medicines for six months, **total sleep decreased 56 minutes per night**.[36] The most restful stage of sleep decreased 18 minutes per night.

Points to remember:

- Benzodiazepines aren't good to use for more than three months.
- Antidepressants, sleep hygiene, and psychotherapy have better long-term results than benzodiazepines.

Our goal is to help you with your symptoms and help you have a healthier life. We do not want to harm your concentration and memory or worsen your sleep by prescribing medicines that can harm you if used too long. Together, we need to talk about better options for treating your symptoms.

Keep in mind that other medications may be used for other reasons and may still be very good treatment for PTS(D). Common reasons why people may be on other medications, even these bad ones, include psychosis, personality disorders, severe anger or rage, debilitating anxiety, panic attacks, and bipolar disorder.

MEDICATION TRIALS

For a medication to actually help, you need two things: 1) to be able to tolerate the drug at its full, therapeutic dose, and 2) to stay on the medication long enough for a full treatment trial in order to know if it helps or not. You have to give the medication a fighting chance. If you've been on a lot of different medications, then you know how hard it is to remember what you've taken, what the dose was, and how long you took it. Imagine how hard it is for doctors to ask patients these questions every day. Many patients don't even know the answer, forcing the physician to make assumptions and represcribe a previous medication or skip past potentially good, safe ones and reach for a more powerful one with bad side effects.

Furthermore, if physicians don't document the details of the patient's past medication trials, insurance companies won't pay for newer, more expensive medications. They will require "prior

---

population-based retrospective cohort study." Public Library of Science ONE 7(11): e49113.doi:10.1371/journal.pone.0049113

[35] Riemann D, Perlis M. "The treatments of chronic insomnia: a review of benzodiazepine receptor agonists and psychological and behavioral therapies." *Sleep Medicine Reviews* (2008),doi:10.1016/j.smrv.2008.06.001

[36] Sivertsen B, Omvik S, Pallesen S, Bjorvatn B, Havik O, Kvale G, et al. "Cognitive behavioral therapy vs. zopiclone for treatment of chronic primary insomnia in older adults." *Journal of the American Medical Association 2006*; 295: 2851–2858.

authorizations" to determine if they'll pay for it, which is a cumbersome process for a physician and clinic staff, requiring them to call in or fax information detailing what the past medication trials have been.

Do yourself a favor: Fill out the worksheet on the following page and make a photocopy for all of your physicians to see. Be sure to keep the original, and update it over time so that it becomes a living record.

My Medication Trials

Name: _____

Date of birth: _____

Medication Name	Dose Used	Dates Used	Comments: Was it helpful? Side effects?

MODULE XV: MILITARY END STATE

Intent: To help better gain a different perspective on your challenges based on the future instead of the past.

Context: Military members often shift their *perspective* from why they joined the military (noble, honorable, or financial reasons) to what they then experienced in a combat zone (evil intent, trauma, and death). They are also taught the Western mindset of working your way toward something as compared with starting with the end first, which can often mean that you miss your target.

Example: Find the letter *C* in a row of *O*'s.

```
OOOOOOOOOOOOOOOOOOOOOOOOOOOOO
OOOOOOOOOOOOOOOOOOOOOOOOOOOO
OOOOOOOOOOOOOOOOOOOOOOOOOOOO
OOOOOOOOOOOOOOOOOOOOOOOOOOOO
OOOOOOOOOOOOOOOOOOOOOOOOOOOO
OOOOOOOOOOOOOOOOOOOOOOOOOOOO
OOOOOCOOOOOOOOOOOOOOOOOOOOOO
OOOOOOOOOOOOOOOOOOOOOOOOOOOO
OOOOOOOOOOOOOOOOOOOOOOOOOOOO
OOOOOOOOOOOOOOOOOOOCOOOOOOOO
OOOOOOOOOOOOOOOOOOOOOOOCOO
OOOOOOOOOOOOOOOOOOOOOOOOOOOO
```

When psychologists test people's ability to think outside the box, they often have to give a test that challenges "conventional" thinking. Why? The military needs people who can both take orders and think creatively on their feet (adapt and overcome). For example, we need people who can quickly adapt to changing circumstances and adjust their COAs as new information is received.

A higher-IQ person will realize that, if they simply start with the first *O* and go sequentially, they will get to the answer, but it may take a while. A big-picture person will step back and look at the overall picture (terrain) and scan for any discrepancies (*C*). Finally, another approach is to look at the key difference between a *C* and an *O* and realize that the left side is exactly the same, but it's the right side that is different. The *C* is open to the right. If you look at this sequentially, you see the left side is closed for BOTH the C and the O, and this makes it hard to differentiate. If you look at it from the right and scan left, however, the open part is easier to detect, thus making it easier to find the solution.

Are you now exhausted (frustrated) or rejuvenated (intrigued)? If you are exhausted, you are probably the type of person who likes things clear, precise, and sequential, and you do an amazing job at following orders and getting things done! If, on the other hand, you are intrigued by the exercise and actually realized the solution before the explanation, you are more of an "out-of-the-box" thinker who likes to know the answer to questions, tries to figure out a different way of doing things, is more of a maverick, and sees "big-picture" ideas.

The key is that we need BOTH types of people in the military and in the civilian world, but most people don't even realize what type of person they are until they are exposed to such tests.

Strategy: When planning at the strategic level, people who are responsible for large numbers of troops and have a significant leadership role need to have the right person in the right place at the right time. You don't want someone who likes to think outside the box when time is limited and you need people to simply follow orders. Can you imagine being a commander who is in a firefight with an enemy, trying to deal with a troop who wants to "figure out" the best strategy, look at the big picture, spend time considering all the COAs, etc.? That would take critical and valuable time, which the commander most likely cannot afford at that moment.

Commanders need people who can follow orders when necessary, but they also need troop leaders who can see the big picture, assess COAs quickly, and be decisive on the battleground to lead others. Knowing people's strengths and weaknesses is essential to being a good leader. Influencing people to think differently than their God-given bent is important for being a strategic leader. This is where you can begin to strengthen your resolve toward brain flexibility.

 Key Takeaway: Having brain-flexible people creates resiliency within a group. They can adapt and overcome quickly and easily, see different solutions to problems, and complete risk assessment and mitigation in a timely fashion. Doing these same things post-military is key to getting through PTS(D). Therefore, the ability to see things from a different perspective matters in your overall wellness and transition into civilian life.

Now that we have a foundation for understanding the importance of perspective and brain flexibility, let's talk about how we "see" the world, which makes a significant impact on our personal and corporate decision-making.

Congress and the President should keep in mind two key words before going to war. This concept drives military decisions and influences the will of the American people throughout any conflict. This concept tells us how we will know if we have been successful when all is said and done.

What two words would you think describe the goals of the military, Congress, and the President before going to war? Give this some serious thought, and write your possible answers below:

_____   _____

_____   _____

_____   _____

Here's a hint: there are actually two possibilities, and both of the words start with *E* and *S*, respectively. When going to war (and in life), to be completely successful, you must have an End State or an Exit Strategy. You have to know when you are finished—when the mission is accomplished. Why? If you don't, in war, you don't know when to bring your troops home. The American people will go to war for a just cause, but over time, they will also become tired of casualties and demand we bring people home. Thus, you have to not only know your End State for purposes of troop decision-making, but you also need it for your mission.

> Key Idea: When shooting a weapon, the ultimate goal is to hit your target—plain and simple. Hit the target. But what if you don't know your target? Then you are shooting aimlessly and have no control over your intentions. Unfortunately, people who have PTS(D) often feel as if they are aimless. They have no purpose in life, no direction, no intent, no mission. If you were to tell a military member to go out and qualify with his or her weapon, that person would need not only the weapon, but also a target in sight. Sometimes people lose sight of their target on the qualifying range and accidently cross fire. In life, we cannot afford to miss our target.

Unfortunately, in many of the wars that we have fought, we did not clearly delineate our true target or End State. Thus, we are left fighting aimlessly with no end in sight. Sound familiar? If history is prologue, then we need to learn from it so as not to repeat it.

PRESIDENT BUSH AND IRAQ

When President George W. Bush went to war in Iraq, the End State, the American people were told, was to find weapons of mass destruction (WMD)—clear, precise, simple. Find the WMD, and we can then prove the evil intent of Saddam Hussein. Unfortunately, the answer was confusing as to the issue of WMD. The case for WMD was anything but clear and precise. Please do not lose focus on the main point of the analogy, which is not whether or not WMD existed—it's that the END STATE was lost.

WMD was not found in the amounts that most Americans expected. As a leader, how do you fix this problem? You change your End State. If you do not, you have no justification for war, and you saw this play out in the media. People on both sides of the war were arguing. People wanted us out of Iraq, and others were arguing that Hussein's ability to hide WMD was the real issue. Thus, the threat to the U.S. continued. What was at stake? The intent of the U.S. to continue to wage war!

If you don't think your End State matters, then why would you deploy? Because the President and Commander in Chief says you will. What does he base this on? His End State. People in leadership are trained to consider the consequences of their decisions and the impact they will have on individual lives. Most leaders do not take this lightly. As a matter of fact, they may even agonize over it. In the end, however, they still have decisions that must be made. It is no surprise that President George W. Bush's book was entitled *Decision Points*. In the case of WMD, it missed the mark. So, what do you do then? If you wish to continue to prosecute a war, you change your End State.

A CHANGE IN END STATE

At this point, a *new* End State from the administration was offered. If you remember, our End State seems to have changed from WMD to the Global War on Terror (GWOT). Why is this so important? By definition, the End State must end. It has an ending. By definition, it tells us when we can cease military operations, which has a tremendous impact on those of us in the military. Deploying to a war zone is all about an End State and your role in accomplishing that End State. I hope you can see how the GWOT as an End State impacts deployments, affects military family lives, and ultimately directly affects you.

Why did they change the End State to GWOT? I teach my children that, when they are uncertain about particular phrases or words, they should parse them (break them) down into components, so let's do just that.

First, GLOBAL: Why did the most powerful leader in the free world, the President of the United States, decide to use the word *global*? This gives him, and us, the right to go anyplace, anywhere, anytime. It's called global reach. There is no place that terrorists can hide that we cannot go, AND we have the End State and justification to do just that. In essence, this notion is at the core of sovereignty. If you are hiding in Pakistan, we have announced our claim of the right to go there. Somalia, we're going there. Egypt, we will find you. Horn of Africa, watch out. It doesn't matter. We are justified to go anywhere. Think about the power of the End State. We didn't have this power with WMD, but we do with GWOT. Let's just say that they didn't come up with this term for fun. It was strategic—just like we will teach you in using your new End State to become resilient.

Second, WAR: We have declared war, which requires the authority of the President and Congress. Although the President can go it alone, he is wise to get the backing of Congress and the American people. Building coalitions isn't just for NATO; it happens at home first.

Third, ON TERROR: What is this about? Why would the U.S. administration and those in power make an argument for war on terror? First of all, in war, we often set it up as good vs. evil. We always see ourselves on the side of good, even so much so that we will justify our actions on many fronts, even to the point of arguing that God is on our side.

In psychology, we have discussed what it means to be ego-syntonic with things. We have to feel as if what we are doing is right and good. To kill people, which many who grew up in an era of Judeo-Christian values were taught to believe is wrong because it is forbidden in the Ten Commandments ("Thou shalt not kill."), we have to tell ourselves something to justify killing. Otherwise, we are now in a dilemma with our thoughts and beliefs or what is called ego-dystonic. To get to a point that we can handle this ethical/moral dilemma psychologically, we justify our actions by saying that there is a bigger purpose, a better End State, a more noble cause, and that killing is the only solution.

Here's the problem (or is it?): leadership called it the Global War on Terror, but will we always have evil in the world? Will there always be people with ill will or evil intent? The answer is a resounding <u>YES!</u> By definition, we are clear that terrorism will never end.

Critical question: At the same time, by definition, an End State ENDS. When will terror end? It never does. Think about that for a moment. As a country, we created an End State that never ends. Let me repeat that: <u>AS A COUNTRY, WE CREATED AN END STATE THAT NEVER ENDS</u>. And we wonder why we are in the "Long War."

End States matter. They mattered regarding your deployment(s), and they matter as an issue of national policy. They probably took you halfway around the world and cost you. They also cost many of us our brothers and sisters in arms. One's End State can be very costly if it is not established correctly, so let's make it personal.

YOU AND YOUR END STATE

Do you even have an End State? What do you want at the end of your life? What are the most important things to you? As an example, an accomplished sniper needs training and a weapon, but he also needs one very important thing: a target. Without a target, a sniper is aimless. He cannot achieve his goals, his purpose, his mission. Although a sniper could shoot aimlessly, it makes no sense, so why would you live your life aimlessly without a clearly defined target in your life? If you are, maybe that's why you are having a hard time hitting it. This is the same concept addressed in such books as *Who Moved My Cheese?* The book is about climbing the corporate ladder only to find out that the ladder you climbed was up against the wrong wall.

Although you may be resistant, it is imperative that you determine what your End State is in your life. Who wants to live their life not accomplishing the most important things to them? It's time to take time and figure that out.

For help in guiding you through writing an End State, we are providing some suggestions.

You may wish to consider such things as:

- ☐ Family
- ☐ Health
- ☐ Money
- ☐ Relationships

What are the important things in your life? Remember that if you don't have an End State, it's like shooting without a target. Will you hit it? Probably not. You may get lucky, but why risk your life on luck? Be strategic! As you write, make choices about what you want your new mission and your End State to be. It is your life, after all.

My End State:

_____

_____

_____

_____

_____

Here is my challenge to you: you have a new mission in life—to get healthy. That starts with the end in mind.

In the military, we start with the end first and work our way back to where we are. This is very clear and precise because it makes life much easier. However, most people are trained in the opposite direction, to work their way toward their goals. The problem is that this view can veer off from one's intended target if you are not sure where you are going. Ask any college student who has changed majors multiple times; they will tell you they weren't sure what they wanted to do with their life. The same concept applies here. If you know exactly what degree or license you are after, you won't waste time trying out different classes or approaches in life. You will have your target, and every decision will be based on hitting that End State. This reduces the waste of time and energy and cuts down on frustration.

Simply put, you have to know where you are going to get there. My wife and I joke a lot about her tendency to start talking about one subject and then completely change to a different topic, and she fully expects me to "get" her train of thought. I explain, "Honey, you went on a trip in your head, but you forgot to take me, so I have no idea what you are even talking about."

I encourage you to get to your End State and be decisive about your goals and the journey that will get you there. We are taught over and over not to leave anyone behind. In your End State, think about the people who matter the most and what you want out of life.

EVALUATE YOUR END STATE

Let's take a little test. Since we are so good at checking boxes, check off the characteristics of your End State:

☐ Clear
☐ Precise
☐ Meaningful
☐ Fulfilling
☐ Goal-directed
☐ Purposeful

Did you write it from a positive or a negative point of view? Is your goal to aim at something (positive) or to get away from something (negative)? If you wrote something such as "get off my medications," think about rewriting your answer as, "to find better and healthier ways for symptom reduction." If you wrote, "get over my divorce," think about instead, "finding a new, healthy, and fulfilling relationship." How you view and how you write your End State matter. Remember that it's what got you deployed. If an End State is good enough for the President and Congress, it's good enough for you to state your new mission and End State.

Now that you have written your End State, the next step is defining how you will actually accomplish your mission. You need a tactical plan. You have the strategy, and now it's time to implement it.

Review what you wrote, and now break it down. For each topic, write a plan for how you will tactically "get there." Sometimes, the most successful missions are the ones that have been thought out clearly, create different COAs, and how they can be implemented. Think about how you would create at least two COAs for each goal you have in your End State.

In your planning, think about how you can ensure that the COAs will be effective.

My End State Goal #1:

_____

_____

_____

COA #1:

_____

_____

_____

COA #2:

_____

_____

_____

My End State Goal #2:

_____

_____

_____

COA #1:

_____

_____

_____

COA #2:

_____

_____

_____

My End State Goal #3:

_____

_____

_____

COA #1:

_____

_____

_____

COA #2:

_____

_____

_____

My End State Goal #4:

_____

_____

_____

COA #1:

_____

_____

_____

COA #2:

_____

_____

_____

My End State Goal #5:

_____

_____

_____

COA #1:

_____

_____

_____

COA #2:

_____

_____

_____

The End State changes your perspective on life. It pulls you toward something. It gives you a different frame of reference. It helps you focus on your future instead of your past. Resiliency is about putting your new life into your new goals and creating your new End State. Congratulations on completing your End State. Take a break, relax, and go do something you enjoy before we embark on what we call your New Mission (Module XVII).

By now, you have hopefully learned how to change your perspective, understand your nodal points and how they have affected your life, understood the importance of seeing things through a non-threatening lens, and resetting your homeostasis from high risk/adrenaline choices to more calm and compassionate positions. This will in turn calm down your amygdala and reset your state of vigilance back to a more "normal" range. Perhaps you've already enjoyed some peace of mind, if only for moments at a time.

You have considered the goal of terrorism and the enemy's *frame of reference*. Secular and political groups may kill civilians and military personnel to achieve a political goal. Religious groups often try to kill as many people as possible if their goal is global jihad.

Regardless of the goal, force is used to instill fear. The End State for the Islamic terrorist is for "infidels" to convert to Islam or die and live in fear in the meantime. What they do not want is free people living in peace of mind, body, and spirit regardless of what terrorists do.

Now it's time to really clarify for yourself what your life values will be. After all, you will need to sustain your progress in achieving more peace of mind, and it, too, will come with a price and some effort. As you learn more about this new way of life, we urge you to share this resource and your experience with others who have had similar experiences to yours.

Let's consider the values espoused by the various military branches and list them alongside, "the fruit of the Spirit [which] is love, joy, peace, forbearance, kindness, goodness, faithfulness, gentleness, and self-control." (Gal. 5.22–23).

Fruit of the Spirit	Military Values	Trauma Themes	Other alternatives:
Faithfulness	*Semper fidelis* Faithfulness Commitment Excellence	Avoidance/Disloyalty	
Joy	Duty	Guilt/Loss/Shame	
Kindness	Respect	Anger	
Self-control	Integrity	Cognitive distortions	
Love	Selfless service Commitment	Intimacy boundaries	
Forbearance	Honor	Revenge	
Gentleness	Respect Excellence	Power/Control	
Goodness	Personal courage	Fear	
Peace	Peace (the goal)	Hyperarousal	

MODULE XVI: NEW MISSION

Intent: To help warriors understand that not only were missions a significant part of their military experience, but also that part of the solution to their PTS(D) is to utilize their extensive training and integrate it into our resiliency formation.

Context: Similar to the problem of not having a clear End State, without a purpose or mission in life, many people feel as if they are living aimlessly. If you are trying to hit a target, the last thing you want is to be aimless. When you ask warriors what their mission or purpose is in life, most of them shake their heads as if to say, "I don't know," "to get better," or "I have none." If that is the case, we need to determine precisely what your mission is in life so that, at the end of your life, you will feel that it has been a life worth living.

INTERNAL VS. EXTERNAL LOCUS OF CONTROL/MOTIVATION

From boot camp on, combat veterans are told where to go, what to wear, how long (or rather short) our hair can be, how to hold our posture, how we address higher-ranking military personnel, where to live, what job we have, what to eat—pretty much everything. There is not a lot of room for discussion. As a matter of fact, a "discussion" can lead to an Article 15. Typically, in the military, people do not require a lot of internal locus of control. It is done quite well by others, but this has its strengths and its weaknesses. For example, you don't have to think. Others do that for you. Your job is to follow and follow without question. That is the reason the military goes after those who are 18–22 years old. They are strong, pliable, willing, and able.

As we mature with age, we seem to become more opinionated. If you haven't noticed, when in the military, you are not really allowed to have your own opinions. As a matter of fact, expressing those opinions could land you in hot water—or kitchen duty. As you leave the military, you may find yourself expressing a lot more of your thoughts and feelings, sometimes precisely because you weren't really allowed to express them while in the military, and, if you did, there might be a fear of retribution.

When you have been repeatedly conditioned not to think for yourself, do as you are told, follow the rules, and be a good troop, now that you are no longer in the military, sometimes this can be a difficult transition. Not only does your motivation have to shift regarding doing things for yourself, but you also have to take on the role and responsibility of those decisions and the subsequent consequences.

Let's bring this home. For example, let's take a quiz to see how you did regarding behaviors when it came to the military and how you are doing now in civilian society.

Rate the following questions on a scale from 1–10, 1 being *not at all* to 10 being *completely*:	In the past	Currently
1. Working out		
2. Eating healthy		
3. Having a purpose/mission		
4. Feeling useful		
5. Having internal motivation		
6. Forthcoming with issues		
7. Maintaining appearance		
8. Motivation		
9. Mental health challenges		
10. Financial security		
11. Occupational satisfaction		
12. Self-esteem		
13. Relationship success		
14. Relationship satisfaction		
15. Trust		
16. Security		
17. Anxiety		
18. Depression		
19. Voicing opinions		
20. Becoming more political		

Does anything surprise you when you look at your numbers?

A LIFE WORTH LIVING

Do you value your life? Yes, I actually asked the question. Do you value your life? This question raises many eschatological issues—for example, "Why am I here?" "What am I supposed to be doing?" "Does what I do matter to anyone?" "Am I of value or worth and to whom?" "Does anyone care if I am alive?" The answer to this is a resounding *YES*, even if you don't feel it. Your life is so important that God created you. He created you in His image for a reason, for a purpose. You just have to determine that purpose, and a life lived with meaning and purpose is a life worth living. How do you find that purpose or meaning in life? That is what we are about to discover.

YOU GET TO DECIDE

Here's the great thing about living in a free country and being given free will: you get to decide. Remember when others told you what to do, where to go, and what to think? Now that is no longer the case. It is up to you to decide, and this can be either good stress (eustress) or bad stress (distress). If you have been used to having other people make decisions for you, this may be an adjustment.

It's probably important to assess what you want out of life. Some people have a hard time seeing their life from the next moment, let alone from an eschatological (End State) perspective. Let me illustrate how what we think affects how we behave.

If, for example, you hold to a philosophy that says you never know what is going to happen and tomorrow you may die, how would you live today? Would you "eat, drink, and be merry," as the Proverbs say, "for tomorrow we shall die"? If you feel, though, that God has a purpose for you and that you are called to fulfill it, you have a more long-term view of life, and your behavior will be such that you sacrifice the short-term (instant gratification) for the long-term (purpose, mission, rewards). How you perceive your life, and your mission and purpose, and how long you have will determine what you do with your life.

Do you believe you see things more from an instant gratification standpoint or more from an eschatological standpoint? _____

How does your view affect the following?

1.   Finances:

    _____

2.   Relationships:

    _____

3.   Health:

    _____

4.   Work ethic:

    _____

5.   Spiritualty:

    _____

6.   Career:

    _____

FORESHORTENED FUTURE

The challenge with seeing people live and die in a war zone is that we get this false belief that we are going to die earlier than we would normally. It's called a sense of foreshortened future. This contributes to our thinking, our decisions, our impulsivity, our high-risk behaviors—all of it. But the question concerning how long you will live still remains. The answer is that you have no idea. We do know, though, that there is a high correlation between people enjoying high-risk behaviors and death, which leads us into a very difficult topic. Is it possible that some people actually live their lives in such a manner that they feel that things are going so badly they would rather not be here? Or they no longer want to be a burden? The answer is *yes*.

Unfortunately, people sometimes feel that the world would be better off without them. It's not that they necessarily want to die; it's that they want to save others the pain that they know they can cause. They have convinced themselves that others would be better off without them. This is the total opposite of a person who has a purpose and mission for their life.

THE IMPORTANCE OF NODAL POINTS

Nodal points are significant points in time that you will never forget. They are often attached to emotional significance and are permanently embedded in your brain. In Module III, we discussed memory, epinephrine, and how it affects memory consolidation, etc., but, for now, let's just focus on the fact that nodal points do occur.

When people spiral down into depression, a sense of helplessness and hopelessness, and suicidal thinking, it's not often that just one thing brought them to that point. A set or series of nodal points is responsible, so let's take a look at what nodal points have brought you to where you are today.

SIGNIFICANT NODAL POINTS

First, what symptom or challenges are you struggling with the most? Write it down here:

_____

Now, let's take a look at some of the nodal points that have contributed to this situation. Think about the most significant events that have impacted your life and brought you to this place or this thought or feeling. Some nodal points may include the following: people getting killed, having a very difficult upbringing (possibly including abuse or neglect), relationship difficulties, financial challenges, and emotional scars.

Please utilize the topics listed below and talk about what comes to the top of your mind. When you think about these things, if it is attached to an emotional experience, chances are you will notice that your eyes drop down. That's because you're getting in touch with your hippocampus (long-term memory) that was encoded by your amygdala (which is triggered during highly emotional states).

- Nodal Point #1: Military experiences

  _____

  _____

- Nodal Point #2: Financial pressures

  _____

  _____

- Nodal Point #3: Relationship issues

  _____

  _____

- Nodal Point #4: Legal difficulties

  _____

  _____

- Nodal Point # 5: Job difficulties

  _____

  _____

For each one of these nodal points, go back and list specific emotions that are attached to it. For example, it could be sadness, grief, loss, anger, frustration, or depression. How do you think these nodal points affect what you think? For example, people often have negative thoughts about themselves after they have experienced enough negative nodal points. You may believe that you are worthless because you couldn't stop someone from getting killed in theater, you cannot keep a job, or you've lost relationships.

Let's now list some of the thoughts that you believe about yourself, and which probably aren't positive. Here is just one example:

"I believe <u>that I am a failure</u>

because <u>I made a bad decision in the AOR, and it cost someone their life;</u>
therefore, I <u>no longer make decisions, and people get frustrated with me, but I don't care</u>."

Now it's your turn to write down some examples you can think of.

"I believe _____,
because _____;
therefore, I _____."

"I believe _____,
because _____;
therefore, I _____."

"I believe _____,
because _____;
therefore, I _____."

"I believe _____,
because _____;
therefore, I _____."

"I believe _____,
because _____;
therefore, I _____."

The more precise you can get with these negative nodal points, the more easily you can attack them.

POSITIVE SELF-AFFIRMATIONS

Now that you most likely are aware of some negative internal dialogue (self-talk) about yourself, it's time to come home and enjoy some real healing. Others may see you differently from how you see yourself.

What positive things have they told you, and who said it?

_____

_____

_____

_____

_____

_____

Was it difficult to write down positive things? If so, this is pretty indicative of the challenge you face, but you can do it.

When I ask people to write down what they want out of life as their New Mission, they often write in such a way as to remove something negative. In essence, it's what they don't want. For example, "I want to have less depression." That's a great goal, but what about putting it in the positive: "I want to have a vibrant, exciting life." A positive alternative is to state, "I want peaceful dreams and to wake up rested." Just that small shift can make a huge difference. It's time to begin thinking about what you want as a New Mission. I suggest the following: write down what you want in each category of your life (for starters), and then finish with anything else you feel may be important.

NEW MISSION

Family: I want _____

_____

_____

Employment: I want _____

_____

_____

Money: I want _____

_____

_____

Stress: I want _____

_____

_____

Legal: I want _____

_____

_____

Spiritual: I want _____

_____

_____

Passion: I want _____

_____

_____

Once you have listed each of these, you may want to actually create in one paragraph your new mission in life. By writing it down, it also helps to create those long-term neuronal pathways that encode it into memory. You have done amazing work. Let's finish strong.

MY NEW MISSION

_____

_____

_____

_____

_____

_____

_____

In any mission in life, not everything goes to plan. As we have discussed, the enemy has a voice, and sometimes things do not work out, but the person who perseveres under all circumstances eventually wins. List those things that may hinder you in accomplishing your new mission.

_____

_____

_____

_____

_____

_____

_____

_____

Do any of these involve people? If so, write down who or what will affect your New Mission, and begin to think about risk mitigation. Sometimes, people even sabotage things on their own. If that is a risk, you will need to mitigate that as well.

_____

_____

_____

_____

_____

_____

_____

_____

_____

_____

_____

_____

BIBLIOTHERAPY: *The Purpose Driven Life: What on Earth Am I Here For?* Warren, R (2012). Zondervan.

MODULE XVII: RESILIENCY FOR EMOTIONAL AND COGNITIVE HEALTH, VETERANS EDUCATION AND TRAINING SYSTEM (REACH VETS)

Intent: To provide warriors with a process by which they can work through unhealthy mantras and create a more accurate, positive lens through which to view the world.

Context: One of the biggest challenges that warriors face is actually changing both unhealthy thoughts (cognitions) and feelings (emotions). Some believe that thoughts change feelings, and others believe it is the exact opposite. Which way do you lean? Check your response.

_____ I believe that feelings change thoughts.

_____ I believe that thoughts change feelings.

Whichever direction it goes, the point is that it is not either/or, it's *both/and*. We need to change both our unhealthy feelings <u>and</u> our unhealthy thoughts. The following information is provided for you to dive into all the things that you have learned in these modules, apply them to the worksheet (below), and get to a more precisely targeted mantra that is congruent with what you feel and believe to be true. We highly recommend you actually write in this page, so more worksheets are provided at the end of the workbook.

A mantra, by definition, is a statement that we repeatedly tell ourselves. It can be viewed as that core belief system that we accept as who we truly believe we are. And who we truly believe we are comes from our experiences.

Mantras are essentially healthy or unhealthy in nature. Early on, mantras come at us from multiple sources such as our parents, friends, pastors, school officials, boy and girl scout leaders, 4-H, etc. Here are a few examples of mantras:

Healthy	Unhealthy
"You are so sweet and smart."	"You will never amount to anything."
"You are incredibly strong."	"You are such an idiot."
"You are such a caring person."	"I wish you were never born."
"You have the sweetest spirit."	"You were a mistake."

"You are destined for greatness." "God has big plans for you." "There is nothing you cannot do."	"You're lucky to even be alive." "The best thing you could do is kill yourself."

In psychology, there is something called one-trial learning. It's when something so egregious (bad) happens that you never forget it. One such example is touching a hot stove as a child. The intense heat is so painful that you not only won't forget it, but you may also even repeat "hot...hot..." whenever you get near the stove afterwards. Mantras can be much the same. The sting of words can be so intense that even though it may have been a one-time event, they are permanently engrained in your brain. I'm sure you know what that feels like. Someone has said something that is so hurtful that you will never forget it. It's like a deep, penetrating wound, much like what happens in open heart surgery. Although over time it may heal, the scar is ever present.

What's equally devastating is when we are the culprits and say something that we know will forever change another person and how they see themselves. Unfortunately, I've been on both sides of this situation. I wonder if you have, too?

It is no wonder that God says: "All kinds of animals, birds, reptiles and sea creatures are being tamed and have been tamed by mankind, but no human being can tame the tongue. It is a restless evil, full of deadly poison. With the tongue we praise our Lord and Father, and with it we curse human beings, who have been made in God's likeness. Out of the same mouth come praise and cursing."[37]

These mantras, permanently embedded in our brain from even a one-time event, often then get spoken or heard internally within us repeatedly to the point that we now accept them as fact. I believe that these are very much the equivalent of fiery darts that can pierce not only our psyche but also our soul. The devastating impact is no less than that of precision guided JDAM aimed straight at the core of our being. Upon detonation, it is extremely difficult to rebuild. But rebuild we must.

The REACH VETS worksheet can take some serious mental focus to complete. However, by processing your various mantras, you will discover that you have multiple issues that need to be challenged.

Warriors, when accepting unhealthy mantras as facts, may find themselves in a downward spiral of negative self-talk that never seems to end. I draw this as a downward spiral of destruction, much like a tornado. These thoughts can be haunting. This negative self-talk can lead to depression, anxiety, a sense of worthlessness, hopelessness, substance abuse and, for some, suicide. So, how do you get out from under this cloud of unhealthy core beliefs about yourself? You have to work toward a precise and healthy true statement about what happened to you and what you conclude about yourself in the process. This will affect your core being.

---

[37] James 3:7-10a

It's taken some of you years of hearing certain mantras from others and yourself to believe them fully. Trying to change these core beliefs is quite challenging. And in the end, your new conclusions must be **genuine**; otherwise, people feel as if they are only lying to themselves, which is never a healthy response. The other incredibly challenging part of this is that even though people may tell themselves that the healthier, resilient belief system is more precise and accurate, they don't feel it in their core. They have told themselves the lie for so long, they believe it must be true. In essence, I feel it; therefore, it must be true. This is an example of emotional logic.

Let's look at an example: you may believe that you cannot make good decisions in life because you believe you made a "bad" decision in a war zone and you believe it got someone killed. You may start out telling yourself the following: "I believe that I got _____ killed in theater because I made a bad decision. It was clearly my fault."

Over time, other situations may occur that reinforce this belief system to the point that you actually believe that every time you make a decision, something bad happens. You then get to the point that you draw a final conclusion and then have a tendency to generalize it to all of life.

Mantra: "Every time I make a decision, it always turns out bad, so I quit making decisions."

So, how is this a problem? Well, when you refuse, based on past experience, to make decisions, you can see how this would impact your life. You don't decide where you want to eat, where you want to go, what you want to do. Can you imagine being married to someone like this?

Let's look at the real problem. We have to go back to the original issue and the original conclusion. In this case, the basic premise is actually flawed – it is not true that you were the one who got the person killed. You may have made a decision in the heat of battle, but the person who killed them was the adversary. Our intent was to make the best decision we could with the intel we had at the time.

Let me just be as upfront and honest as I can. Unfortunately, you are not omniscient, omnipotent, or omnipresent. And it is our enemy that has the clear intent, at all costs, to kill. And they did. What is difficult to accept is that we sometimes cannot stop this from happening. If we could, we would have no casualties of war. Unfortunately, that is not reality in war.

What *is* reality is that we are not God, and we cannot thwart the enemy's attacks every time because we do not know when they will strike (which would require being omniscient), where they will strike (being omnipresent), or with what force they will strike (being omnipotent). Point blank: the only way we could ultimately 100% thwart an enemy who is intent on killing is to be God. And if that were true, war would be futile.

Unfortunately, we blame ourselves for our inability to stop our enemy from accomplishing their goals. We blame ourselves for our decisions that may have contributed to bad coutcomes, even if that was not our intent. And, in the end, we start believing that we make bad decisions, when in fact, our enemy's intent was to kill at all costs. We draw conclusions about ourselves based on a false premise (that we have the power to stop our enemy from killing 100% of the time). It is simply not possible. If it were, again, we would never suffer even one casualty in war.

Also, don't forget about the impact of attention bias from our training modules. Remember: what you look for, you will find. In this example, after we made a false conclusion about it being our fault, we then begin to <u>look</u> for other areas in which we make other "bad" decisions and this only reinforces our faulty belief system. It is then that we draw conclusions and create negative self-talk that only solidifies our belief system. We tell ourselves things like, "I can never do anything right, I make horrible decisions under pressure. I cannot do this."

Question: How do you unwind all of this mess? Let's first try an illustration. Have you ever gone kite flying and the line gets all tangled up? Or maybe attempt to untangle electrical cords or a hose?

Answer: You have to start at one end and work your way through the maze by loosening that which has a grip on you. Pulling tighter, getting angry or kicking it doesn't help. Some of you can really relate! What does help is beginning the process of loosening and untangling that which has its grip on you and slowly and methodically unwinding it and laying it out for its intended purpose.

We must unwind our faulty belief systems one at a time. This takes energy, willingness, clear thinking and sometimes others to help us see our blind spots. It took time to create the knots in the first place, and now it will take time to undo them. In our example above, instead of looking at things through the faulty lens of making "bad" decisions, we understand that in reality it wasn't our decision that killed a person, <u>it was the intent of our enemy</u>.

As soon as I said that, was your first thought, "But I contributed to it"? If so, do you see how fast we want to take responsibility and blame, even when our intent is good and others' intent is to do harm? It just goes to show the intensity with which we place responsibility on ourselves - even in a war zone where people die and we cannot control it. And again, if we could, there would be no casualties of war.

At this time, think about the mantra that you tell yourself that negatively impacts you the most. We've provided the following worksheet to help you work through how you got to your conclusion in the first place. Each category follows the A-B-C-D-E-F-G-H model. Our intent is to explain each of these categories first, and then have you fill out the sheet on your most challenging mantra.

What we have found over time is that the crux of this worksheet is when you make arguments in the *Differing opinions* section. It is easy to argue why you believe what you believe. What is difficult is arguing against this belief. Sometimes, people have the hardest time because they completely accept the premise and they don't see any alternative way of looking at it. This is where you may have a blind spot. Simply put, you may not be able to see all of the other alternatives, let alone accept them. This is where taking this to your therapist or talking it out with other warriors or family members can help.

Whatever you decide to do, this is the most challenging part of the worksheet for many. The more accurate you make the arguments, the more clearly you will see the unhealthy conclusions. What we are after is precision and accuracy. In the example above, the person concluded that it was impossible to make good decisions. In reality, that person may not have made a good decision in 2004, in Iraq, on that day, but probably made the best decision possible with the time and context given. The truth is that one decision in life cannot make a true mantra any more than believing that you are an Einstein because you got a 100 on one test in college can make you an actual Einstein. Simply put, just because you have some small evidence of something doesn't mean it applies to all of your life.

Let's get started with a quick explanation of the categories, and then move on to actually writing down your mantra on the worksheet provided and then working through the categories.

Title	Description
Aspects of the situation	This tells us what happened.
Belief	This tells us what mantra you have concluded is true in your life.
Context	This helps to understand what was happening at the time.
Differing Opinions	We are our own worst enemy. We draw conclusions often initially based on facts but then incorrectly make them into unhealthy beliefs. It's easy to state facts, but, in reality, we often have blind spots about how things are not true. Put this in the context of a court of law. First argue the prosecution (which is what you will naturally do anyway). This is where first you list out why you believe things to be true and how you concluded your belief. Then, do the opposite and argue for the defense attorney, which is much harder and when others can see things easier than we can. This is often when our blind spots come out. You will probably need others to help you see these blind spots because, by definition, you don't see them. This is actually when other warriors can help tremendously.
Emotional Cost	This is what it has cost you. It could be in life, relationships, jobs, etc. List out specific ways in which it has cost you. For example, it may have cost you in regards to anger, depression, guilt, anxiety, etc. Then list out a percentage from 0 to 100 on each area which reflects how much you believe it has cost you. An example: Depression – 100% Anger – 100% Guilt – 100%
Factors	These are overarching conclusions that you draw. For example, ask yourself, "Am I using all or nothing thinking? If so, how?" Don't just circle the Yes or No: literally think about how you are doing this and how it affects your life.
General themes	Many warriors then see how these beliefs translate into a general theme. For example, many end up getting angry, depressed, feeling guilt, etc.
Healthy resilient thought	Once you realize you have accepted this belief about yourself and begin to challenge that negative belief in **Differing opinions**, you can then choose a healthier belief. Once you do that, think about how this could change the Emotions that you listed. Finally, go back and review your Emotions as if you truly accepted and believed this new healthy mantra.

Resiliency for Emotional and Cognitive Health – Veterans Education Training System (REACH VETS) Worksheet

Aspects of Situation	Belief	Context	Differing Opinions	Emotional cost
Who or what brought me to this point?	I believe	Who was involved?	Reasons why I convinced myself that my belief is true. (Prosecuting attorney arguments: what would JAG say?): 1. 2. 3. 4. 5.	What percentage of time does this issue take away from my life? ___% # of relationships lost ___ # of jobs lost ___ Rate Emotions based on your Belief and what % ___/ ___/ ___/
	Because	When did it happen? 2. 3. 4.	Reasons why my belief is not 100% true. (Defense attorney argument: self-defense): 1.	Factors (please circle): ___/ ___/ ___/
		Where did it happen? 5.		All-or-nothing thinking: Y/N Mind reading: Y/N Emotional logic:Y/N Overgeneralizing: Y/N Defense mechanism: Y/N
	Therefore (consequence, how does this belief affect me or others)	Why did it happen? 2. 3. 4. 5. 6.		General themes (examples): ☐ Anger ☐ Grief & Loss ☐ Avoidance ☐ Guilt ☐ Depression ☐ Safety ☐ Failure ☐ Shame ☐ Fear ☐ Power/Control ☐ Forgiveness ☐ Trust ☐

Healthy Resilient Thought: I now choose to believe _____. Therefore, _____, because _____.

Now, go back to Emotional cost, and rerate your %, assuming that if you could tell yourself this mantra, over time, with genuineness, it could be true.

BUILDING ON YOUR PRIMARY TRAUMA THEME

The Resiliency Formation Graph below visually shows both the Trauma Themes and the healing barriers you will have to work through to achieve resilience. If it appears as if it looks like a target, it is just that. Notice that the outer ring represents the principles that have troubled you, and the inner ring is the antidote.

Think about your top trauma themes that tend to repeat themselves. If you were to rank your top three themes, what would they be?

Trauma Themes:

1. _____

2. _____

3. _____

Trauma "recovery" is the gradual process of moving from the outer ring to the inner ring. In hindsight, you will come to realize that you are more resilient—and this can only happen after future life stress occurs. Yes, life does go on, and it continues to bring its joys and its pains. What we hope is that, #1, you're no longer making your problems worse and, #2, you're regaining the parts of your life that the trauma was stealing from you.

In the military, risk assessments are done in advance of any operation, large or small. Well, this process you've just gone through to identify your Trauma Themes is a risk assessment. It is good, reliable information that, if you get really stressed out again sometime in the future, you are prone to struggle in these specific ways. So, what are you going to do about it? Become the subject matter expert.

The following table outlines the common additional homework (bibliotherapy) and lifestyle mastery commitments for warriors based on specific trauma themes identified during RFT. This is homework that will continue for you, often long after your *Combat PTSD Training Program* time has ended. The best-case scenario is that you discover that growing and healing in the areas where you were previously weaker will become a gift of knowledge and ability that you will use to help other trauma survivors.

So, based on the number-one Trauma Theme from the previous page, read the associated book listed below and begin the next phase of your life journey.

Trauma Theme	Reading	Writing	Arithmetic (Action)
Survivor Guilt & Anger	*Soul Repair: Recovering from Moral Injury after War*, Brock and Lettini	Write letters to the deceased. Write letters from the deceased to you.	Plug in with a local veterans' group, or create your own using the *Combat PTSD Training Program*.
Power & Control	*The Quest for Authentic Power: Getting Past Manipulation, Control, and Self-Limiting Beliefs*, G. Ross Lawford	Conduct an inventory of your patterns of manipulating other people.	Commit yourself to permanent change in this area. Then make amends to the people you have harmed with this behavior.
Fear & Trust	*Selling Fear: Counterterrorism, the Media, and Public Opinion*, Nacos, Bloch-Elkon, and Shapiro	Make a list of trusted news sources that you'd like to use. Identify people who cause you to feel more anxious.	Start an "information diet," limiting your sources of news and interactions with people that perpetuate fear and mistrust.

Trauma Theme	Reading	Writing	Arithmetic (Action)
Esteem & Shame	*Shame and the Origins of Self Esteem: A Jungian Approach*, Mario Jacoby	Write out your values, beliefs, and life purpose—as best as you can today.	Do esteemable things. Revisit your values list regularly and choose to believe healthy things about yourself.
Grief & Loss	*Grief Healing Techniques: Step-by-Step Support for Working Through Grief and Loss*, Calistoga Press	Identify how you could honor the memory of the lost person, belief system, or your sense of self.	Determine to live a life that honors the people and things that were lost, incorporating your life lessons in such a way that serves other people.
Avoidance	*Daring to Trust: Opening Ourselves to Love and Intimacy*, David Richo, PhD	Make a list of things that make you feel anxious, and rank them in numerical order.	Commit to doing the least anxiety-provoking and healthy items first, and progress toward getting your life back.
Distortions & Perspective	*"Stinking Thinking": Think well to live well. Taking on Maladaptive Cognitions and dealing with Cognitive Distortions*, Lawrence Cameron	Identify people in your life who tell you the truth you need to hear and use tact and respect.	Conduct periodic inventories of your thought process and journal so that you can gain perspective on distortions.
Hyperarousal	*Biofeedback: Guided Meditation to Practice Biofeedback Therapy and Neurofeedback for Self-Improvement, Self-Discovery, and Self-Enhancement* (Audible–Original recording), Mayu Kimura	Keep a "trigger log," which lists the various things that bring back memories or cause bad feelings and nightmares. Also make a list of things that make you feel more peaceful and relaxed.	Practice mindfulness and/or guided meditation to improve your conscious awareness of the here and now. Rid yourself of self-judgement as you move toward a life of truth and peace.
Intimacy & Boundaries	*Where to Draw the Line: How to Set Healthy Boundaries Every Day*, Anne Katherine	Make a list of boundary violations in your life and some possible ways to reduce them.	Commit to trying different approaches until you experience relief from improved boundaries.

PHASE 3: REINTEGRATION AND REINVESTMENT

In order to combat PTS(D), hopefully, you have been successful at beginning the reintegration process by using the modules in Phase 2. You will need ongoing support. So, in Phase 3, we will set you up for success by providing you with:

1. Answers. These are possible answers to some of the most difficult questions that warriors face. By thinking through answers to questions that may make you uncomfortable, we hope to decrease anxiety by providing a baseline of answers that will mitigate problematic reactions, thoughts and feelings.

2. Affirmations. These are written by people who were in your Combat PTS(D) group or the support system you have around you, allowing you to review their notes and impressions about you to encourage you during the dark times.

3. Aftercare and Crisis Planner. This quick-reference sheet will have all of the contact information for the people and organizations in your aftercare support plan going forward. Its provocative questions will force you to think about these issues prior to any potential crisis or very bad day so that you can pull it out and commit to calling every phone number on that page if necessary.

ANSWERS

Preparing answers to difficult questions posed to combat veterans...

Perhaps the first and most glaring challenge "treated" trauma survivors face is reintegrating with their family, friends, and colleagues. For each of these groups, there may be different dynamics at play, and different levels of prying questions that they might ask. For example, a coworker might say "Did you kill anyone?" or "Man, it must have been bad over there." Family members might take it even further and want to know the specifics about your Trauma Themes or delve too much into everything you've just stirred up in this giant learning curve we call PTS(D). You will need a guide - a roadmap if you will - to help you prepare for tough questions.

Answering the question, "Did you kill anybody?" and other difficult questions

You will inevitably run across people who will ask you intrusive questions about your military history that can be uncomfortable. One question that a lot of veterans get, even from children, is "Did you kill anyone while you were there?" This can be a really difficult question to answer for some veterans.

You are in control of the information you share. You alone decide when, how much, and how often you share any details of your past—and with whom. Instead of giving a specific answer, we'd like to propose the following technique, which can be helpful in putting you in control of answering life's difficult questions.

The SAR technique is a written exercise in which you describe the:

1. **Situation,**
2. **Actions performed, and**
3. **Results obtained.**

It has a wide application, such as explaining to a potential employer why you got fired from your last job. Here's how it works:

The first step in using this technique is to imagine a question that you might be asked that will be difficult to answer. If someone asks me _____, it will be hard to answer.

Part 1 = **S**ituation. Write 2–3 sentences describing the situation that led to the event, such as your crisis that led to PTS(D) treatment. Put it in the most positive and redeeming light possible. *You don't have to describe any details you're not comfortable disclosing.*

Part 2 = **A**ction. What actions did you contribute to the process? If you were in a treatment program or a particular military unit, what additional duties or contributions did *you* make to the group or organization? Focus on actions you took that were outside of the usual requirements of the experience. For example, did you serve as a leader, volunteer, or organize anything? Brainstorm to think of anything, great or small, that you did that was "above and beyond."

Part 3 = **R**esults. What results did you achieve from your actions? Every little bit counts here. Think back: did you take care of service members? Did you help your group have a cohesive bond together? If so, you need to take credit for your part in the outcome here. As in a job resume, focus on numbers whenever possible.

Let's consider some real-life examples, and then it will be your turn to prepare yourself for reintegration with your family, friends, and colleagues.

Example 1: Imagine someone asking you if you have killed anyone

Tough question veterans often get when they return home: "Did you have to kill anyone?"

SITUATION: I don't discuss things like that. Besides, in my unit, we were responsible for engineers who built buildings, and we didn't always have enemies in the area.

ACTIONS: My role was to serve as a security escort and coordinate with other units moving in and through the theater.

RESULTS: I did achieve the best safety record for the battalion and got an award for my actions.

Example 2: Imagine you got fired for being tardy too many times.

Tough question during a job interview: "What happened at your last job?"

SITUATION: I worked at XYZ auto parts for over a year, filling orders for stores on the assembly line. I had been thinking that it was time to expand my career possibilities, and my family encouraged me to look elsewhere. (Note: Make sure you're telling the truth; don't dig yourself a giant hole of shame you can't crawl out of.)

ACTIONS: I was the fastest part "picker" in the warehouse and was frequently chosen to do additional duties, such as fill in for other overwhelmed or absent workers.

RESULTS: My shelves were the most organized in the entire warehouse, making the semiannual inventory much faster and saving the company $1,500 per inventory in reduced staffing costs.

If your potential employer knows the details of how you were fired for tardiness, don't attempt to conceal it. What is important is that this behavior has changed and that you can help accomplish your employer's goals.

Example 3: Imagine you were arrested for drunk driving and *everyone knows* you went to a PTS(D) treatment program.

Tough question by coworkers on your first day back to work: "Where have you been?"

SITUATION: I was going through a pretty bad time and got plugged into a good program to get some help.

ACTIONS: I've been busy reaching out to other veterans who are struggling, and I'm really enjoying it.

RESULTS: So far, I've had three guys join our local fishing group, and I plan to run the 5K fundraiser coming up in the spring.

Do you see how that changes the tone and directs the conversation? Of course, there will be some people who can't take a hint and will repeatedly ask prying questions that make you feel uncomfortable and, quite possibly, angry. For the hardheaded folks you know, you'll have to establish and maintain some healthy boundaries. Start gently by saying you appreciate their caring enough about you to ask the question and that you also appreciate their respecting that you don't want to go into detail.

If it's a concerned loved one who is annoying you with questions about your trauma experience or therapy, you might be able to reassure them that you're opening up to your support group or therapist and that it's helping a lot. Explain that you don't feel comfortable answering detailed questions right now because you're learning so much so fast, and there are still many things you simply don't yet know. If that's not enough, you may want to limit your exposure to them as it is not helping you to get to your End State.

Ironically, the people we need the most in our lives are often the ones who can annoy or hurt us the most. Keep your End State in mind, and remember this example of what to say:

The Rock
"You know, you really are important to me, and I find a lot of strength in having you around. That said, I need your presence more than anything. When I'm around you, I have really good memories. I don't want to ruin our time together talking about the past. You're my rock, and I need you. I need you to be my stable, quiet rock.
You know, rocks are pretty quiet."

Now that you've seen how the SAR technique works, prepare your own answers for the tough conversations you know you're going to have with family, friends, or colleagues:

Tough Question: _____ from _____

SITUATION:

_____

_____

ACTION:

_____

_____

RESULTS:

_____

_____

Tough Question: _____ from _____

SITUATION:

_____

_____

ACTION:

_____

_____

RESULTS:

_____

_____

Tough Question: _____ from _____

SITUATION:

_____

_____

ACTION:

_____

_____

RESULTS:

_____

_____

AFFIRMATIONS

Personal Feedback Form

There are times when others have told us things that we have accepted as truth, even when those things were extremely negative. For some of you, these things have been drilled into your head since you were a child. For others, it's experiences that you believe reinforced a negative belief. Whatever the case, these negative mantras that we accept can keep us frustrated, exhausted, isolated and in need of encouragement. In a group setting, your peers have seen your strengths and your weaknesses. We already know many of our shortcomings, so this is a time when we encourage group members to specifically write positive comments about characteristics that they have seen in you. You may reject them because they are hard to accept, but the reality is you have much to contribute. Sometimes we need to bask in these positive comments and rid ourselves of the negative thoughts that haunt us.

Team Member's Name: _____

What are some positive characteristics that you see in this person? _____

_____

_____

What do you see as their biggest struggle? _____

_____

_____

What positive mantra do you believe they should accept that will help them move forward?

_____

_____

What is your best story or experience you've had with this person? _____

_____

_____

_____

(signature)

Overcoming Setbacks

Now that you have learned about Post-Traumatic Stress, understand what it means to be normal, are hopefully sleeping better, and have discovered healthier, alternative thoughts and feelings about post-war life, you are likely more hopeful and optimistic than you were when you first started this journey. Many people who complete our program get excited about their future and can't wait to go help others or even write their own books to tell their story. However, most of them fail if they try to do it alone. Did you notice this book has two authors?

When you face a struggle that is beginning to rob you of your joy and stop you from accomplishing your New Mission, you will need a systematic process for dealing with it. Your old temptations will try to drag you back to your old ways of thinking. Your enemy won't let it be as easy as a simple, one-time decision. When you temporarily get stuck in a rut or feel overwhelmed and can't figure out what to do, you are experiencing a resiliency deficit. Your previous level of resiliency is lacking in that moment—and, yes, this will happen to you. This training didn't fail: **resiliency deficits are expected!**

In fact, it's been said that you really don't learn how the Resiliency Formation Training system works until after the training is complete and you face a major life challenge. It will be your first nodal point with your new training and resources. But don't let this scare you. When this happens, fear not. All this means is that you are human and that you're just like the thousands of other recovered trauma survivors in the world. You will be able to draw on your Combat PTS(D) Training, rebuild your resilience, and get back on track relatively quickly. And it is an awesome feeling to have success. Success breeds success. Each successive time you face life's trials, the self-care habits and psychoeducation tools you've learned will become more and more second nature—assuming you practice them heavily until they become habit.

AFTERCARE PLANNER

My New Mantra is . . .

_____

_____

I will live in _____ with _____.

My plans for the future include . . .

_____

_____

The important relationships in my life are with . . .

_____

_____

I plan to use my experiences to help others by serving . . .

_____

_____

_____

Veterans I plan to connect with include . . .

_____

_____

_____

Community Contacts	Name	Phone Number
Psychiatrist		
Psychotherapist		
General Medical Doctor		
Social/Case Worker		
Pharmacy		
Neighbors		
Bank		
Insurance Company		
Mechanic (tow assistance)		
Lawyer		

My Crisis Plan:

_____

_____

_____

_____

Personal Notes:

_____

_____

_____

_____

_____

_____

_____

_____

_____

_____

_____

_____

_____

APPENDIX A: REACH VETS WORKSHEETS

The following REACH VETS worksheets have been included for you to work on your specific mantras. Each person has unique issues that need to be addressed. You can find examples of how to complete the REACH VETS worksheet on our website at ProjectHealingHeroes.org.

Permission is granted to duplicate these sheets as necessary to work on multiple mantras and help other veterans. They they must be copied in their entirety and reference cited.

Resiliency for Emotional and Cognitive Health - Veterans Education Training System (REACH VETS) Worksheet

Aspects of Situation	Belief	Context	Differing Opinions	Emotional cost
Who or what brought me to this point?	I believe _____ _____ _____	Who was involved? _____	Reasons why I convinced myself that my belief is true. (Prosecuting attorney arguments: what would JAG say?): 1. _____	What percentage of time does this issue take away from my life? ____%
			2. _____	# of relationships lost ____
	Because _____ _____ _____	When did it happen? _____	3. _____	# of jobs lost ____
			4. _____	Rate Emotions based on your Belief and what %
		Where did it happen? _____	5. _____	Belief and what % ___
			Reasons why my belief is not 100% true. (Defense attorney argument: self-defense):	___ /___
		Why did it happen? _____	1. _____	___ /___
	Therefore (consequence, how does this belief affect me or others) _____ _____		2. _____	Defense mechanism: Y/N ___ /___
			3. _____	Overgeneralizing: Y/N
				Emotional logic: Y/N
			4. _____	Mind reading: Y/N
				All-or-nothing thinking: Y/N
			5. _____	Factors (please circle):
			6. _____	General themes (examples): ☐ Anger ☐ Grief & Loss ☐ Avoidance ☐ Guilt ☐ Depression ☐ Safety ☐ Failure ☐ Shame ☐ Fear ☐ Power/Control ☐ Forgiveness ☐ Trust ☐

Healthy Resilient Thought: I now **choose** to believe _____. Therefore, _____, because _____.

Now, go back to Emotional cost, and rerate your %, assuming that if you could tell yourself this mantra, over time, with genuineness, it could be true.

Resiliency for Emotional and Cognitive Health – Veterans Education Training System (REACH VETS) Worksheet

Aspects of Situation	Belief	Context	Differing Opinions	Emotional cost
Who or what brought me to this point?	I believe	Who was involved?	Reasons why I convinced myself that my belief is true. (Prosecuting attorney arguments: what would JAG say?): 1. 2. 3. 4. 5.	What percentage of time does this issue take away from my life? _____ % # of relationships lost _____ # of jobs lost _____ Rate Emotions based on your Belief and what % ___/___ ___/___ ___/___ ___/___
	Because	When did it happen?		
		Where did it happen?	Reasons why my belief is not 100% true. (Defense attorney argument: self-defense): 1. 2. 3. 4. 5. 6.	Factors (please circle): All-or-nothing thinking: Y/N Mind reading: Y/N Emotional logic: Y/N Overgeneralizing: Y/N Defense mechanism: Y/N General themes (examples): ☐ Anger ☐ Grief & Loss ☐ Avoidance ☐ Guilt ☐ Depression ☐ Safety ☐ Failure ☐ Shame ☐ Fear ☐ Power/Control ☐ Forgiveness ☐ Trust ☐
	Therefore (consequence, how does this belief affect me or others)	Why did it happen?		

Healthy Resilient Thought: I now **choose** to believe _____. Therefore, _____, because _____.

Now, go back to Emotional cost, and rerate your %, assuming that if you could tell yourself this mantra, over time, with genuineness, it could be true.

Resiliency for Emotional and Cognitive Health – Veterans Education Training System (REACH VETS) Worksheet

Aspects of Situation	Belief	Context	Differing Opinions	Emotional cost
Who or what brought me to this point?	I believe	Who was involved?	Reasons why I convinced myself that my belief is true. (Prosecuting attorney arguments: what would JAG say?):	What percentage of time does this issue take away from my life? _____ %
			1.	# of relationships lost ____
		When did it happen?	2.	# of jobs lost ____
	Because		3.	Rate Emotions based on your Belief and what %
			4.	___ / ___
		Where did it happen?	5.	___ / ___
			Reasons why my belief is not 100% true. (Defense attorney argument: self-defense):	___ / ___
		Why did it happen?	1.	Factors (please circle):
			2.	Defense mechanism: Y/N Overgeneralizing: Y/N Emotional logic: Y/N Mind reading: Y/N All–or–nothing thinking: Y/N
Therefore (consequence, how does this belief affect me or others)			3.	General themes (examples): □ Anger □ Grief & Loss □ Avoidance □ Guilt □ Depression □ Safety □ Failure □ Shame □ Fear □ Power/Control □ Forgiveness □ Trust □
			4.	
			5.	
			6.	

Healthy Resilient Thought: I now **choose** to believe _____, because _____. Therefore, _____.
Now, go back to Emotional cost, and rerate your %, assuming that if you could tell yourself this mantra, over time, with genuineness, it could be true.

APPENDIX B: CAFFEINATED SUBSTANCES (MG)

Coffees	Serving Size	Caffeine (mg)
Starbucks Coffee, Blonde Roast	Venti, 20 oz.	475
Dunkin' Donuts Coffee with Turbo Shot	Large, 20 oz.	398
Starbucks Coffee, Pike Place Roast	Grande, 16 oz.	310
Panera Coffee, Light Roast	Regular, 16 oz.	300
Starbucks Coffee, Pike Place Roast	Tall, 12 oz.	235
Dunkin' Donuts Cappuccino	Large, 20 oz.	233
Starbucks Caffè Americano	Grande, 16 oz.	225
Dunkin' Donuts Coffee	Medium, 14 oz.	210
Starbucks Iced Coffee	Grande, 16 oz.	190
Panera Frozen Mocha	Medium, 16 oz.	188
Starbucks Caffè Mocha	Grande, 16 oz.	175
Starbucks Iced Black Coffee	Bottle, 11 oz.	160
Starbucks—Caffè Latte or Cappuccino	Grande, 16 oz.	150

Starbucks Espresso	Doppio, 2 oz.	150
Starbucks Doubleshot Energy Coffee	Can, 15 oz.	145
Starbucks Coffee Frappuccino	Bottle, 14 oz.	130
Nespresso Kazaar Capsule	1 capsule, makes 1 oz.	120
Starbucks Mocha Frappuccino	Grande, 16 oz.	110
Maxwell House Light Ground Coffee	2 Tbs., makes 12 oz.	50–100
Starbucks Coffee Frappuccino	Grande, 16 oz.	95
Folgers Ground Coffee, House Blend	2 Tbs., makes 12 oz.	60–80
Nespresso Capsule (except Kazaar)	1 capsule, makes 1 oz.	50–80
Green Mountain Keurig K-Cup—Breakfast Blend or Nantucket Blend	1 pod, makes 8 oz.	75
Maxwell House Lite Ground Coffee	2 Tbs., makes 12 oz.	50–70
International Delight—Iced Coffee or Iced Coffee Light	8 oz.	55–65
Califia Farms Café Latte Cold Brew Coffee	8 oz.	50
Dunkin' Donuts, Panera, or Starbucks Decaf Coffee	16 oz.	10–25
Maxwell House Decaf Ground Coffee	2 Tbs., makes 12 oz.	2–10
Teas	**Serving Size**	**Caffeine (mg)**
Starbucks Chai Latte—iced or regular	Grande, 16 oz.	95

Honest Tea Organic Lemon Tea	17 oz.	90
Starbucks Green Tea Latte—iced or regular	Grande, 16 oz.	80
KeVita Master Brew Kombucha	15 oz.	80
Black tea, brewed	8 oz.	47
Tazo Organic Iced Black Tea, bottle	14 oz.	45
Snapple Lemon Tea	16 oz.	37
Arizona Iced Tea, black	16 oz.	30
Green tea, brewed	8 oz.	29
Lipton Lemon Iced Tea	20 oz.	25
Gold Peak Unsweetened Tea	19 oz.	23
Arizona Iced Tea, green	16 oz.	15
Lipton Decaffeinated Tea, black, brewed	8 oz.	5
Herbal tea, brewed	8 oz.	0
Soft Drinks	**Serving Size**	**Caffeine (mg)**
FDA official limit for cola and pepper soft drinks	12 oz.	71 (200 parts per million)
Pepsi Zero Sugar	20 oz.	115
Mountain Dew—diet or regular	20 oz.	91

Diet Coke	20 oz.	76
Surge	16 oz.	69
Pepsi Zero Sugar	12 oz.	69
Dr Pepper or Sunkist—diet or regular	20 oz.	68
Pepsi	20 oz.	63
Coca-Cola, Coke Zero, or Diet Pepsi	20 oz.	56–57
Mountain Zevia (Zevia)	12 oz.	55
Mountain Dew—diet or regular	12 oz.	54
Coca-Cola Life	20 oz.	47
Diet Coke	12 oz.	46
Dr Pepper or Sunkist—diet or regular	12 oz.	41
Pepsi	12 oz.	38
Pepsi True	12 oz.	38
Barq's Root Beer, regular	20 oz.	38
Coca-Cola, Coke Zero, or Diet Pepsi	12 oz.	34
Coca-Cola Life	12 oz.	28
Pepsi True	7.5 oz.	24
Barq's Root Beer, regular	12 oz.	22

7-Up, Fanta, Fresca, ginger ale, or Sprite	12 oz.	0
Root beer, most brands—diet or regular	12 oz.	0
Energy Drinks	**Serving Size**	**Caffeine (mg)**
Bang Energy	16 oz.	357
5-hour Energy	2 oz.	200
Redline Energy	4 oz. (1/2 bottle)	163
Full Throttle	16 oz.	160
Hiball—Organic Energy Drink or Sparkling Energy Water	16 oz.	160
Monster Energy	16 oz.	160
NOS Energy	16 oz.	160
Rockstar Energy	16 oz.	160
Venom Energy	16 oz.	160
AMP Zero Energy	16 oz.	157
AMP Energy Boost Original	16 oz.	142
ávitāe Caffeine + Water	17 oz.	45–125
Mountain Dew Kick Start	16 oz.	90–92
Red Bull	8 oz.	80

V8 V-Fusion+Energy	8 oz.	80
Bai Antioxidant Infusion	16 oz.	70
Mountain Dew Kickstart Hydrating Boost	12 oz.	68
Crystal Light Energy	1 packet, makes 16 oz.	60
MiO Energy, all flavors	½ tsp., makes 8 oz.	60
Ocean Spray Cran-Energy	8 oz.	55
Glacéau Vitaminwater Energy	20 oz.	50
Starbucks Refreshers	Can, 12 oz.	50
Caffeinated Snack Foods	**Serving Size**	**Caffeine (mg)**
STEEM Caffeinated Peanut Butter	2 Tbs., 36g	150
Awake Energy Chocolate	1 bar, 1.55 oz.	101
Jelly Belly Extreme Sport Beans	1 package, 1 oz.	50
Run Gum	1 piece	50
Awake Energy Granola	1 bar, 34g	50
GU Energy Chews Raspberry	4 chews	40
GU Energy Gel—Espresso Love, Caramel Macchiato, or Jet Blackberry	1 packet	40
Blue Diamond Café Mocha Almonds	1 oz.	24

	Serving Size	Caffeine (mg)
GU Energy Stroopwafel—Caramel Coffee or Wild Berries	1 waffle	20
GU Energy Chews—Strawberry or Black Cherry	4 chews	20

Ice Cream & Yogurt	Serving Size	Caffeine (mg)
Bang!! Caffeinated Ice Cream	4 oz.	125
Dannon Coffee Yogurt	1 container, 6 oz.	30
Häagen-Dazs Coffee Ice Cream	4 oz.	29
Stonyfield Gotta Have Java Nonfat Frozen Yogurt	4 oz.	28
Dreyer's or Edy's Slow Churned Coffee Ice Cream	4 oz.	15
Breyers Coffee Ice Cream	4 oz.	11
Häagen-Dazs Chocolate Ice Cream	4 oz.	less than 1
Dannon Oikos Café Latte Greek Yogurt	1 container, 5 oz.	less than 1

Chocolate Candy & Chocolate Drinks	Serving Size	Caffeine (mg)
Crackheads⌧ Gourmet Chocolate Coffee Caffeine	1 box, 40g	600
Crackheads Espresso Bean Candies	1 package, 28 pieces	200
Awake Caffeinated Chocolate Bar	1.55 oz.	101
Starbucks Hot Chocolate	Grande, 16 oz.	25
Hershey's Milk Chocolate Bar	1.6 oz.	9

Hershey's Milk Chocolate Kisses	9 pieces, 1.4 oz.	9
Hershey's Cocoa	1 Tbs.	8
Silk Soymilk—Chocolate or Light Chocolate	8 oz.	4
Silk Dark Chocolate Almondmilk	8 oz.	4
Hershey's Chocolate Lowfat Milk	12 oz.	2

Over-The-Counter Pills	**Serving Size**	**Caffeine (mg)**
Zantrex-3 weight-loss supplement	2 capsules	300
NoDoz or Vivarin	1 caplet or tablet	200
Excedrin Migraine	2 tablets	130
Midol Complete	2 caplets	120
Bayer Back & Body	2 caplets	65
Anacin	2 tablets	64

Pure Caffeine	**Serving Size**	**Caffeine (mg)**
Caffeine powder	1/16 or 1/32 tsp.	200
Liquid Caffeine (brand)	1 tsp.	83

Made in the USA
Columbia, SC
01 May 2022

59683610R00126